I haven't heard.

All I've ever heard has

Do they write songs?

They used to be good.

never hear about them any more.

They're still singing? What kind of songs
do they do now?

The Everlys are musical geniuses whose success is
due to their deep moral dedicaton to their work, and
who, in fact, have also given up their fame for the
same reason.

Aren't They Sissies?

THE EVERLY BROTHERS

Ladies Love Outlaws

Consuelo Dodge

CIN-DAV, Inc.
Route 1, Box 778
Starke, Florida 32091

Consuelo Dodge

Grateful acknowledgement is made for permission to reprint the following:

Elizabeth Taylor: The Last Star, copyright 1981 by H. B. Productions, Inc. Reprinted by permission of Simon & Schuster, Inc.

Permission to print partial script from the Johnny Cash Presents The Everly Brothers Summer Replacement Show granted by Harold D. Cohen, President of Halcyon Productions, Inc. in association with Screen Gems, Inc.

Recipe from "Country Stars Cookbook," copyright 1977 by H. Jackson Brown, Jr. Used by permission of End, Inc., Nashville, Tennessee.

KMA Guide permission courtesy of Evelyn Birkby, KMA Radio, Shenandoah, Iowa 51601.

Cover: AP/Wide World Photos

Includes Photographs, Chronology, Bibliography and Index.

Library of Congress Catalogue Card Number: 90-085691
Printed in the United States of America
First Edition

Publisher's Cataloging in Publication

Dodge, Consuelo, 1942-
 The Everly Brothers : ladies love outlaws / by Consuelo Dodge. --

 p. cm.
 Includes bibliographical references and index.
 ISBN 1-879347-09-1 (pbk.)

 1. Everly Brothers.   2. Everly, Phil, 1939- 3. Everly, Don,
1937- 4. Rock musicians--United States--Biography.   I. Title.

ML421.E8   782.42166'092'2
                                           90-85691

<u>DEDICATION</u>

This book is dedicated to my wonderful husband David, who has withstood near financial catastrophe, burned dinners (or no dinner at all), days bordering on insanity, nights with no sleep, long hours of driving to strange places, strange food, and strange people, with an even stranger wife.

His love, infinite patience and support made this project possible and it is amazing that he never stopped believing in me and knowing I could do it - even when I was ready to quit.

If he ever thought he took a back seat to the Everly Brothers, he was wrong.

This is also dedicated to my daughter Jennifer, who was possibly not given the attention she deserved during this hectic period.

APPENDIX

FOREWORD

This book was written without any comment or endorsement, one way or the other, from the Everly Brothers.

I began writing this book because of my profound admiration and love for the Everly Brothers. I was in awe of their talents and, being a sometime-performer myself, I was aware of some of the trials and tribulations which most performers encounter.

Not only was I aware of them, I realized that these two guys were survivors in a rough, tough business that chews young people up and spits them out without a backwards glance. "The Business" had tried to do this numerous times with the Everlys and yet they persisted.

Couple this with the personal aspect of their claustrophobic togetherness and you have an almost impossible situation. The word "almost" is the key, for if there was a glimmer of a chance, the Everlys dove for that chance and took it. They had a ten year hiatus from each other and used that time to grow and mature, coming back with the strength and force of a locomotive crashing full steam ahead. The Everly train could not be stopped.

I began this book wanting only to look at the Everlys from afar as the men that they had become, and also to delve into their futures as entertainers. It astonished me when I was told by complete strangers that "enough" had been written on the duo. Nothing could be farther from the truth! All entertainers need exposure and publicity.

This book then has become a book for the reader who was not cognizant of the fact that the Everly Brothers still exist and perform regularly. I asked multitudes of people about the Everlys, and was amazed by answers that proved to me the general public was not fully aware of their vast contributions to the world of music today. For these people, I write this book.

As word spread, some people actually demanded that I stop writing this book. I suppose the birds peck at the best fruit, don't they? Apparently no one told them that this is the United States of America, the Land of the Free and the Home of the Brave. Indeed, I needed to be brave to get this accomplished. After all, what do the last four letters in the word "American" spell? I CAN!!! Anyone is free to write a book if they care to, as long as it is an honest rendition. I have tried to make it as honest as I could.

PREFACE

Once upon a time I entered a large University's library to get a biography to read on the fantastic singing duo called the Everly Brothers. To my utter amazement, there were none available! I couldn't believe it, and yelled at the librarian that these men have been in show business for over forty years, so this could not be true. She assured me that it was, and then said, "If you're so upset, why don't you write your own book?" I replied, "OK, I will!" And that is how it all started.

I began writing this book the same as a young bride enters a new marriage. There were stars in my eyes (two in particular) and I was going to extol their virtues *ad nauseam*. Along the way, however, a few people tried to stop me, but I failed to see why, so I didn't. I was told not to write a book because I did not have the Everlys' permission. Gee. This is America. If I wrote a book about Hitler, I wouldn't have his permission, either. I was told I had to get permission from the fan club. Gosh. Who are they? I was told there would be no market for my book. I don't agree. I know there are many people who would be delighted to read a simple little book about the Everly Brothers. Besides, since I was financing the entire project myself, it's nobody's business but mine, anyway. I was told enough had been written about them. Wow. Marilyn Monroe has had over fifty books written on her, and she's not even alive. I won't even venture a guess as to how many books are out on Elvis, the Beatles, the Rolling Stones, etc. I was told I could not find out anything new on my own. On the contrary, I found out quite a lot. I was accused of not telling the Everlys of my intentions. This also is not true. I notified them at the onset and also delivered a note into their own hands at dinner (Donald's, to be precise), informed their office in Nashville as well as their publicist, and their cousin Ted Everly, exactly who

I was and what my intentions were. I received no answers, nor did I expect to, but they were very informed. It is their choice not to respond, and as I said before, this is America. The same rules work for all of us.

Ted Everly contacted me, however, and offered to help in any way that he could. That was very nice and I really appreciated it. Unfortunately, the help was offered two years after it was requested, and the horse had already left the barn.

I will not forget, however, the people who believed in me and were so very encouraging. To these strong, admirable friends I will be eternally grateful. In particular I wish to thank my marvelous, supportive husband David, Nancy Godfrey in Greenwich, Jeanette Blackstone in Indianapolis and Teresia Sheppard who remained so close even though she lives in Alaska.

Those were the conditions under which I wrote this book. I can only liken it to a soldier who, under fire from all sides, runs through an opening in the middle of the shelling towards a ray of beautiful, glorious sunlight.

I present you, therefore, with my small ray of sunshine.

ACKNOWLEDGEMENTS

My heartfelt thanks extend to the following. I have placed them in alphabetical order so that no one would feel slighted. You know what you did.

Eddy Arnold, Evelyn Birkby, Doris Brandt, George Brezina, Jr., Esq., Arline Broome, Bryn Brydenthall, Dee Dee Caidin, Martin Caidin, Glen Campbell, Chris Church, Everett Corbin, Harold D. Cohen of Halcyon Productions, Inc., Neomia Compton, Professor Don Cusic, Peggy Carney, Phil Cranham, Marsha Denny of Group 5, Randy DeMarco of Rose Printing, Polly DeBose, David Langston Dodge, Jennifer Consuelo Dodge, EBI, Sharon Eldred, Donald Everly, Phillip Everly, Ted Everly, Professor Paul Feehan, Warren Franz, Esq., Glenda Frederick, Peter S. Godfrey, Dr. Mary Hartigan, Bill Hollingshead, KMA Radio, Mike LeTourneau of AP, Cathy Langer, Robert W. Lloyd, Esq., Larrie Londin, Cristina Martinez, Esq., Professor Bill McKeen, Reverand Dwight McQueen, Doreen Milne, Kari Moore, Tammy Murray, Nashville Courthouse Staff, "Nathan Nashville," Rich Newsome, Esq., Lavern Outlaw, Patricia Patterson, Johnnie Potts of The Sutler, Celeste Racano, Renee at Tootsie's Orchid Lounge, Marian T. Rigney, Dale Evans Rogers, Lansing Roy, Esq., Pat Shore, Ruud Schakel, Mitch Schneider, Sharing & Caring, Teresia Sheppard, Joseph W. Smith, Jerry Spies, Wilma Staakman, Joe Stewart, Terry Stokes, Larry Strauss, Steven Thornton, The University of Florida, Peter Van Calck, Terry Vaughn, John Waters, Reverand Ballard Wilson, and all my other "informants" who wished to remain anonymous.

To my dear friend Jeanette Blackstone, words cannot thank you enough for all your help, support, faith and encouragement. Just think - if it hadn't been for the Everly Brothers, we would never have met!

Special thanks go to my readers: Nancy Godfrey, Jeanette Blackstone, Jacquie Gordon, and Esther Hardy.

Last but certainly not least, my deep appreciation and love go to David L. Dodge for his editing expertise as well as his undying support of me and my lofty aspirations, not only with this publication, but in every area of my wacky life.

1
ONE CONCERT

*"Music is harmony, harmony is perfection,
perfection is our dream, and our dream is heaven."*
- Amiel

I have been to quite a few Everly Brothers concerts, from the most casual in Central City, Kentucky to "Big Time Showbiz." I would like to take the reader through one in-between concert: Chastain Park in Atlanta, Georgia.

Chastain Park is a very large outdoor amphitheater, built on the side of a steep hill. There is a level area at the bottom of the hill with picnic tables, and just beyond that lies a building with well lit stage and backstage areas. Regular "theatre" type seats are installed on the hill itself and the arena seats approximately 4,000 people. Single seats sell for twenty-five to thirty dollars, while the tables for six on the "floor" go for approximately one hundred and seventy five dollars a night. Chastain Park is definitely "Yuppie Heaven." No one sits on the ground as one might have to do at a more rural outdoor concert!

Patrons who go to Chastain Park, it appears, try to outdo their neighbors in picnic basket elegance. This is clearly a social event with a little entertainment thrown in for good measure. The picnic baskets are huge and varied, but almost all contain (especially at the tables on the "floor"), linen tablecloths and napkins, silver candlesticks, silver service for six, crystal goblets for wine, (some people bring beer, though), vases with real flowers in them, elegant hors d'oeuvres, and catered meals such as lobster, crab, or fancy tea sandwiches. Of course, desserts can be French pastries and/or various cheeses and crackers. This is definitely MY kind of picnic!

I'm not so slow that I did not gather that the audience was there to picnic and not necessarily to pay attention to the "guys singing." After all, many top notch entertainers come here and these people have seen the best. Except for the Everly Brothers, apparently. I don't think the audience was quite ready for them.

I started talking to the people around me, and they to me when they saw my note pad and pen! I was questioned extensively as to who I was and what I was doing-and who were these guys anyway-old "has-beens" from the 50's? Yes, several admitted that they were good 'way back when, but now? I politely reminded them that you can't really call people has-beens when they've never been washed up in the first place, but an alcoholic fog by now had started to take hold and they didn't hear much of what I said. To put it bluntly, they were all a bit "looped." Of course I was "on the floor" near the most fervent party goers. I kept hoping there were some sober fans in the upper hemispheres.

Poor Katy Mofatt, the Everlys' opening act. She is an extremely talented singer and really attacks that guitar with gusto. She smiles a lot and is quite charming. The crowd that night, however, was thoroughly rude to her and I really was embarrassed to be sitting amongst them. The conversation never let up and people continued walking, eating, drinking, talking and shouting during her whole performance of eight songs. I ached for her. Lord knows it's hard enough to get up on a stage and sing with people not appreciating a thing that you're doing. It's damn hard to get up on a stage and do anything without an appreciative audience. I really wondered how the Everly Brothers would handle this rowdy crowd!

I needn't have even begun to concern myself. These two have been standing before all kinds of audiences for over thirty years, performing approximately one hundred shows a year. They know exactly what to do and how to do it.

To begin with, after Katy left, the rock 'n roll music was turned up to the maximum, so all those "talkers" were prevented from talking. That was smart as hell. Next, out marched one of the best bands in the world, and when they start playing, you can't help but listen. Then two tuxedo-clad

Everly Brothers quietly took the stage, opened their mouths and did what they do best. A couple of brave souls started to say a few words during their first song, but they were overwhelmed, to put it mildly. After that, there was silence, and then awe. The Everlys told them and showed them what they sang: Heterosexual Rock!

When the Everlys quietly walked up to their individual microphones, the audience erupted in applause, but the two men hardly acknowledged the sound. It was as though they normally expected such adoration. After all, they have heard welcomes like that for many, many years.

When they sang, they looked at each other mostly, intent on fine-tuning their performances. Donald stands stage left, Phillip stage right, and they at first seem like twins because of the identical guitars and tuxedos, but Donald, the older brother, is heavier and Phillip has a one inch advantage in height. When they sing together, it is like one voice, and although they are unable to hit as many high notes as before, their voices are almost the same, except that today, their voices are far mellower and better than ever.

They opened with "The Price Of Love," and then continued with "Walk Right Back" and "Claudette." They told their little joke about all their songs having girls' names in them, and that they had been married to half of them, and the Beach Boys had married the other half. A quite breathless Donald sang "Crying In The Rain" with Phillip, and then they did a rather different rendition of Phillip's composition, "When Will I Be Loved." Next followed a medley of three songs, "Devoted To You," "Love Hurts" and "Brown Eyes."

At this point a few people were standing up and dancing in the aisles. Donald reassured them by telling them to go ahead and do whatever they wanted to do, "we've seen it all." That I can really believe! Many people had sparklers, and the entire hillside was further illuminated by people's candlesticks, making the moment appear magical. Phillip had come out on the stage originally without his tie on. Whether this was a personal Phillip Rebellion or he had just lost it, I don't know, but neither of them had flowers in their buttonholes either, which is pretty rare. At any rate, after a few songs, Donald's tie disappeared also. I began to wonder if anything else was going to be discarded!

Next they sang their old standby, "Bye Bye, Love," Phillip broke one of his guitar strings which he frequently does, and threw his guitar backstage, sailing through the air to Equipment Manager John Earl, who caught it and immediately started restringing it. This is always a complete surprise to first time audiences, and I heard a lot of Ooooohhhhhhs. The Everlys followed this stunt (which Donald ignores completely) with "All I Have To Do Is Dream," then they left the stage while the band played a terrific interim song. I guess the Everlys left to dry their hair or something, as after three songs, both were completely drenched. Donald has a distinct advantage here, as he can dry his hair with a towel and the curls stay, but Phillip just drips. His hair is straight and if he messed his hair up with a towel, he would look very strange indeed.

The brothers returned, sang "Why Worry" (this was where Donald removed his tie), "(Til) I Kissed You," and "Cathy's Clown."

By this time Phillip's hair was again plastered to his head. They continued with "Wake Up, Little Susie," then "Lucille" which Donald announced as one of his favorites, and then their favorite ballad, "Let It Be Me." That was it.

The Everly Brothers rarely do encores, as they seem to want to leave their audiences wanting more. And wanting more, they did. People were going absolutely crazy, yelling, screaming and stomping. Lo and behold, they encored with "Be-Bop-

A-Lula," left and then were brought out again with "You Send Me," a quiet song to calm the restless natives.

Talk about a professional show! The Everly Brothers whacked that newly-sobered audience right between the eyes. They didn't know what hit them. The people around me who couldn't have cared less before the show, were asking me a million questions about the duo, asking everything that came into their heads. They were hooked. Everyone was hooked. My husband and I became re-hooked, if that is a word.

The Everly Brothers' performances resemble a runaway train barrelling down the track, never stopping. They really out-did themselves that night, but then they usually give one hundred and ten percent every time they get on a stage. It is a good lesson for performers to remember. It works, and it has worked for the Everly Brothers for many, many years. They are the best.

It wasn't always like this.

2
YOUNGSTERS

*"They are able because
they think they are able."*
- Virgil

Their people were coal miners and railroad workers in Western Kentucky, but there was music in their genes. Their parents played and sang, as did their uncles, their aunts and their grandparents. They were born to music and have been performing their special brand of it all over the world for fifty years. They are the Everly Brothers.

They were not the original Everly Brothers, however. The Everlys' grandfather was a French harp player and an old time left handed fiddler with that thumb-picking style so uniquely native to Kentucky. Their grandmother sang and played the fiddle, too. This couple had nine children, four boys and five girls, all of whom played the guitar. One of these nine children was named Ike (short for Isaac) and he was to become the father of Donald and Phillip Everly.

In and around Cleaton, Kentucky, (walking distance from Central City), Ike Everly and Merle Travis learned to play guitar in the local style from Mose Rager. Mose, in turn, had learned it from a man by the name of Kennedy Jones. Mr. Jones died recently on September 6, 1990 in an Ohio nursing home at the age of 90.

In the rural parts of the south, children do not have many toys, so they pick up their parents' musical instruments and play with those. The instrument is usually a fiddle, dobro, mandolin, dulcimer or a guitar, and since there are always a lot of children and there are not a lot of instruments available, they are passed around from child to child. Hardly any of them remembers learning how to play, but play they do, and that is how the great music from that part of the country is passed on from generation to generation. It is interesting to note that while children in the north ask Santa for sleds and skis, many Kentucky children ask for guitars.

As a young man, Ike and his friends would play the guitar at church socials and other gatherings, just for the sheer joy of playing. It never even entered their minds that someone could actually get paid for doing what was such a natural function in their lives. Since almost everyone who worked in the coal mines was pretty broke, this was their main entertainment, their fun, their joy, and their excuse to forget the dirty, stinking mines for a few brief hours.

Ike's father had been a coal miner and like most Kentucky youngsters, he and his brothers imitated their fathers and started working in the mines at around thirteen years of age. They were employed by the Peabody Mining Association which is still in existence today.

When mine fires and cave-ins became too dangerous, however, Ike and two of his brothers, Charlie and Leonard, relocated to Chicago. Ike worked days for the WPA (Works Progress Administsration) and at night was part of a group called the North Carolina Boys, on KXEL radio. He also performed what Donald termed "white blues" with his brothers. They began a career in music, utilizing their unique talents as harmony singers. These original Everly Brothers sang much the same style of harmony that was later passed on to Donald and Phillip.

In 1935, Ike married Margaret Embry. Ike was twenty-seven and Margaret was only fifteen. She had been Ike's next door neighbor all of her life, and they had walked home together a couple of times from church. She was really quite smitten by a "man" who had actually been out of the Central City area! Margaret herself played the bass fiddle and sang. They stayed together through thick and thin for forty one years until Ike's death in 1975. Working together, they produced and trained the two finest harmony singers on the planet.

Even though none of the original Everlys could read music, Phillip inherited his Uncle Charlie's rhythm guitar expertise and exquisite voice, and many relatives insisted that you

Consuelo Dodge

could not tell the difference between the two. Donald on the other hand, inherited his Uncle Leonard's guitar playing, using a regular straight pick instead of the finger picks which were native to the area. These men formed the basis of Donald and Phillip's southern musical roots. It seems as though they were born to carry on this musical family tradition, and carry it on, they do.

Ike, Leonard and Charlie had a trick they did, where all three of them played on the same guitar at one time. Donald and Phillip demonstrated this unique method of playing on the Tennessee Ernie Ford TV show in the late 1950s. It is a strange talent for someone to display, but a talent nevertheless.

After a while, the original Everly Brothers were having their own difficulties. Unable to get along with each other, they disbanded. Apparently Ike wanted to be the head man because he was the oldest, and Charlie was the best musician, so he thought he should be the most important, and so on. It is amazing that these three brothers couldn't stay together for more than a couple of years, but when Donald and Phillip Everly broke up after some thirty-odd years of claustrophobic togetherness, no one could "understand why." What I don't understand is how they stayed together for as long as they did. That's the real miracle. Perhaps their extreme differences in temperament, abilities, likes and dislikes saved them from an early extinction.

In 1944, Ike, Charlie (Chuck) and Leonard (Len) split up their act, and Ike and Margaret moved to Waterloo, Iowa to sing with a country and western band on radio station KASL. Ike's two brothers remained in Chicago playing the Madison Street clubs and honky tonks. Charlie at one time played for Xavier Cugat's band, but when they found out he was unable to read music, he was fired. All three brothers eventually died

10

of some form of lung disease brought on by working in the mines in their youths.

When the family moved to Waterloo, the boys who would become the famous Everly Brothers were only five and seven years of age.

Isaac Donald Everly was born February 1, 1937 at home in Brownie, Kentucky. The place where he was born has since been levelled, and there is nothing left but a bunch of smokestacks. The town of Brownie was located at the end of Old Brownie Road in Central City, Kentucky. The road is now overgrown so that one is basically unable to continue to Donald's specific place of birth, but Old Brownie Road does still exist.

Phillip Everly was born in Chicago in Cook County Hospital on January 19, 1939, where the Everly family had moved to pursue a career in music. He once said he thought he was named for Phil Harris who was playing Chicago at the time of his birth.

Around that time, many other southern musicians and singers were travelling to the Chicago area to perform in the various clubs. Many of them played for a while to earn money, and then returned to their home states to live for a while on what they had earned.

Although as a child Donald liked to cook (and still does), the boys also played baseball with their parents and friends, went squirrel hunting in the woods and fished in the streams. This was all fine for growing up, but since their parents were entertainers, it was instilled in them early on that they must practice their music first in order to enjoy the other things later. Every day Ike made them practice for long periods of time, and of course, they worked hard.

When they were very young, according to custom, their father was their guitar and singing teacher. He taught Donald first and then Phillip, and since he was the eldest, Donald usually got to the guitar first. Phillip seems to feel that's why he didn't learn to play as well as Donald. It was darned near impossible to wrestle the guitar from his older brother.

As one story goes, at one point in their early lessons Donald was not keeping good time to the music. His father stopped him and told him that he would not sing with a boy who could not mark time. Donald left and came back many hours later promising his dad that it would not be a problem again, that he could keep time from now on. And he did. No one ever knew what he did during that time, but whatever it was, it worked and worked well. Donald also remembered that his father sometimes paid him twenty-five cents an hour to practice the guitar, and quipped in a 1987 interview in *Country Musicians Magazine*, "it paid off for him, I guess."

Donald recalls also that his father wouldn't let him touch his guitar too much because he was a southpaw and he would pick it up upside down. Like their grandfather, both Donald and Phillip were left handed, but Ike taught them to play guitar with their right hands as he thought that it would be too much trouble to be changing strings all the time, and people would call them funny names like "lefty." Of course there is nothing wrong with being left handed. About ten percent of the population is left handed, and this includes lots of Presidents of the United States, like Garfield, Truman, Ford and George Bush. Interestingly enough, Paul McCartney is left handed and does actually play a left handed guitar. It didn't seem to hold him back too much! As a left handed attorney friend of mine once stated, "Every person I have ever met that is left handed has been unusual in one way or another."

The first time Donald made a recording was in Chicago when he was about five years old. His father took him into a street recording booth complete with a guitar, and sang,

"Paper Doll" which had just been made popular by the Mills Brothers. Unfortunately Donald forgot a word and ended the session with, "Aw, shucks." I guess that was his first musical disaster!

As they were not very happy in Waterloo, in 1945 Ike, Margaret and their two young sons moved to Shenandoah, Iowa, where Ike had found work on Radio Station KMA. When the children were a little older, they also sang with their parents on the radio. Growing up in Shenandoah was an idyllic experience. That small town feeling was there, and the boys had room to run and play, hunt and yell. Donald still seems to yell a lot, which must be a carryover from his more youthful days.

The following are reprints from several *KMA Guide* issues which give a hint of what family life was like when the Everlys were growing boys in Iowa:

"The Everlys are real outdoor folks and just about as swell people as you'd meet anywhere. Ike says he hunted a lot when he was a kid and he's been at it ever since. Margaret isn't one of those wives who just goes along and carries a gun either. She always hunted with her brothers and can certainly hold up her end of the bargain when it comes to killing game. The family came home with nine squirrels just the other day and the way we got the story, five of them were Margaret's. Donnie is a fairly good shot...but Phil hasn't quite 'got his eye' as yet." (*KMA Guide*, November, 1946)

"Ike's favorite pastime these sunny days is playing baseball. Margaret, his wife, chooses half of the neighbor boys, and Ike chooses half. Don, their older son, usually is on Margaret's team, and Phillip, the younger son, is on Ike's. The other day one of the boys asked Phillip what the score was. He replied,

`15 to 0 - but just wait `till we get to bat!'" (*KMA Guide*, April, 1948)

"Yes, Ike Everly's sons...are really `chips off the ole block'. They are shown at their favorite pastime - singing with dad. The microphone which Phil is holding is part of a home recording machine which the boys use to check their musical progress. They have been making home records for four years and now these have become treasured family keepsakes...Don (12 years old, gray eyes, brown hair) is studying the violin. Moreover, like dad he is a painter...Don is also a Boy Scout. Phil (10 years old, blue eyes, sandy hair) is learning to play the flute and, in his spare time, helping Ike care for their acreage on the outskirts of Shenandoah." (*KMA Guide*, April, 1949)

"Mrs. Ike Everly was mighty proud of her birthday cake this year...The reason? Because her 12 year old son Donnie had baked it! Mrs. Everly says she hasn't any daughters to help with the cooking, but Donnie is proving he's going to make as good a cook as any girl." (*KMA Guide*, January, 1949)

"...entertainer Ike Everly has decided it's NOT too late to learn football. Not that he wants to play the game...he only wants to learn the rules of the game. So he promised his two sons...he would accompany them to a junior high football game, if they would explain the plays to him! So off they went. But Dad soon discovered he was going to have to find some-one else to teach him. The boys got so enthused over the game, they forgot all about their promise!" (*KMA Guide*, October, 1949)

"Both boys are left-handed, but learned to play right-handed guitars and mandolins. Donald has been playing the guitar for some time but made his first public appearance only last January in Council Bluffs - before 800 people! Phil, practicing mandolin, has not yet played it on the air, but he sings with the family on the radio." (*KMA Guide*, October, 1950)

"Donald, 13, has inherited the art abilities of his father, Ike, another KMA radio artist. He likes to draw and someday wants to attend college where he can study art and dramatics. His blond-headed brother Phil, 11, sings on the Everly Family programs and is learning how to play the mandolin. Margaret, the boys' mother, claims that Phil is handy around the house with a hammer and saw. Phil wants to go to college and study dramatics." (*KMA Guide*, January, 1951)

When Phillip was just a little boy and first began to sing, Donald sang harmony to his lead, but after a while when it became apparent that Phillip's voice was higher than Donald's, they switched parts and Phillip was taught harmony singing. Phillip has admitted that at first it was a tremendously difficult thing to learn to do, but after so many years, it is now second nature to him and quite effortless. As to their early singing career, Donald remembered, "Phil and I have been singing together all our lives. When we were kids, I started singing harmony with my father. When Phil's voice matured, his was higher, so he started harmony. We've got a good voice blend. If I change melody, Phil changes right with me. Being related helps immensely as far as the sound goes. It has been a tradition in country music that family members sing together."

To Donald it didn't seem at all unnatural to be working hard at the ages of seven and eight. He was of the opinion that since families naturally sing together, that's what they should do. The fact that these two little boys held permanent jobs and were required to be at work at all hours of the day and early morn-

15

ing, without fail - rain or shine, snow or sleet - seemed normal and not really worthy of any special attention.

To say that their voices blend is the understatement of the year. Sometimes even the Everlys themselves admit that it is hard to tell where one voice leaves off and the other begins. To many people they sound like one voice at times, but at other times they are so complementary to the other brother's voice that their creation is that famous "third" voice which is the very essence of the Everly Brothers.

When they were still quite young and had visitors, they would frequently ask the two little boys to sing them a song. Donald and Phillip would always oblige. Their friends and relatives knew even when they were little that they would be famous some day.

When at school, however, the boys did not tell their friends what they did, as their line of work was looked down upon. At the time it was called "hillbilly" and it wasn't "cool" according to the kids. Perhaps that's why Donald and Phillip started out at a very young age sporting unusual hairstyles and wearing strange clothes. I guess they thought that if they were going to be considered "different," then they might as well go all the way and BE different. Actually all of this is a contradiction in terms. On the one hand the boys tried to remain anonymous in regards to their radio "profession," but on the other hand, they were screaming for recognition. Which way did they actually want to have it? They still don't know! They're still playing the same game, i.e., go to my shows and buy my records, but I won't give interviews or be accessible. You can't have your cake and eat it, too, guys!

When the boys got to be a little older, sometimes there wasn't enough money for two new jackets or suits for an event such as a dance or special evening, so their parents would buy one and they would share it. Phillip would go to the function for the first half of the night and Donald the second half. At other times, if Donald wanted something new, he was told that it wasn't fair to Phillip and he had to wait until there was enough money or Phillip was old enough to get it, too. This could have been one of the reasons for years of jealously and discontentment between the two brothers, Donald especially. Who on earth would want to wait for a kid brother to grow up so you could do or have something? On the other hand, poor Phillip never had a ghost of a chance with the girls if Donald was around. He was OLDER, and all the girls liked OLDER MEN!

One significant societal/behavioral problem was the fact that from birth on, the boys were almost always dressed alike, like twins. In fact, many, many people thought they were twins since they were always together and were dressed alike. Even their guitars were identical, and still are to this day. Some of their album covers even had little arrows pointing to Donald and Phillip, labelling them, so the fans would know which was which. Later on, Phillip quipped that that was also to show THEM who was who! At any rate, when you are young, two years makes a hell of a difference and Donald must have wanted everyone to know that he was two years older. He jokes about it even now, even though when you are in your fifties, two years makes little difference, but it must have been a sore bone of contention when they were youngsters. Every time they perform, Donald mentions that he is the "eldest" of the Everly Brothers. Why is it so important at this late date? Is it still a holdover from those days as children when they were not allowed to be "two years apart in age"?

As their careers progressed, it seemed that Donald was always in command and Phillip kind of followed along as the "little brother." This practice created frequent blow ups when Phillip insisted that he was not a lesser Everly Brother but fifty percent of the Everly Brothers team. Unfortunately, he was being bossed around by his big brother who in turn was always reminding the world that he was older. Later on when they were both married, their wives did not think it was such a wonderful mode of operation either, and Phillip's wives especially resented this treatment and goaded him into complaining and being highly dissatisfied with his position in the group.

Phillip hardly talked at all on stage, did not sing solos, didn't tell jokes, and to boot, his very talent, that of harmonizing, was in itself none other than following Donald's every move, literally. When they sang, Phillip would watch Donald's mouth so as to know exactly what changes in tempo, lyrics or whatever else Donald would be throwing in for good measure. This has to be a difficult task, as Donald changes his lyrics, tempos and keys whenever the feeling descends upon him. He insists it keeps the music fresh, and he's correct. Phillip is supposed to know what is going on in Donald's mind at almost the same time Donald thinks of it. He does an excellent job, amazingly enough.

Although they are not commonly thought of or known as such, they were child stars, and like most child stars, they were treated as adults. They had adult responsibilities to their public and adult working conditions. One would assume that this would mature a person, but sometimes just the opposite occurs. When the child finally becomes an adult, he has already been an "adult" for so long that now he acts like a child, refusing to be responsible and take charge. I think this has happened in more than one instance in the Everlys' personal lives.

In the early 1950s, their Uncle Emmett and Aunt Dimple owned a twenty-four hour restaurant called the D&W, where Donald and Phillip would perform sometimes with Phillip singing tenor and Donald singing baritone. The other teenagers would come listen to them sing, but, because their hair was long instead of cut in the crew cut style of the day, they would laugh at Donald and Phillip's rather bizarre appearance.

As their cousin Reverend Ted Everly stated, "The sound was sincere and genuine and original. They had a God-given talent and they tried to express it without any hypocrisy at all. Their music was them, and young people identify with something that's real."

The Everly kids were still out there working hard for a living when other kids were sitting at home worrying about things like dating and terminal acne.

Although their father was a wonderful teacher to his sons, Ike reportedly wasn't exactly overly endowed with ambition. He was usually content to just sit around playing his guitar and, if there was enough food to eat and a roof over their heads, he was content. Margaret, however, was the real "Commander" behind the family troop, because when all three of her "men" would get discouraged and be ready to quit, she never would. She was constantly telling them how good they were and that success was just around the corner. She would tell them they were wonderful and talented, over and over again, and that they would be big stars some day and that they should never give up. Never. Thank God for Margaret. If it weren't for her persistence, we might not have had the joy of the Everly Brothers all these many years!

The Everly Family Show

3
RADIO DAYS

*"Children must receive musical instruction as
naturally as food, and with as much pleasure
as they derive from a ball game...Only then
will we produce a generation prepared to
receive the larger musical experience, and to
have the passion to probe even more deeply."
- Leonard Bernstein*

Like Scandinavian children knowing how to ski almost before they can walk, the Everly children knew how to sing almost before they could talk. Ever since he could remember, Donald knew what he wanted to be when he grew up. Aside from singing, he wanted to write songs like Hank Williams, and he was forever writing when he was young. As teenagers, they didn't need a radio in the car, because they just drove along singing and playing and writing. When they composed, they wrote of familiar human emotions and desires. Their talents were a combination of simplicity and power. Their innate sense of purpose was very strong.

Donald and Phillip Everly joined their parents' radio show at the Earl E. May Seed Company in Shenandoah, Iowa when Phillip was six and Donald was eight. In addition to being a radio station, the Earl May Seed Company sold seed and other goods behind the counter and out in the field. Phillip was tagged with the (awful) name of "Baby Boy Phil" and Donald was known as "Little Donnie." It soon became The Everly Family Radio Show. The show aired from 5:30 to 6:30 a.m. daily except Sundays, and the boys would sometimes do a show in the morning before going to school and then again at noon-time. As Donald later stated in a *Playboy* interview by Jean Penn, "We had morning shows and noon shows, and there really wasn't much time for a social life...ours was not a normal childhood."

When questioned later on about what kind of children they thought they were, Phillip quipped, "I was adorable" but Donald said (a little too seriously), "Precocious. I think anybody on radio at that time had to be. You know, we had to be pre-cocious because you were put in precocious positions. You talked to an imaginary audience, you know? You were very innate. You were told there were thousands of people listening to you over the radio, please send cards and letters to this microphone. So you had to be precocious, knowing they're really there."

Shenandoah, Iowa was the nursery center of the world. Its two biggest industries were two seed companies, both of which had their own radio stations. The seed company business has been entrenched in Shenandoah history, however, since before the turn of the century, pioneered by companies such as David S. Lake's Shenandoah Nurseries, the Henry Field Seed Company and E. S. Welch's Mount Arbor Nurseries.

Earl Ernest May was born in 1890 and founded the Earl E. May Seed and Nursery Company in Shenandoah in 1919, after having been employed in the seed business for several years at the Mount Arbor Nurseries. Mr. May was a futuristic type of guy however, and thought it important to broadcast farm and marketing reports. So on August 12, 1925, the first radio broadcasts were begun. The station was called Radio Station KMA, its call letters standing for "Keep Millions Advised." It's slogan was "The Cornbelt Station in the Heart of the Nation," and in 1926 Mr. May won Radio Digest's gold cup for being "The World's Most Popular Radio Announcer."

Lavish showman that he was, Mr. May had big ideas and in 1927 he built the Mayfair Auditorium. This theatre could seat one thousand people at a time, nine hundred downstairs and an additional one hundred in the balcony. Because it was an actual broadcast studio, the stage was soundproofed by having a huge sheet of glass lowered, to separate the performers from the audience. The piece of glass used was six feet high, twenty-four feet long, and was reportedly the largest single piece of glass ever made. It weighed three tons. A movie screen was lowered in front of the glass so motion pictures could be shown. The decor was quite elaborate, and included curved ceilings, floating cloud illusions and stars at night, all replicating an outdoor Moorish garden. This became the symbol of KMA Radio.

During Jubilee Week, a thousand people would watch a one hour broadcast, then be ushered out so another thousand people could replace them. Those who had just finished seeing the show were treated to free pancakes, sausage, bacon and Mama's Choice coffee in the basement where twenty two tables were set up to handle the crowds. The Earl May Seed & Nursery Company's business that year increased a staggering four hundred and twenty five percent! This meteoric rise was attributed to KMA Radio.

The Mayfair Auditorium was the largest radio hall between the Mississippi and the Rockies, and it stood there for the next thirty six years, when it was unfortunately demolished in 1963 to make room for the May Company's new corporate offices.

The station gradually became a mecca for live music and live musicians gravitated towards Shenandoah. Of these musicians, some were extremely talented, and others could hardly carry a tune, but they came from the Ozarks, Texas, Tennessee, Alabama and Kentucky, to perform on the radio.

After a couple of years of Ike playing gigs in Chicago honky tonks and bars, Ike and Margaret knew that they didn't want their little boys to grow up in a large, dirty city. They desperately wanted their children to grow up as they did, in a clean, small country town. They first moved to Waterloo, Iowa, and Ike formed a band called the Blackhoff Boys and played on radio station KASL, but the Everlys had the feeling that Waterloo wasn't where they wanted to raise their family, so they continued on to Shenandoah.

While employed at Station KMA, Ike Everly, among other things, played in the "Stump Us Gang": a listener would name a song, the musicians would play the tune, and they usually succeeded. If however, the listener "stumped" them, he or she would win a small prize like a set of dishes or more likely a package of Waldorf Crackers or something equally as exciting. Johnny Carson often plays this game on The Tonight Show. Since he is from Nebraska, I often wonder if he heard this game played first on radio station KMA.

In the beginning, Ike and Margaret had difficulty trying to find a place to live. First they got a trailer, then found a little place out in the country with a few acres. They encountered a problem, however, because Ike was forced to commute into "town." This would have been alright except for the fact that Ike was terrified of driving. The junker/clunker that he bought needed a lot of work, and it took a lot of huffing and puffing and pushing to get it started in the morning. Margaret remembers it well. "Of a morning, the happiest moment of my day was when that car got out of hearing distance. I knew that if I heard it stop, I'd have to go help Ike get it going again. I was elated when it was beyond earshot." At night when it was time to go home, Ike's friends at KMA helped get him started, and at long last, the harrowing commute was accomplished.

Eventually, the Everlys moved back into town and rented a small house which consisted of one large room, one bedroom and one bath. The rent was $12.00 a month, and the boys slept together on the couch in the "big" room. The house was so small that Margaret commented that if you wanted to go into the bedroom, you could almost get there by just staying where you were, and if you wanted to go into the kitchen, the same rule applied. A friend of theirs said the house was so small, they didn't have room enough to change their minds. Phillip, recalling those early couch days said that it was an interesting way to grow up - with Donald's feet in his face.

Ike and Margaret also managed to tend a small garden, and to this day Phillip enjoys gardening. Donald's hobbies, however are fishing, photography, cooking and art, all of which he still pursues. As a matter of fact, Ike was pretty heavily into oils

25

and landscapes, and Donald has followed in his footsteps. The entire family enjoyed hunting and entertaining at dances, revivals and harvest festivals where sometimes the children were given free coffee and pancakes. The hunting helped to supplement their table and the entertainment helped to supplement their meager income.

Ike was content to be a KMA entertainer, but Margaret was not content with his paycheck. She saw the money that other duets were making, and she kept harping at him to do duets with her. The determined Margaret then proceeded to go out and buy a Wilcox-Gay recording machine from Montgomery Ward. She and Ike would fool around on that, and sometimes Phillip and Donald would join in.

Now that Ike was a regular at KMA, he was in a position to let Donald and Phillip sing a song or two. They started doing this at ages six and eight, respectively. Although Donald could sing and play a little by now, "Baby Boy Phil" was still too young, so he would tell jokes. Ike remembered that Phillip had the best memory in the world and never flubbed up. Donald soon was singing on the KMA Country School segment. In 1946, on Christmas Day, all of the performers' children got to be a part of the show, and since it was live, obviously a lot of crazy things happened. A recording of that 1946 Christmas show has survived, however, and it is very cute. "Little Donnie" sings "Santa Claus Is Coming To Town" (although it sounds more like "Sandy Claws"), and Phillip, age seven, sings "Silent Night" - quite well, I might add, for such a small boy.

The Everly Family Program began at 5:30 a.m. and was varied. Margaret would read the ads and give cooking and gardening tips, and Donald would guest on the show as a musician. After a while, he would sing the theme song. Phillip began to make appearances on the Country School segment, and began to sing duets with his brother. Later on, they sang a duet which was such a success that they began to receive fan mail. Margaret remembers, "In the winter it might be sixteen below zero outside, but we never missed a show. I think we would have crawled to the studio to put that show on."

Donald was soon given his own Saturday morning show, The Little Donnie Show which had as its theme song, "Free As A Little Bird As I Can Be." It was fifteen minutes long and went on the air before the movie was shown in the Mayfair Auditorium. Donald would sing three or four songs, do a commercial, and then go home. In order to earn some much needed money, he had his picture taken too, and sold copies for fifty cents each. He would also autograph them for his young fans, and pretty soon he had earned enough money to buy a bicycle. His mother, however, thought that he should "share his money with his brother" and so Donald bought Phillip a bicycle, also. Since Donald now had his own "fans," the radio station reluctantly began to pay him the grand total of five dollars per show. Donald Everly was now a bona fide paid working musician before he reached the age of ten.

Since The Everly Family Show was a success, the family managed to rent a larger farmhouse in the country where they had seven acres of fields for the kids to play in. At school, Phillip joined the glee club and basketball and track teams, they both ran lemonade stands, had paper routes, and along with all the other kids in town, worked seasonally detassling corn in Mr. May's corn fields. Phillip stated once that he learned to read music while in the glee club.

The Everlys lived in Shenandoah for eight years, which was enough to give the children a feeling of stability and home. As Margaret said, "They got to go to school with the other kids and be a part of things." How sad. I guess that was the last time in their lives they ever did anything the "normal" way.

All this small town stability wasn't as "normal" as it sounds, though. Phillip recalled summers that were far from idyllic. He vividly remembered that the jobs in Iowa were based on a farm economy, which was OK in the winter when all the farmers listened to the radio while in the barn with the cows, but during the summer they were all out planting crops. As a result, the Everlys were fired every summer, which could get pretty disheartening after a while. The family would pack up the car with instruments and go auditioning, but this became more and more difficult as live radio was on its way out. Finally, they connected with Chet Atkins, and according to Phillip, "he helped us get a recording contract that was a mess."

The boys' popularity was not assured either, as the type of singing they did on the radio was not the type of crooning which was popular in the early 1950s. The other kids, in fact, considered Donald and Phillip nothing more than hicks and hillbillies. They tried to keep their job a secret for fear of constant teasing.

Earl May died December 19, 1946 of a heart attack, at the age of 58. His son, Ed May took over, but the times themselves were changing fast. Live entertainment on radio was being taken over by the disc jockey, and TV was becoming a force to be reckoned with. Gradually the live radio entertainers were let go and in 1951, the Everlys met the same fate. They transferred to the smaller station in town, Station KFNF, where they had a morning and a noon show, and in between shows Margaret worked at the candy counter and at the fountain in the seed house, filled seed sacks and at one time held a job in a glove factory. Ike worked with shrubbery and seeds.

The Everlys were about the last live musicians to be employed by radio station KFNF. When they were finally let go, they decided rather than stay there and let the boys finish school, to move to Tennessee. Margaret told the local newspaper that they had a job in Knoxville (even though they didn't), because she was embarrassed to leave Iowa a failure. She never could accept failure. Her sons felt the same way. According to Margaret, "the boys wouldn't tell their friends they lost their jobs. They still left the house early and left school at noon so their friends wouldn't know. I hated putting the boys through that." The day they left Shenandoah, their departure was delayed because the parents couldn't find their sons, and had to cruise around town searching for them. As Donald remembered, "I didn't want to go. It was my home." Years later he spoke of the Midwest with much love, saying "It's like its own ocean...it's a part of me."

In the summer of 1951, the Everlys got a job in Evansville, Indiana, on Radio Station WIKY, FM-104.1, which paid only $35.00 per week, but was the first place that the boys started to attract a following of girls, and the first place that girls lined up for their autographs. Their sponsor was the NUNN-Better Flour Company, which is still in business today. After that job, in the summer of 1953, they moved on to Knoxville, Tennessee where the family was hired to work on radio station WROL. They were paid $90.00 a week, and did a morning show, a show at noon, and one on Wednesday evenings. Their shows were truly a family affair and usually consisted of a duet by Donald and Phillip, a solo or two, a quartet with the whole family, perhaps a trio with Ike, some instrumentals and of course, jokes and commercials in between.

The boys attended West High School, where they had their share of problems. All of the teachers and administrators were on their case about their hair and tight pants and their strange clothes, and they were accused of being rebels and/or gay because of the length of their hair. When Phillip joined the glee club, he had a lot of trouble with his music teachers. He surmises now that since he was singing professionally

29

at the time, they must have been jealous. Towards the middle of high school, however, the hair styles and pants styles changed, and all of a sudden they went from "ugly delinquent" to "handsome."

At this same time, rock 'n roll was beginning to be "the" sound, and the boys latched on to it immediately. Ike, however, couldn't follow very well on the guitar, and the station manager where they were working got angry, called them bad names like "bobby soxers" and it became obvious that the parents and children were moving in opposite directions musically. In 1954 the whole family was fired from WROL. They were unable to find other work, and Donald in particular was afraid of starving to death. By 1955, American live radio had finally died.

After their few years in Knoxville, Margaret and Ike tried to support the family as a beautician and a barber. They might have been good at it, but they didn't account for the time needed to build up a loyal clientele, and before long, they were forced to apply for welfare. As Margaret told a reporter for The Shenandoah Evening Sentinel none of the checks came and they waited and waited. Finally, she wrote a letter to the agency, and pretty soon six checks came in the mail. Thank God someone paid attention to her letter! Soon after came "Bye Bye, Love" and the rest is history. Failures? Anything but. They were an extremely talented and ambitious family, and they were determined to make it. And make it they did.

After all those many years of singing on the radio with their mother and father, it became obvious that the boys were ready to go on to bigger and better things as a duo. So at the tender young ages of sixteen and eighteen, Donald and Phillip Everly left for Nashville to seek their fortunes.

Ike contacted guitarist Chet Atkins (who became an integral part of "The Nashville Sound"), introduced his sons to him and asked Chet to listen to them. Chet agreed, and when it was obvious that the Everly Family was not going to make it, the Everly Brothers became a reality.

Actually, Donald had started writing songs when he was very young, the first of which was entitled "Lightening By Glove." However, he began in earnest at age sixteen when he wrote "Thou Shalt Not Steal (Another Man's Wife)," a precocious song to say the least, for a young teenager to write. Chet Atkins helped them sell the song to Kitty Wells who recorded it and it made the top 10! Donald also had written a song entitled "Here We Are Again" which was recorded by Anita Carter. In "making it," however, they were forced to sing country songs that they really didn't want to sing because they had to play by the rules and the rules in Nashville said "Country."

The Everlys signed their first recording contract with Columbia Records on November 8, 1955 and then on November 9 they cut a record which consisted of four sides penned by Donald, "The Sun Keeps Shining/Keep A` Lovin' Me/If Her Love Isn't True/That's The Life I Have To Live." The session musicians had just arrived in town after driving from California. They were in an awful hurry to get home, so they did the set as quickly as possible, and all four sides were recorded at the unheard of record time of twenty two minutes, and the boys were back out on the streets again. Phillip later on likened the experience to "the first time you get laid" and how young people usually wonder afterwards what all the fuss was about. Poor Donald and Phillip. A lifetime of dreams and hardships and performances were hanging on this session. It was over before they knew it, and although Phillip thought he sang sharp on three of the songs and Donald had really wanted to have a pedal steel guitar used, it seemed immaterial to Carl Smith's Tunesmiths, who couldn't have cared less about these two young kids with high voices.

The first two sides were released, but the record was obviously a flop, and the Everly kids decided to go home and forget Nashville and help support the family, as all good country boys should.

Looking back on that year, Margaret says she worried a lot about her sons because they were just thrown out into the world and looking back she admits that she didn't prepare them well enough for that world. She adds, however, that she did "the best she knew how."

Photo Courtesy of KMA Radio

Mr. May at KMA Radio

4
YOUNG POP ARTISTS

"If a man does not keep pace with his companions, perhaps it is because he hears a different drummer. Let him step to the music which he hears, however measured or far away."
- Henry David Thoreau

When they were still basically children, the Everlys journeyed to Nashville to become songwriters and recording artists. It took a couple of extremely hard years, but amazingly enough, they did it. Imagine two teenagers who were expected to act like adults, travelling that tough road to the top in Music City, trying to become "nuevo famous." It's a good thing that they had each other, as well as some inherited characteristics. After all, each parent had given his offspring his or her best. Ike contributed his tremendous talent, and Margaret gave them her unwavering faith and determination. Both of these wonderful characteristics were ingrained in their sons from the day they were born.

Of course their goals were the same as all the other young, up-and-coming singers in Nashville, the first being to appear on the Grand Ole Opry. Until they reached that point, they would hang out in the back alley behind the old Ryman Auditorium, hoping that someone would notice them. There was usually a bunch of artists going up and down that alley from the Opry to Tootsie's Orchid Lounge, a still famous "establishment" (more like a hole-in-the wall), at 422 Broadway, (it really is painted purple, folks!) which was owned at the time by Tootsie Bess. Tootsie died around 1978 and the bar has been sold a couple of times since then. Robert Moore is its present owner. Before Tootsie took over the place, it was simply called "Moms."

Just when things were looking pretty grim, Donald and Phillip were offered a songwriting contract with a publishing company called Hill and Range, and they decided to stay in Nashville just a little while longer. This contract might have changed the course of music history. They were advanced $200.00, and became very excited about having all that money. They immediately had two thousand cards printed up promoting two of their soon-to-be-released songs, "If Her Love Isn't

True" and "That's The Life I Have To Live," and sent the cards out to all the local deejays. Unfortunately, the songs were never released by the record company and the entire amount was lost. After this disappointment, they planned to leave Nashville to go home, as they had been offered a construction job with their uncle in Indiana. Once again they were persuaded to stay just a little bit longer. This one week did change the course of musical history.

It was at that all time low point in their young lives that someone mentioned to Wesley Rose, President of Acuff-Rose Publications, that the Everly Brothers were leaving town because they had basically given up, and Wesley decided to talk to them. Acuff-Rose Publishing was the largest publishing house in Nashville, founded in 1942 by Roy Acuff and Fred Rose, Wesley's father.

Fred Rose, born August 24, 1897, was an extremely talented songwriter who sometimes penned his songs under pseudonyms such as Bart Dawson and Floyd Jenkins. He had started out in show business as a honky tonk pianist and had also been a member of Paul Whiteman's orchestra. During Gene Autry's movie career, Fred Rose wrote sixteen movie songs for the cowboy star, and he was one of the first members of the Country Music Hall of Fame. In 1945 he handed Acuff-Rose over to his son Wesley, so he could pursue multiple careers of songwriting, publishing, producing and record executive. Fred Rose died in 1954 from a heart attack.

Wesley Rose, a former accountant for an oil firm, was one of the main forces in establishing the Nashville known today as Music City. He soon formed his own record label, Hickory Records, and his was the first publishing company to have its own recording studio, booking/management agency, the first to hire record promoters, to print its own sheet music, and to have worldwide music ties. One of the founders of the

Country Music Association, Wesley Rose was the Country Music Association's Chairman of the Board three times, and was very active in various charitable organizations. Wesley Rose died on April 26, 1990 at the age of 72 from complications relating to Alzheimer's disease.

Another side of Wesley, however, was seen by Bobby Blackburn, a friend of the late Roy Orbison, as related in Roy's biography, *Dark Star*. Bobby ran into Wesley at Claudette Orbison's funeral, and said that Wesley wailed to him, "I've lost the Everly Brothers! I put so much into them and then they run off and left us. You can't invest in talent - you have to invest in people."

At the time the Everlys were starting out, Archie Bleyer had been working with Wesley Rose and just happened to be starting up a Country Division for his New York label, Cadence Record Company. At first Archie was very reluctant to sign the Everly Brothers, because he had not been favorably impressed with their earlier Columbia recordings, but at the insistence of Wesley Rose, he finally relented. He had decided earlier to use a couple of country acts anyway, so he signed up the Everly Brothers, Gordon Terry and Anita Carter. At this time the Everlys were also offered the recording session for "Bye Bye, Love" which about forty other acts had turned down. The boys took it because they were so hungry by now, they would have sung anything for the $64.00 session fee. The song was an instant hit (probably in part because of Donald's innovative guitar intro). After this recording, Wesley Rose became the Everlys' first manager. Among other things, Phillip had not yet graduated from high school and someone had to see to it that he did some studying while working and travelling on the road. He eventually received his diploma through the mail.

Two of Acuff-Rose's top staff writers were Boudleaux and Felice Bryant, who became one of the greatest songwriting teams in Nashville history. They wrote many, many songs for the Everlys (it is said that Boudleaux did his best writing in the car) and as a matter of fact, they "kind of" adopted the Everly kids. In the 1960s they lived in Hendersonville, Tennessee where they raised their own sons and entertained a lot out by their swimming pool. They helped the Everlys along socially as well as professionally.

Born in 1920, Boudleaux was originally a classical violinist from Georgia who had played with the Atlanta Philharmonic. His wife Felice had been previously employed as an elevator operator at the Shrader Hotel in Milwaukee, Wisconsin. Both Boudleaux and Felice started writing songs in 1949 and enjoyed a lucrative career. In 1974 *Billboard Magazine* published a list of over four hundred artists who had recorded material of theirs. Not only that, they penned the song "Rocky Top" (in a mere ten minutes) which is now the state song of the State of Tennessee. I might add that the Everly Brothers' rendition of this much sung tune is the very best that I have heard anywhere. Of course, when Boudleaux started out hacking songs, he would stand outside the Grand Ole Opry and try to sell them right there in the street to the stars coming off stage. They would ask him if he had anything new, and he always would say, "yes, of course!" Even though he sometimes didn't have anything, he knew he could always whip something up in the car on the way to the studio. He was that talented and prolific.

Generally, Boudleaux wrote the music and Felice the lyrics to their songs. Boudleaux Bryant passed away in June of 1987, and his extraordinary talent will be greatly missed. Phillip paid tribute to Boudleaux by saying simply, "Without Boudleaux Bryant, we'd be doing some heavy lifting somewhere." Felice Bryant still resides in Nashville.

After recording "Bye Bye, Love," things happened very fast. First, the young Everlys were booked on a 'Grand Ole Opry' tent show tour with Bill Monroe, "The Father of Bluegrass Music." Bill Monroe supposedly "invented" bluegrass, as well as naming it for his home state of Kentucky. The Everlys received $90.00 per week, and thought they were in entertainment heaven. Others in the group included singer Jimmy C. Newman, fiddler Rufus Thibodeaus, stuttering songwriter Mel Tillis from Florida, and two Cajun performers. The audiences on this tour were very rough.

Apparently the audience was admitted for one admission fee, which entitled them to view the "country" show. After they were seated, they were hit again for an additional fee so they wouldn't have to sit in the colored section. This made them a bit angry, even though apparently nobody told them that as a general rule the "colored folks" didn't attend country tent shows in the first place. No matter. After the show, the audience was again hit up for more money to see the "second show," which was called a "rock & roll" show. Actually this show consisted of all the same performers from the first show doing the same songs and music but lying down instead of standing, or with some sort of other foolish minor difference. By then the audience had paid three times for one short (and usually not very good) show, and they were quite hostile. These were the audiences the young Everly boys had to face.

The group of thirteen entertainers travelled from town to town in an old, beat up Cadillac limousine. They would do their show and then leave that night for the next place. This maneuver was commonly referred to as a "hit and run." I saw Bill Monroe in Nashville in 1989 and he was still entertaining and going pretty strong.

While the Everlys were away doing the tent shows, their recording of "Bye Bye, Love" was quietly becoming a hit, and when they pulled into Nashville, it was being played on the radio. This was a complete surprise to the Everlys, and they were elated! Success at last. Someone was actually finally listening to them!

Of course, the boys realized they could not support themselves just because their record was being played on the radio, so two days after the end of that tour, and because of the amazing success of their first hit record, the Everly Brothers were on a Greyhound bus en route to Cleveland for their first big TV appearance on The Julius La Rosa Show. In addition to making other television appearances, they also played sock hops all over the country. Shortly afterward, Ed Sullivan started calling, the producers gave them $5,000.00 advances, money for a 1957 Oldsmobile, and off they went feeling rich and happy on a promotional tour with Johnny Cash. The money machine had kicked into passing gear.

On September 6, they departed on yet another tour accompanied by Chuck Berry, Fats Domino, the Crickets, the Drifters, LaVern Baker ("Tweedle Dee"), Clyde McPhatter, Eddie Cochran, Paul Anka and Frankie Lymon and the Teenagers. The all-black orchestra was led by Paul Williams.

At first their music was called "Rockabilly" which later on Donald was quick to point out was an undesirable title, because to him it was the same as being called a hillbilly and some people seemed to think that everyone from Kentucky was a hillbilly. They did insist that they were rock 'n roll innovators, and they were. Of course rock 'n roll was more than just singing. It was the cut and tightness of the pants, the tilt of the guitar, the sneer or leer, the long haircuts, sideburns, and of course some eye contact with the audience, along with good body movements on stage. Their songwriting depicted lots of romantic agony which drew sympathy from their largely female audiences.

The two young boys with their impeccable harmonization were naturals for the pop scene. Phillip had such a "little lost boy" look to him that females naturally wanted to take him home and make him happy. He was a good looking lad standing five foot ten inches tall with blue eyes and straight, sandy blond hair. Donald was five foot nine inches tall and had dark brown, curly hair and beautiful gray eyes like his father, Ike. He seemed like the kind of guy you would be afraid to take home. He was, well - all male. They haven't changed much in thirty years.

It is amazing to me how "Kentucky" and countrified their accents are when speaking and singing country songs, but the bad English and the pronunciation of "git-tars" and "kay-settes" all give that homey, down-to-earth Everly Boys touch. Don't be fooled! Imagine the surprise of the listening audience when they heard them in 1972 introduce the judges for the Miss U.S.A. Pageant. There is hardly a trace of accent anywhere. Then we have an inside peek at the two knowledgeable, sophisticated entertainers and cosmopolitan world travellers that they have become. Simple country boys? Hell, no. These two men are as smart as anyone, and tough as nails. Don't let them fool you for a moment.

Donald's description of themselves found in a 1986 *Playboy* interview, went as follows: "Both of us were late bloomers. We never got into trouble and were always the cleanest-cut kids. I didn't say 'Hell' until I was 20. From then on, I guess, I made up for lost time."

The female fans went wild over Donald and Phillip for several reasons. One was that (in public, anyway) they were so sweet and shy. They sang romantic songs that related to teenagers, because they were little more than teenagers themselves. Also because their music was so different and beautiful, they were liked by more males than a lot of the other teen idols were. Let's face it. Their music was unique, and plainly wonderful. Phillip commented once that a few female fans would sometimes bare their boobs for the Everlys to sign, but even that got old after a while. The changes which were so hard in coming, are prevalent today. As Phillip told an interviewer from the Kansas City Star in August of 1986, "They call me 'Mister' now, if that means anything. In the '50s they just wouldn't call you anything. They thought you were outlandish because of your long hair, you dressed different, and they threw you out of town."

In 1957 their music was considered radical and their hair was considered ridiculous. Donald remembers one incident with obvious disgust, as he recounted in an interview by Floyd Mattson, "Buddy Holly and you and me, and they got a couple of the other guys on the tour. The photographer and the press man came to the show and all they wanted was a picture of the profiles of the guys and girls. The girls were a sister act, the Sheppards, and they wanted to make a picture of how the guys looked like the girls. And all of this was the hair. I mean, they were only interested in the length of your hair. And it wasn't that long anyway."

Phillip interjected with, "The caption of the picture was, 'The Only Way You Can Tell The Difference Between Rock 'n Roll Boys and Rock 'n Roll Girls Is The Rock 'n Roll Boys Have Longer Hair.'"

Phillip continued with, "In the early days of rock 'n roll, ... we were fighting the current, because people were always asking you what were you going to do when it's over, all those kinds of pressures and fears and I think that all contributed to a lot of the hard times with everybody and a lot of pressure. Don't you think so, Don?" To which Donald replied, "Yeah, well rock 'n roll wasn't respectable at all. I mean, they really wondered if you were outside stealing hubcaps between shows." To which Phillip answered, "And we all did, occasionally!"

Of their first recording, Phillip stated, "T. Tommy Latraire was a disc jockey on WSM, Nashville, in fact we knew him quite well. Webb Pierce also had a version of "Bye Bye, Love" too. Webb heard it on the radio on the way to session, and made him get the record is the way I heard it. It's all hearsay. And T. Tommy heard about it when it was coming out. I've often thought about it and I think that mainly what it really meant was that everybody felt that something had happened, which is more than I knew about it. We were working in Mississippi in a tent show in a shifty kind of a situation show. It wasn't a very good show. And we heard that Webb Pierce had covered "Bye Bye, Love" and we figured that it was all over. He had twenty four number one records in a row and when he covered an act, it was the end. At that time Mel Tillis wasn't famous. Mel had written a lot of Webb's songs. But every time Mel would get a good record out, Webb would cover it and Mel would disappear. And then we told Mel Tillis and Mel said, "well that's it, boys." But it didn't work out that way."

When they first were popular in 1957, they would make numerous appearances on other television programs. They were told right up front, however, that they weren't liked by adults, but adults had to have them on the show because of the kids in the audience. They were treated very rudely, especially on shows such as the Arthur Murray Dance Party, and they thought that Ed Sullivan didn't know what was going on. They do recall, however that Perry Como was the first decent "star" that they met, and he treated them kindly. I'm not surprised. That would be typical of a man like Perry Como. Part of his extreme popularity over the years has come from the kindness he expresses. To this day you can still see it in his face.

They were not alone with their hostility, and perhaps they could have gained some comfort from a humorous quote by J.B. Priestly who stated, "There was no respect for youth when I was young, and now that I am old, there is no respect for age. I missed it coming and going."

On May 10, the Everly Brothers first appeared on the Grand Ole Opry and the audience went wild. They had to encore about four times, which was almost unheard of for that stage. They were invited back the next night and the same thing happened. They felt that at this point in their lives they had really arrived! After a while, they were signed up as regulars which meant they had to appear on the Opry every fourth weekend. This they dutifully did for about two years, until the pace of their bookings and schedules necessitated their dropping out of the Grand Ole Soap Opry. In addition, there was a problem with the Opry people accepting their kind of music. At the time it was not considered country enough, and they more or less agreed that their music was not the same as the other country music being performed on the show, (in particular "Bird Dog") which probably was not the worst thing that could have happened to these two innovative singers. They do, however, to this day still have their original Country Music Association Cards, and renew them annually. Donald's card is Number 11 and Phillip's is Number 12.

They did do a couple of unusual things on the Opry. They were the first act to wear suits, they were not another "hat act," they claim to be the first "county" stars to use drums (played by Buddy Harmon) on the Grand Ole Opry stage, even though it is said that Buddy had to hide his drums behind a bass fiddle. Apparently drums were a no-no up until that point in country music. Loretta Lynn, however, also recently claimed this distinction on the Grand Ole Opry's 64th Anniversary Special in 1989. It's anyone's guess as to who is correct.

In addition to those early appearances, the Everly Brothers were invited to be on The Ed Sullivan Show about five times and this, in the late '50s, meant you had really arrived. The Music Machine was now controlling them entirely. They never had to carry money. If they wanted something they would just charge it, and as Donald explains it, "Number one you were working and earning phenomenal fees. The first year I paid income tax, I probably paid more than my father and grand-father and great-grandfather had earned in their lifetimes." Phillip added, "You really get a distorted value of money." Donald explained it further, "You call up on the phone and you get your meals and liquor sent up and ... you never even see the money. You just live it."

After the phenomenal success of "Bye Bye, Love," the boys were in great demand. According to Stephen Citron, author of *Songwriting: A Complete Guide to the Craft*, at about this time, there was a hard-of-hearing deejay from Cleveland's station WJW by the name of Alan Freed who began playing what was then called "race" music on his daily radio show. He got most of his music from radio stations in Harlem and he had noticed that white teenagers were really going for it. After a while, he renamed this new sound "rock and roll," which at the time was a slang term referring to sex. (Roll was short for jelly-roll which had long been a black term for sexual intercourse.) The sound was typified by a driving beat which worked its audiences into a tizzy. The sound was also as loud as it could be, and the music was interspaced by person-al messages which the teens thought were directed right at them. The anger that the teens felt was addressed, and they went for it all in a big way. Alan Freed went on to become known as the "Father of Rock 'n Roll."

In December of 1957 the Everlys participated in Alan Freed's "Show of Stars Tour," which was basically a two and a half month's bus trip with no days off. Every night they were in a different place. Sometimes they had a hotel room to sleep in for a couple of hours, other times they slept on the bus. Most nights they did two stage shows, and then would return to the bus, travel all night to the next spot and perform again. It was a perpetual travelling show, a perpetual high filled with adrenaline and heaven knows what else. But they were young, and when you are that age, you can handle it. Most of the time it was a lot of laughing and fooling around.

It is interesting to note that when the show went to such places as Chattanooga, Columbus (Georgia), Birmingham, New Orleans and Memphis, the white acts were canceled as it was the law then in the south that blacks and whites were not allowed to appear together on the same stage.

According to the *Rock 'N Roll Encyclopedia*, the South was very anti rock 'n roll at this time and various notices were sent to radio stations and other public places, which tried to keep racism active. One such bulletin proclaimed, "Notice! Stop! Help save the youth of America. Don't buy Negro records. If you don't want to serve Negroes in your place of business, then don't have Negro records on your jukebox or listen to Negro records on the radio. The screaming idiotic words and savage music of these records are undermining the morals of our white youth in America. Call the advertisers of radio stations that play this type of music and complain to them!"

On radio and television, rock 'n roll was also called the Devil's music, and radio and television personalities made it a point to physically break records and throw them in the trash "where they belonged."

Alan Freed also staged a twelve day holiday show at the Paramount Theatre in New York City, called the "Holiday of Stars Twelve Days of Christmas Show." It was put on by WINS radio and the shows were continuous live rock and roll marathons. They consisted of approximately fourteen acts playing in a two hour period of time, back-to-back, playing six or seven shows a day. Most of the acts only had five or ten minutes to perform, and if they did not have their own musicians or if they couldn't play music, Mr. Freed had his own Rock 'n Roll Orchestra to accompany them.

As the story goes, the first night Fats Domino had top billing which apparently upset Jerry Lee Lewis no end, as he considered himself The King of Rock and Roll. He asked Alan Freed to put him at the top, but Freed said no. Jerry Lee apparently thought that he would have to do something about the situation.

The show began with Terry Noland, followed by Lee Andrews, The Hearts, The Twin Tones, Jo Anne Campbell, Paul Anka, and Danny and The Juniors singing "At the Hop." Then Buddy Holly played. Next came the Everly Brothers who sedated the audience with their smooth harmonies. Some in the audience remembered that they looked like twins as they were dressed alike. Young, bright, innocent twins, who seemed to be wishing they were somewhere else instead of on that crazy stage. After the Everlys came Jerry Lee Lewis who dressed outrageously, pounded the piano with his hands, head and feet, ended his "act" standing on top of the piano, and then set the entire thing on fire. All of this started an insane riot. People screamed, girls fainted, and the crowd started running out of the theatre. The entire show had to be stopped for about ten minutes until normalcy returned. After all this, Fats Domino came out, but most of the people had left or were leaving the theatre, and he told Alan Freed later that he would prefer not to follow Jerry Lee Lewis again in the future. Jerry Lee got his top billing, and the next day the marquis was changed to read: Jerry Lee Lewis, Fats Domino, the Everly Brothers and Buddy Holly.

Sadly, Alan Freed was later indicted and accused of various payola schemes. The media harassed him unmercifully, and he died without the public having been made aware of his great contribution to the world of music.

In October of 1963 the Everly Brothers headlined a British tour promoted by Don Arden Enterprises, Ltd. They were supported by some pretty impressive folks, namely Bo Diddley, Julie Grant, Mickie Most, The Flintstones, and an up-and-coming group which called itself The Rolling Stones.

Buddy Holly became a good, close friend of the Everlys, and it was around this time that Phillip took Buddy out and made him buy the thick, black, curved glasses that became his trademark. It was Phillip's idea that since Buddy had to wear glasses anyway, then he should WEAR GLASSES. They also helped Buddy and his band, the Crickets, choose some clothes so they wouldn't look so goofy in New York. The Crickets admitted that they didn't know how to dress, and they let the Everlys guide them. To me it sounds more like the blind leading the blind, because the Everlys at that time were just young country kids, too.

Jerry Allison, Buddy Holly's drummer once said that the girls would come around to get their autographs, but if the Everly Brothers appeared, the girls would throw theirs away and go after the Everlys'.

It must have been quite an artistic feat to go from singing one night at the Paramount Theatre in New York, which featured a fifty-piece orchestra, and then the next night sing on the Grand Ole Opry stage with only four pieces. In addition, one audience was made up of screaming teenagers, while the next night the audience consisted mostly of adults. Although they would perform the same music, they would, of course, receive far different reactions to their performances. In one place rock 'n roll would be accepted and in another place,

47

perhaps even in the same city, it was not accepted and the audience didn't like it at all. Still these two brave young men sang and entertained and gave every audience all that they had to give. The ability to handle themselves well in any venue is what helped make the Everly Brothers the professionals that you see today. Of course show business is hard. That's why it's called show business. If it was easy, it would probably be called show play or show games.

At most shows, usually there were many screaming girls in the audience, but the rest of the audience consisted of adults with their hands over their ears because of the shrieking girls. That's surely called a mixed reaction!

Outside the stage door, another wild show would be staged as hundreds of teenage girls would scream and chase the Everlys. One time in New York Donald was literally jumped on by a mob of girls, and the police stood by, laughing. He was damn near killed, but the police somehow thought it was funny. Also, for years they were unable to wear watches, as they would have been torn off their wrists. Their clothes were torn many times and then identical outfits would have to be made for them. It reminds me a little bit of a story in the book *Richard Burton: A Life* by Melvyn Bragg, when Richard Burton and Elizabeth Taylor went through the same "fan mobbings," Richard once turned to Elizabeth and asked, "Why?!" to which Elizabeth Taylor answered, "Because they're sex maniacs."

They did run into the King of Hysteria - Elvis Presley - once or twice. Phillip remembered it quite well, "The only opportunity I had was in Nashville, backstage at the Ryman Auditorium for the Grand Ole Opry. He was backstage. But wherever he went he caused such a riot that it was a quick handshake and kind of a quick look in the eye. We weren't in the same boat - he was on a steamliner and we were in a rowboat by comparison. Presley was the King and always will be." Although they were not Elvis fans, they did give him the respect he deserved for many things, including the fact that he paved the road and opened some doors for acts that wanted to wear their hair long. Phillip also said, "... having lived an existence similar to Elvis, it's not that fantastic an existence, that fishbowl kind of life. And he even led a tighter one."

Although the kids liked them, the adults did not. Rock 'n rollers were looked down on, and tolerated only because of the big bucks they were bringing in. As Phillip once commented, "We were an abomination to the ear and a blight to the eye." One can't tell what the young Everly Brothers thought of all this, but it had to have terrified them on one or two occasions. I would worry about their mental health if they weren't frightened from time to time. That sort of screaming and clawing of hysterical females would turn me off of women for the rest of my life.

These early days of rock 'n roll were a time of constant fear and uncertainly for all the rock stars. To start with, rock and roll was condemned by everyone over twenty five years of age, and the stars only lasted five years at the most. Every time the Everlys recorded a new single, they were terrified that it wouldn't be a hit, and this could signal the end of their careers. Also the Everlys were one of the first in the rock 'n roll business, so they really had no one to follow, nor anyone to emulate. They had to create their own style, their own mood, their own demands, their own pace and their own standards. It must have been terribly hard for two young boys out on their own, and gradually their careers started taking over their personal lives.

Life on the road was not too glamorous. Sometimes it was terribly difficult for most artists. Patsy Cline described it in Roy Orbison's book, *Dark Star* as "singing in clubs and sleazy

49

joints, travelling on dusty, rutted roads, and staying in motels that have seen better days. It's also signing autographs, doing the very best job you can, and meaning something special to a whole bunch of strangers who suddenly become like family to you."

After a while, according to Donald, they realized that they couldn't stay Number One in the world forever, nor could they physically remain working at such a feverish pitch. They had reached the point where the only way to go was to go down. That's not much to look forward to when you're young and just starting out. What happens to two talented young men when they realize that this must eventually happen?

In the 1960s their popularity waned and Donald was pretty upset about the whole thing. "I was frustrated because Phil and I couldn't seem to be accepted with our music at that point. Music seemed to have to have sort of a hidden meaning. I wanted to hear us on the radio, too. And I said, 'Gee, well we can do that. We can do this, we can do that.' I mean, it just never...I don't think I ever heard a record of ours during the late '60s on the radio."

He also said that they literally tried everything to get back on the charts including going into the recording studio stoned, but even that didn't work.

Phillip had a timetable worked out. "If you were in the business, a very hot act, you'll have about a five year intensity run. And then there's a levelling period. And if ... you've done good work during the five years, you'll be here twenty five years." He was pretty accurate in his estimation.

The funny thing about the Everlys was that they were so shy and "small town" that they really didn't realize for the longest time the financial and creative impacts that they were making in the world.

Some circulating stories imply this. In the beginning they had a lot of car problems and thought they didn't have the money to fix the car, so, as the story goes, one day in Nashville another recording artist walked into Archie Bleyer's office and stated that he had just seen the number one act in the world thumbing a ride! Again, they were too proud to ask anyone for help.

As time passed, tension grew between the two brothers. After all, they had been living, working, and touring together for years, and they began to have a lot of fights backstage. Some were serious and some were just "brotherly," but they could be heard occasionally by fans and associates, and this could hardly be ignored. One obvious reason for the in-fighting was the fact that they were together much too much. No two men should have to spend that much time together, but if you are half of an act, you have no choice. There was also friction because their creative juices clashed at times. Donald would say something like, "I'm not singing that shit" and Phillip would counter with, "I really like it." Something as simple as that can, in itself produce friction. Also, brothers normally fight! That's natural, too! Both of the Everlys went through their own private ups and downs in their professional lives and in their personal lives, and one would blame the other for women or money problems. Much of the time, the Everlys' wives were not getting along either, as they too were competing. The brothers also had separate managers, thus creating more animosity between them. In addition, Donald and Phillip each liked different types of concert halls and performing venues and had different ways of doing things, but when one wanted to do something creative, he only had half a say in whether it was to be done or not.

The press wasn't much help, either. The press constantly compared their looks, sex appeal, singing, guitar playing and their composition skills, as well as who was bigger, brighter, older, better, etc. All of these things had to have some effect on their thinking and their stability. They were well aware by this time that you either eat life or you are eaten.

Often the fighting was just verbal abuse hurled back and forth. After a while it got so that they were screaming insults at each other from one dressing room to the other, and the people working backstage really were at a loss as to what to do about it. The only thing that everyone agreed on was that they should be kept separated at all costs.

Once as the story goes, a sound engineer was half listening to them singing in the recording booth, when he heard a thump, it suddenly became quiet and there was only one Everly standing there. Apparently Phillip had gotten angry at Donald for something, had just punched him out, and Donald was flat on the floor. But incidents such as these were pretty rare.

Everly-type people are creative people, and creativity is not measured with the same kind of yardstick as intelligence. In fact, standard intelligence tests often fail to recognize creative people. They are really in a class by themselves. Usually they are self-confident and highly motivated towards success. They are committed to their creative work, and can work long hours without breaks or vacations, because their creativity is what they live for and they would rather be doing that than anything else in the world. Other than being highly independent, creative people sometimes tend not to place too much importance on pleasing others. They are often termed "crazier" than the rest of the world and at times they are identified as "living close to the edge of insanity." Singer James Brown summed up 'the business' this way: "It's designed for you not to make it. And if you make it, it's designed for you not to keep it." Such pressure is bound to cause an explosion sooner or later. I am personally very surprised that the Everly Brothers stayed together as long as they did.

Donald has minimized all the brouhaha by saying, "We're brothers. We've been working together all our lives and, although we argue plenty, we need each other."

Oh yes, they were good, but as Garrison Keillor once mentioned to a member of the Associated Press, "The worst possible thing is when all your dreams come true."

Phillip definitely summed it all up by saying once that if there had ever been an Olympic Singing Event, he and Donald would have won a gold medal.

Throughout all of this, the brothers continued to sing on stage as if they were angels. Sometimes in our lives there are rare moments that allow us to escape our earthly shells. Things like a sight of incredible beauty, the ultimate moments of making love or sometimes that magical note of music. I thank the Everly Brothers for many moments such as these; moments which lift you, however briefly, from this earth.

THE MARINE CORPS RESERVE

On November 25, 1961 Donald and Phillip joined the Marine Corps Reserve. They were twenty three and twenty five years old at the time, and it was either enlist in the Reserves or be drafted. Since they were at the pinnacle of their careers, they thought it intelligent to join the Reserves, so off they went to Camp Pendleton in San Diego, California.

Active reserve training at Camp Pendleton lasted six months, and the Marine Corps routines were difficult. Fortunately life on the road had also been difficult, and that rigorous regimen helped them get through the Marine Corps training. Also, since they had to report for duty annually for the next six years, it was always in the back of their minds that they would have to keep in shape and stay healthy, or they would have to practically whip themselves into shape annually.

An attorney friend of ours, Lansing Roy, was in boot camp with the Everlys. Even though he was in a class one week ahead of theirs, he remembers them well. Although the latrine story cannot be repeated, he did state that both men were extremely popular with all of the men at camp, and that they had their Hollywood friends join them in giving a fantastic outdoor concert at the base.

On February 13, 1962 their active tour of duty ended. Phillip graduated as a Private First Class and Donald as a Squad Leader. That very same day Donald married actress Venetia Stevenson with Phillip (of course) serving as best man. Five days later on February 18, the two brothers appeared on the Ed Sullivan Show in Miami, where they sang "Crying In The Rain."

For eight months, they produced many hit records and LPs, toured hard and made many personal appearances on radio, television and stage. Then in October, Donald finally succumbed to the drugs that were keeping him going at such a frantic pace. Donald's "drug overdose" should have killed him, but even today he thanks the Marine Corps and their rigorous routine for saving his life. He contends that without that gruelling training he was put through, his body would not have been strong enough to fight the drug battle and stay alive. God bless the United States Marine Corps!

THE DOWNWARD SPIRAL

After you have been on top for so long, there is nowhere to go but down. The Everlys' records were not being played over the radio, and their personal appearances were becoming quite scarce. They tried everything to get back on top, but the going was rough.

There were many, many reasons for this downward trend. In the first place, their required stint in the U.S. Marine Corps put a damper on their swirling upward progress. During this short six month span also, Donald got a divorce and was getting ready to marry again, and Phillip was preparing to marry, also. While they were ensconced in boot camp, they were virtually out of the public eye and in the music business, it's really out of sight, out of mind. Audiences are extremely fickle and forget very quickly.

In addition, Donald's battles with drugs virtually stopped most of their momentum, because they were only performing off and on for about three years. Although he was really "out of it" for only four months or so, he was actually affected by drugs for a very long time. This, in turn, affected his personal and professional life as well as his brother's, who was fighting his own less difficult battle with drugs. Also with both of the brothers married, the wives reportedly got into the fray from time to time and stirred up some fires that had been smoldering under the ashes for a long, long time.

The biggest influence of all, however, was the British Invasion. When the Beatles hit America, the world knew pop music would never be the same. "The British Invasion," says Phillip, "had to do with the inability of Americans to accept their own music. We Americans have always had this inferiority complex about the British. Their accents made us think they're more cultured, so when they came along everybody was so overwhelmed that they started ignoring American artists, which I always resented." Phillip continued, "It's just the eventual flux of things. You lose your newness, and people at that time were just so busy being psychedelic. Also the rock press, which was born in the sixties, wasn't interested in yesterday's performers.

They all wanted to show how up to date they were, which is all bullshit anyway."

The truth is that they just weren't sexy enough. Elvis was sexy, the Beatles were adorable, but the Everlys were just great singers. I remember it well.

There was no relief after the British Invasion, either. The disco phase hit and this was no time for romantic love ballads. It seems that music had really taken a turn for the worse.

With all of this going on all at once, it is nothing short of a miracle that the Everly Brothers hung on as long and as tenaciously as they did. It is this tenacity that we now can look back on and recognize for the force that it is. The feelings of betrayal though, have stayed, contributing to the resentment they feel today.

5
THE CRASH

"Out of suffering have emerged the strongest souls."
- Edwin Hubbel Chapin

The Everly Brothers had been performing at a frantic pace for years; the craziness finally began to take its toll. No matter how young and energetic you are, you just can't go on forever, and in the entertainment business, enough is never enough. The bigger you get, the more people there are who get higher and higher cuts of the money you're making. Everyone wants a ride on the fabulous music-go-round. This lifestyle was accurately summed up once by the great Louis Armstrong who said, "You don't have no fun at all, you know, if you get too famous."

Also the bigger an act gets, the more hangers-on there are, the more food, liquor, women, drugs, airline tickets, bus miles, hotel rooms, etc. Sometimes getting "bigger" doesn't necessarily mean you are getting richer, as the expenses can kill you. Many times you could find yourself singing for free. And some of the really big acts of today have to support not only managers, but assistants to these managers, bodyguards, book-keepers, valets, chauffeurs, etc. All of this gobbles up the profits. Then there are always those who want to "travel with the band." They think it's great fun and games, wild and a wonderful vacation. These people must really be in the way, because the bottom line is that "the band" is a working group of professional artists who are literally killing themselves out there every night. They are not playing games.

In addition, it becomes harder and harder for a performer to live up the public's image of him. Those public images sometimes become further and further from the truth, until one can't hide any more.

The Everlys each weighed about one hundred and fifty pounds when they were at their peaks, a little thin for their heights of five foot nine and ten perhaps, but all right for young men working at the top. After years of grueling work, staying on top became more and more of a challenge however, and they couldn't maintain their energy levels at the necessary plateaus. As they were touring, recording and performing regularly, they had too many commitments made on them, they had too much responsibility heaped on their young shoulders, and there were just too many people making too much money off of them. At this point they should have taken a long rest, but of course that was impossible. In this business, if you neglect your audience even for a short period of time, they are quick to forget.

Coupled with all this, there were some Wesley Rose lawsuits, Donald was in the middle of a divorce, and they joined the U.S. Marine Corps Reserves. According to Phillip, Donald as the older brother, seemed to take the brunt of everything and forged ahead carrying the heaviest part of the load. As most older brothers do, they sometimes feel a natural responsibility for their younger siblings, and an attitude such as this can last a lifetime. There must have been many times when Donald felt he had enough responsibility just to survive himself, without the added burden of a "kid" brother to worry about, also.

In order to keep going for long hours on end, the Everlys started to see Dr. Max Jacobsen, a Jewish refugee from Hitler's Germany, also known as the "celebrity doctor" who had offices on East 72nd Street in New York. Among various celebrities he was known as "Dr. Miracle," "Dr. Needles," "Dr. Feelgood," or just plain Max, and he was personal physician to many famous people, up to and including President John F. Kennedy and First Lady Jacqueline Kennedy. The President was in constant pain from his back injuries and needed something to keep him going strong. Reportedly, the President even took Dr. Jacobsen with him to the summit meeting he had in 1961 in Vienna with Nikita Kruschev.

Although it's not known exactly what the Everly Brothers' treatments consisted of, no one was given the same concoction, as the doctor experimented continuously on his patients who he considered to be no more than laboratory rats, but the Everly Brothers were told that their treatment was Ritalin Therapy and that it was harmless. Dr. Jacobsen said his "Magic Elixir" contained only vitamins and minerals. The good doctor's infamous formulas, which were intramuscularly injected by hypodermic needle either in the arm or buttocks, included various personalized combinations of ingredients such as: amphetamines, (methamphetamine in particular), or dextromethamphetamine, riboflavin, placenta, bone, liver cells, vitamin B2, vitamin B12, celestone, procaine, silicone, steroids, hormones such as testosterone, some antibiotics, enzymes, purified water, and various animal organ cells. Calcium was added at the last minute as a buffer, and it was the calcium that was responsible for the initial immediate hot flash throughout the entire body. The "meth" gave out the incredible energy. About twenty minutes after such an injection, the patient can go strong for the next seventy two hours or so without stopping. The recipient feels terrific! In addition, there was an almost total loss of appetite and sometimes slight tremors of the hands, but most entertainers were used to not having enough time to eat, so this was considered a benefit, and the tremors were hardly noticeable. What was not explained, however, was the fact that when the drug wore off, there was a horrible letdown. Truman Capote likened the experience to falling down a well, 72 hours after the "instant euphoria." The patients would soon have to get another injection in order to continue the hectic paces that they were subjected to. The actual label for this medicine, of course, is "speed," and those who become addicted to these frequent dosages are now commonly referred to as "speed freaks."

As reported in C. David Heymann's biography called *A Woman Named Jackie*, one of Dr. Jacobsen's nurses, Ruth Mosse, thought he was an absolute quack, totally off the wall, and wondered why so many people were willing to be treated by him. She assumed people believed in him the same way that some fanatics believe in religion.

Max Jacobsen was a macabre looking, barrel chested man who wore thick horned rimmed glasses, had dark hair and a deep voice with a heavy German accent. His fingernails were dirty and stained from chemicals. Somehow, people said he could be charming and very funny. At any rate, you either hated him or loved him. Mike Todd hated him, and Eddie Fisher loved him, at least for a while.

In addition to reportedly having an insatiable desire for women, Dr. Jacobsen also took his own drugs, and was frequently drowsy, slovenly and his speech was slurred. He was able to sleep anywhere at any time, and as a matter of fact sometimes he would go to sleep in the middle of administering an injection. He didn't care about his appearance or what came out of his mouth. His suits were almost always dirty and rumpled, and his pockets were usually filled to overflowing with needles and vials. He always had his black "miracle" bag with him. His offices were a complete disaster, with bottles all over, and his trash overflowed onto the floor. Cleanliness had been completely forgotten. His lab procedures were haphazard at best, and he kept few medical records. Because of his dealings with his patients who were some of the richest people on earth, he had an income of about $500,000 a year, but he spent most of it on chemicals, drugs and his various lab experiments. Later on he became involved in complicated experiments dealing with rejuvenation. As the years progressed, he became more and more tyrannical and erratic in his own behavior, and he, like many of his patients, had wide mood swings. He would be charming and entertaining one minute and the next he could be cruel and abusive. The man was, in short, a monster, but a monster who had the ability to handle the neurotic insecurities of show business personalities.

Why did people go to him? It was accepted practice at that time to get "medication" from a doctor as long as he was a legitimate physician, which Dr. Jacobsen was, although he was not known to be accredited by any hospital. Also, it was easy to argue the fact that if the President of the United States went to him, then there must be nothing wrong with him. The sad truth is that at that time, there was nothing illegal about the doctor's drug administrations.

Not only were the Everly Brothers taking Dr. Jacobsen's treatments, but reportedly so were other notables, including Judy Garland, Winston Churchill, Prince Radziwill (Jacqueline Kennedy's brother-in-law), Mark Shaw, Cecil B. DeMille, Kurt Frings, (Elizabeth Taylor's agent), Zero Mostel, Tennessee Williams, Milton Blackstone, Anthony Quinn, Margaret Leighton, Johnny Mathis, Andy Williams, Truman Capote and Alan Jay Lerner.

In 1972 The New York Times did an expose of Max Jacobsen, the Federal Drug Administration began investigating him in earnest, and on April 25, 1975, his medical license to practice was revoked, due to "unprofessional conduct." He died in 1978.

One of the cruelest stories was that of singer Eddie Fisher who for years would not go out on a stage without a shot from Dr. Jacobsen. By 1968 his "injections" had turned him into a hopeless addict, with uppers in the morning and downers at night. In 1972 he was declared bankrupt in Federal Court in San Juan, Puerto Rico. Reportedly, his debts totalled one million dollars. What a horrible thing to happen to someone who had earned over $20 million during his lucrative career.

The press wasn't much help to Mr. Fisher either, as they openly reported an on-stage battle he had with Buddy Hackett. As Mr. Fisher stated in his biography, he apparently publicly returned a "present" Buddy had given him one night for his forty-eighth birthday, a watch with the inscription, "Dear Eddie: Fuck you on your birthday. Hate, Buddy Hackett." The press forgot to mention what the watch had said, and concentrated only on Eddie's public words with Buddy on stage.

One of Eddie's former wives, Debbie Reynolds, despised Dr. Jacobsen, called him "Dr. Needles" and referred quite negatively to him in her biography, *Debbie: My Life*, as a "ruiner of lives." She stated that she would not let him so much as touch her, and she always wondered why a healthy young man of twenty six needed to have "vitamins" injected into him every time he performed.

On the positive side, if there is one, the drugs at first produce wonderful energy, self confidence, great singing voices, loss of pain, weight loss for those who need it; in short, a life that is on the edge and speeded up. Thinking and ideas and movements are all profound and brilliant, or so you think. You are being fooled, of course. Prolonged use of this therapy produces memory loss, insomnia, hallucinations, shaking, unpredictability, depression, slurred speech and paranoia, all of which affected Donald Everly. Many people become short tempered and abusive to their families and friends, and rude and critical to their audiences and fellow co-workers. Something to be kept in mind, however, is that the injections for different people contained different ingredients, and different people were affected in different ways. Phillip somehow endured his treatments with less ill effect, and managed to kick his habit successfully, even though he went through several bouts of severe depression. After a while, it seems the ups and downs start spiraling downward, as it is harder and harder to achieve the ups and the downs become deeper and longer. In short, you lose control.

While under the influence of drugs, the two brothers were at each other's throats constantly. It was a confusing, maddening (and totally mad) period in their lives.

On October 13, 1962, while on tour in London, Donald overdosed on barbiturates and was wished off to Charing Cross Hospital where they pumped his stomach and released him, stating it was nothing more than acute food poisoning. He returned to his room at the Savoy, but tried it again by gulping down more pills. He was then rushed by ambulance to Middlesex Hospital where the diagnosis finally stated: "Don Everly - Drug Overdose." Reportedly at the time he was so high he didn't care if he lived or died.

When Donald and his wife Venetia flew back to America on October 15, 1962, Donald was committed to the mental ward of a New York hospital for a "nervous breakdown." He was exhausted, depressed, and suffered from hallucinations and insomnia. He was given electroshock treatments but later he adamantly denied it was a "nervous breakdown." On his way to the airport heading back to America, when questioned by the press, all he said was, "I don't feel good. I wanna' go home." Not only didn't he feel good, he didn't look too hot, either as evidenced by a photograph snapped of him and published in The London Daily Express. Donald by this time had lost twenty pounds, bringing his weight down to a low of only one hundred and thirty pounds. Donald Everly was a very sick young man.

In a *Playboy* interview, Donald remembered the shock treatments. "They say shock therapy is good for some things, but it didn't do me any good. It was a pretty primitive treatment at the time - once they gave it to you, you couldn't remember how long you'd been there. It knocked me back for a long time. I thought I'd never write again."

When questioned by a European radio station about whether his collapse was a nervous breakdown or whether he was hooked on speed, Donald replied, "No, no. I'd rather be hooked on speed than have a nervous breakdown. At least there's a reason. I legitimately went to a doctor. It wasn't like I had to go to back alleys."

Phillip was forced to perform alone for the rest of the tour, which was something he had never done before in his life. He did an admirable job, although he was extremely worried about Donald and mentioned him frequently during the shows. One British journalist, however, criticized him for his frequent "sickening references" to his brother. Unfortunately some people have no empathy when others are in pain. Phillip described his lone voice as "a little voice in a big barrel," and he continued the entire tour solo, meeting with good reception and appreciative audiences throughout.

As Donald recalled in an interview at the Amsterdam Hilton in 1971, "I didn't kick speed for three years after that. It's very difficult. Yes, I did. I kicked it. If anybody says it can't be done, they're wrong. It can be done. You can do it." He also added, "I don't think the drugs have that much to do with the pop scene. Not as much as people would like to think that it does. I don't think that you have to be a drugger to be in the pop music field."

It did take about three years to conquer the drug problem, but Donald did it. I admire him for that, for so many don't make it. *Playboy* reported, however, that a later album entitled *Don Everly* was recorded after the close of the 1970 Johnny Cash Presents The Everly Brothers Summer Replacement Show. The article stated that the LP was recorded "with the assistance of much booze and reefer." In addition, Donald openly admitted in the 1970s that he had smoked pot and took LSD ("Owsley's orange sunshine," he called it), during a period in the early 1960s when he was running around New York with the likes of Jimi Hendrix (a left handed guitar player who played a right handed guitar upside down) and Joni Mitchell.

The name "Owsley" referred to an amateur chemist in the Bay Area of California whose real name was Augustus Owsley Stanley III. He could mix up a dazzling array of high-quality hallucinogens which were given to his friends and acquaintances. This was a strange life to be leading when all the songs the Everlys sang on stage were innocently done wearing suits. Looks can be deceiving.

All of this must have been extremely difficult for Venetia, because in 1963 she sued for divorce. They reconciled later, but the rest of their marriage must have been pretty rocky. Their final divorce decree was granted eight years and three children later, on January 14, 1971.

In 1974 Phillip stated to The Daily Express, "Maybe one reason I never collapsed is because I'm not sensitive enough. I'm a survivor." I see him as a survivor, all right, but certainly not insensitive.

6
THE
UNCOUPLING

"The greater the feeling of inferiority that has been experienced, the more powerful is the urge to conquest and the more violent the emotional agitation."
- Alfred Adler

On July 12, 1973, Donald and Phillip were scheduled to do their last performance together at Knott's Berry Farm in Buena Park, California. At times labelled "The Bickersons," it was obvious that they had not been getting along for years. They had had entirely too much togetherness and both men needed room to breathe and grow as individuals. As Donald stated in a May 3, 1977 Detroit Free Press interview, "It was all getting weird toward the end. Very weird. Phil and I had separate everything - managers, lawyers, agents, dressing rooms, cars, everything. We'd even stay in different hotels. Offstage, we hardly spoke to each other."

Donald further explained, "When we did split up, we'd been working twenty five or thirty years already. I haven't even counted them up, but we've been in show business since we were very young. Phil and I, I was seven (when) we really started working at it and Phil was five and a half. And so when we split up we needed some time to really basically find out who we were as individuals and I think it's wonderful. I mean, it's crazy and everything but it's still an experience. Because it's not really, I don't think it's normal to spend your life completely that close actually. And we were close. I mean, we survived four marriages, and we needed the time alone."

Bill Hollingshead, former Entertainment Director of the John Wayne Theatre at Knott's Berry farm, remembers the kind of relationship they had during that period.

"They arrived in separate cars, had separate personal managers and requested separate dressing rooms. If the show was 6:00 or 7:00 they both would open their doors and one would go out first and he would go to the edge of the stage and the other would follow behind a few minutes later and then when there came the announcement, they would both walk out."

During the 1973 gig, the Everly Brothers were booked for a six day run, Monday through Saturday, and there were three scheduled thirty minute daily shows, one at 6:30, one at 8:30 and one at 10:30. By mid-week Donald had casually mentioned to Bill Hollingshead, "By the way, this is our last engagement. We're breaking up after this week is over." Mr. Hollingshead also casually replied, "Oh, well that's sort of historical. Can I call someone and make mention of that and get an article in the paper?" Donald agreed, so Robert Hilburn, the entertainment critic from The Los Angeles Times was notified that this was basically the end of the Everly Brothers as we know them. As a result, fans and friends travelled from far and wide to see them. What the audience saw was a show, alright. It certainly was not the one they expected, however. The show they saw was far from pleasant.

As usual, the Everlys arrived separately, but Donald apparently had had a few Margaritas on an empty stomach. He felt he had been drinking because he was quite distressed about the impending breakup with his brother. He has since stated that it was the only time in his career that he had ever had anything to drink before a show, and I believe him. One cannot adhere to a touring schedule such as they have and drink before shows. It just isn't done. Now AFTER the show is another story.

During the first show it was obvious that Donald was not singing in his usual manner. Mr. Hollingshead stated that "when he has a little bit to drink, he sings about one-eighth to one-quarter tone flat." His timing was also off, and he forgot the lyrics and names of people, and he kept saying nutty and insulting things to the audience like, "I don't even know why you're in here, you ought to be over there riding the burro ride." The audience was getting restless, embarrassed, ill at ease, and they started gradually getting up and leaving, literally walking out on the Everly Brothers! Phillip was obviously in agony, but didn't know what to do or how to end the fiasco and exit the stage. They had finally gotten through five of their scheduled ten songs. Ironically, their sixth song was to be "So Sad (To Watch Good Love Go Bad)."

Mr. Bill Hollingshead is a sharp professional, President of Bill Hollingshead Productions, Inc. in Santa Ana, California. He said of himself, "I'm a commodities dealer. I don't worry about what goes on backstage." He soon realized, however, that they had an emergency situation happening out there on the stage. He was in "the tunnel" at the theatre, with Tom (T.J.) Johnson, the stage manager, and said, "I'm going to pull the plug on this. This is awful." They decided to end the show by starting the fountains, which dump 22,000 gallons of water into a trough, thus signaling the end of the show. Since the water begins to flow after a thirty second delay, they waited until the Everlys were just finishing up a song, and then one of them went out and loudly announced, "THERE THEY ARE, LADIES AND GENTLEMEN, LET'S HEAR IT FOR THE EVERLY BROTHERS! THE EVERLY BROTHERS, LADIES AND GENTLEMEN. HOW ABOUT THAT, FOLKS! THE EVERLY BROTHERS! Phillip understood immediately what was going on, and he was off that stage as fast as his legs could take him. He was so furious, he walked off the stage in a fit of rage and frustration, and then smashed his $1,200 black Everly Brothers Gibson guitar on the edge of the stage. (The latest price I've been quoted for this guitar was $4,800!) Later reports said that he smashed his guitar over his brother's head, which sounds far more dramatic and exciting, but that wasn't true at all.

According to Mr. Hollingshead, after Phillip stormed off, he stated most emphatically, "I will never go back on the stage again with that man." He didn't refer to him by his first name or as his brother, just "that man." Later on in his dressing room, Phillip said to Mr. Hollingshead, "Bill, I gotta' go. I just can't stay." To which Mr. Hollingshead replied, "Phil, we've got two more shows!" And Phillip answered, "You don't understand. I've got to leave. This is it. It's over." He then promptly packed up his things and left the building with his wife, Patricia. He was not to sing with his brother again for ten long years.

Donald in the meantime for some strange reason, thought he was doing a terrific job and was still out there bowing, apparently oblivious to the audience's reaction. Maybe he wasn't leaving, but they sure were!

After Donald finally realized what had taken place and had left the stage, he apologized to Mr. Hollingshead. Bill Hollingshead said, "Well, what the heck are we going to do? You know, we have two thousand people lined up there for the second show." Donald replied, "Well, I'll go on by myself."

It was obvious at this point that Donald had to sober up. Karen Prettyman, who was his girlfriend at the time, said that he hadn't had anything to eat all day and if they could just get some food into him, he'd be OK in about thirty minutes. The scenario seem familiar to her. So they all rushed out to Mrs. Knott's Chicken Dinner Restaurant (which has been in existence since 1934) and brought back some chicken, mashed potatoes and vegetables. Donald ate his entire dinner.

After the recent events of the evening, who could blame Mr. Hollingshead for insisting, "I'm not putting anything on that stage unless I audition it." So he sat there all alone in the front row of a 2,000 seat theatre, and auditioned Donald Everly. It must have been a long time since that had happened!

About 7:30 that evening, Robert Hilburn from The Los Angeles Times called up and innocently asked, "Well, how are things going?" The conversation progressed as follows according to Bill Hollingshead:

Bill: Do you want the second scoop on the Everlys?

Robert: My God, what is that?

Bill: They broke up in the middle of the stage.

Robert: What are you going to do?

Bill: Well, we are premiering The Don Everly Show.

Robert: Oh, my God! I'll be over to review the 10:30 show!

Mr. Hollingshead and Mr. Jim Enos, the Operations Manager, were in direct radio contact that evening. Bill called Jim and said, "Jim, get all of your people together and change the show to The Don Everly Show." Jim shouted, "What?!!!"

The marquee was quickly changed to read "The Don Everly Show," and Donald came back and completed two shows without his brother. Although the show completely lacked all the usual songs the Everly Brothers sang together, those who saw it say that it was surprisingly good under the circumstances. Mr. Hollingshead's personal opinion was that it was just OK. It's truly amazing that Donald was able to pull himself together and give the audience a good night's entertainment. I really have to give him a lot of credit.

Later on, Bill Hollingshead received a very apologetic note from Donald, with pain between every line. Mr. Hollingshead, too, remembers the incident with a lot of pain, as he reflected, "Yes, I was the main person in the evening of the breakup, and I will remember every detail for many years."

A drunken scenario is a performer's worst nightmare, and it happened to the Everlys only once during their forty years of entertaining. Actually I hate to even bring it up, but it goes with the territory of being the Everly Brothers, and should be kept in perspective. My point is that since this is probably the only time they embarrassed themselves in such a long period of performance time, I think that these road warriors should be given a great deal of credit. One unfortunate night out of about one hundred performances a year for close to forty years ain't bad, folks. It ain't bad at all.

Unfortunately the main thing that people seem to always remember about these two men is "The Breakup." After all that they have done since 1974, let's forget this one night and concentrate on the hundreds of other magical evenings that these two singers have given to the world. They're surely not the first or the last to make mistakes or to be embarrassed in front of others. The Practically Perfect People can criticize and smirk all they want, but those people are usually dull and boring in the first place.

Donald and Phillip also think it is a shame that they are so famous for their split, because they have really been closer and together longer than any brothers they can think of. Phillip also knows that in order to sing harmony like he does, one almost has to climb inside the other person. He once said that harmony is the ultimate in love.

Donald also stressed the need for both of them to have those years apart, and that actually it wasn't a bad thing after all. Five of the years were pretty good and the other five weren't so bad. It gave them time to mature and develop as individuals. It didn't kill them and they didn't wind up with any brain damage, so what was the big deal? He also insisted that they didn't break up; he left. Well, that's debatable, but the point is that they both just needed to have the whole stifling togetherness of it all to be over.

In the July 16, 1973 edition of The Los Angeles Times Donald said, "After eight to nine months a year, for twenty years, travelling together, being big worldwide for years, there was too much pressure with being such a successful duet - such close harmony, nose to nose on stage every night - it's got to put a strain on the relationship. We needed a rest. And I had never lived an 'ordinary' life before."

Donald continued, "I can't tell you why or tell you what changed it, but I think that time takes care of things. We'd been working together for twenty five years already before we quit. And here we were two guys singing six inches apart into one microphone, living in the same room on the road, and survivors of three marriages, numerous other tragedies and good and bad times. I just think we needed a rest away from each other. We needed a life of our own."

The true sadness of the situation was stated by Donald in an interview by Kurt Loder in *Rolling Stone Magazine*, wherein he summed it up as follows: "People thought that night was just some brouhaha between Phil and me. They didn't realize we had been working our buns off for years. We had never been anywhere without working; had never known any freedom. We were just strapped together like a team of horses."

At another time he said, "When folks mention the feud I ask them how often they see their brothers. They usually reply 'Once a year, if that.' Try and figure out what it's like spending forty years with your brother, day in and day out, with guys sticking cameras in your faces wanting photos of you practically kissing each other."

The women who were around them at that time adamantly declared that the Everlys had hated the very sight of each other for about ten years, so it was not a surprise at all to anyone. Their mother Margaret Everly, on the other hand, blamed it on "women and managers."

Phillip was convinced that their type of lifestyle was sort of normal and defended it by saying that they did what people normally would do when you go away to college at the age of eighteen, but that they went on the road instead when he was eighteen. "You were singing on one mike, you were staying in one room together. It's been a long time - you can figure that out. One toothbrush, one everything, one bicycle. I saw the Smothers Brothers the other night on TV. They weren't getting along either!"

Once when he was being (a bit unfairly) criticized in the British press, Donald shot back with, "Well, there's gonna' be problems, but that happens constantly in families. Even the Royal Family I think has had problems over the years, haven't they? People always say (things) about my family. I turn to them and say, 'What's your family like? What about your brothers, your sisters?` and everybody has problems in their family." Phillip wondered what the big deal was, too.

Donald thinks they did more together than any other brothers. "Phil and I have probably spent more time together as far as brothers go and, maybe the Mills Brothers could top us, but very few people could say that they spent more time with their brother than me."

Phillip remembers it all well, as reported by *Playboy*, "It was an awfully big factory to close down. It took a lot of balls, and Donald's got them. I think I'm a little less serious than

Donald. He was always kind of out front, having to do the heavy lifting."

In case anyone thinks this existence is a simple one, they should watch the film, The Fabulous Baker Boys a couple of times, to gain some added insight. This terrific movie touches on many of the tiny details which make up a working/sibling/professional relationship and the more one views this film, the more one feels the multitude of emotions which the two men in the film harbor. It is made even more interesting because of the fact that the two actors, Jeff and Beau Bridges are brothers in real life, and in order to make the film, they had to live and work together.

Former child actor/photographer Roddy McDowall agrees that there are big problems with being too successful, and said, "I've always found it much harder to survive success than to achieve it." Perhaps the Everlys would tend to agree.

7
THE SOLO
YEARS

"Let there be spaces in your togetherness."
- Kahlil Gibran

After the Knott's Berry Farm Spectacular in 1973, the Everly Brothers did not see or speak to each other for ten long years. The only time they crossed paths was at their father's funeral in October of 1975, where they both admitted that they "didn't exactly hang out together."

In retrospect, one can easily see that they needed this hiatus from each other. The claustrophobic atmosphere which they had existed in was finally broken and a sense of well earned freedom enveloped both brothers. Phillip likened it a bit to "getting out of school" and Donald said that it was the first time in his life he had been free to do just what he alone wanted to do. It was all new to both of them and for a couple of years they really didn't know what to do with themselves and all their "independent time."

For starters, Donald and Karen left California and set up housekeeping in Nashville. It took Donald a couple of years to get the "California" out of his system and become "just folks" like Nashville seems to make one. Phillip loved California and enjoyed that lifestyle. He stayed in his North Hollywood house, swam in his pool, tended his garden, and helped raise his two sons, as well as his nieces and his nephew who all lived nearby.

At this point in their lives, Phillip had two sons, Jason and Christopher, and Donald was the father of three daughters, Venetia, Stacy and Erin, and a son, Edan.

As both of their recording contracts were eventually canceled, Donald re-acquainted himself with his Nashville friends and did a bit of backup singing for some other groups, as well as spending a lot of time fishing in Florida and just "hanging out."

Ever so gradually, Phillip started composing a few songs, and began to get together with friends who wrote and sang. In 1975 he began recording his solo albums, which were entitled, *Living Alone, Phil Everly, Star Spangled Springer, Phil's Diner* and *Mystic Line.*

Donald also was composing, and one of the first songs he worked on was "Asleep" which he insisted would never be sung unless it was sung as a duet by Phillip and himself. I think he assumed this "hiatus" would only last a short while. I think everyone did. No one thought it would go on for ten long years, but it did.

Donald got together a bunch of associates and formed his own band called "The Dead Cowboys," and they performed a few times at The Sutler, a restaurant/bar on Franklin Road in Nashville, which brags about its great hamburgers. The man who has owned The Sutler since 1976, Johnny Potts, had known Donald since before he decided to try out his new band, but he told me he has not seen him for years, except for an occasional path crossing in various restaurants around Nashville. Mr. Potts described Donald as a very strong per-sonality who is able to talk about a variety of subjects, as opposed to some musicians who can only talk about music. Mr. Potts said that their three or four appearances packed the house (of course) and it was a happy time, mixed with a lot of personal therapy for Donald. Donald, wearing his jeans extremely well, and the band had accumulated a fan following of their own who called themselves "The Dead Buckeroos." Those perfor-mances at The Sutler were casual, gratifying and successful. So successful, in fact, that in 1980 the band set out to tour England. This tour was also a big success. Members of the Dead Cowboys included Philip Donnelly on lead guitar, Rachel Peer on bass, Tony Newman on drums, and Lamar Hill on key-boards.

Rachael Peer also sang harmony with Donald and she did a superb job. According to Mr. Potts, Rachel used to be married to singer/songwriter John Prine, but they are now divorced.

Phillip on the other hand, decided to perform a bit on his own, and after a while did a few informal appearances at the Palomino Club which was very close to his home in North Hollywood. The general idea was to try some of his newly created songs out on an audience, which is the only true test of a song there is. An audience cannot be fooled, and if their reactions are carefully observed, small changes can be made and the song can become finalized.

Phillip had a lot of fun at this local club, and he often would bring all of the Everly kids up on stage, along with some of the musicians' kids. I have heard him introduce Erin as his niece saying, "This is Donald's girl" which must be the way they say it in Kentucky. In addition, cousins Jason and Edan Everly would sometimes play together, which seemed so natural. After all, they were Everly boys, and when Everly boys get together, they play guitars. Both Jason and Edan are very accomplished guitar players, and Phillip has said that his oldest boy played quite a lot and he thought that Jason was pretty darn good, maybe even better than Phillip himself. Edan, however, is the only Everly who has taken music up professionally. Although he can sing, he doesn't particularly want to, preferring to just play. In 1989 and in 1990 Edan joined his father and his uncle on stage when their tour got to California, playing lead guitar on "Be-Bop-A-Lula." The fact that the two cousins have played together gets little attention from their fathers however, and as far as Jason and Edan becoming the "New Everlys," Donald squashed that idea with, "There's a second generation. Our father was really the original Everly Brothers, our father, Chuck and Leonard, his two brothers. There was three of them. So we're actually second generation ourselves." Phillip ended the discussion with, "There's two of us already, you know?" I guess the kids don't get the spotlight, at least for a while.

Throughout this solo period, both men travelled all over the United States and Europe doing interviews and participating in various shows. They kept their hands on the pulse of the music industry, for it was all they ever knew. Donald in particular spent a lot of time in England.

Phillip let a lot of his yearning for normalcy show when he said, "I basically stayed home. I guess you could either call me lazy or semi-retired. I just sort of took life easy. And I have children and I just watched them grow up and did all the good things. The things that people take for granted that from all the years on the road that we had been travelling so much that we had kind of missed."

A close associate thought that Phillip could either take it or leave it (the business) but if Donald was ever deprived of his music, he would be like a tiger trapped in a cage.

Both of them could easily make it as solo artists, but the public has it in its mind that they are the Everly Brothers, and so refuse to believe they can go it alone. Once on the first segment of The Johnny Cash Presents The Everly Brothers Summer Replacement Show, Phillip demonstrated his unique solo style with a song entitled, "The Last Thing On My Mind," which was sung without much backup instrumentation, just a string or two, and was simply gorgeous as sung by Phillip. Not only that, towards the end - in front of millions of viewers - the man broke down and cried throughout the end of the song. I don't know about anyone else, but it almost tore my heart out. The audience response, of course, was thunderous.

Musician Warren Zevon, in reflecting on his experiences while working with the Everly Brothers told Michael Donahue of The Hawk Eye, "They always sang the same which was as well as they could, which was incredibly good. They didn't get along with each other, and that was real understandable. And I stopped feeling bad about not having made it before I was twenty, from seeing that you don't really have anywhere to go. The saddest part is that individually they still sing better than anyone else...the other great but sad part is that they're the kind of guys who would do the set and then go back to their rooms and play their guitars all night."

8
FAILURES

"Our greatest glory consists not in never failing, but in rising every time we fail."
- Oliver Goldsmith

The only people who succeed a lot are those who fail a lot. Everyone knows that someone who sits on his ass doing nothing all of his life never fails. Hell, they've never tried!

So it is to the credit of the Everly Brothers that they have had a few failures and dreams that didn't come true. Hopes and wishes surface throughout their lives, and I just want to touch on a couple of them. My point is not to gloat, but to sympathize with their failures and to praise them for having the courage to not only fail, but to pick themselves up and try something else. I really am in awe of such men.

There was that rather grim tour in Australia in 1985 when the fans did not flock to the Everly concerts for various reasons, and a great deal of money was lost. The press blamed "The Elderly Brothers," and Actors Equity blamed the tour company. At any rate, a lot of people worked very hard and, according to reports, didn't get paid. One report has it, however, that the band did get paid. Even if you lose a few dollars yourself, you pay the band! Since this was the only tour in their lives to be termed a failure, other factors must have been hard at work, and even if they were not, they've got a damned clean record overall.

Calliope Records, their own record company formed in 1961, was a mild disaster simply because it probably was musically too far ahead of its time. It was more or less Donald's venture, and its concept was to take ordinary songs and give them a different treatment. He wanted a lot of brass and a big band sound. His version of "Pomp and Circumstance" was particularly notable (and decidedly juvenile) and strange with its cheerleader-type girl vocals in the middle. It seemed almost a sacrilege to the British who are extremely formal in situations that call for pomp. The British were horrified. Calliope also put out three more records, namely "When You Wish Upon A Star," Draggin', Dragon," and a rock and roll rendition of "God Bless

America." These were all produced under the name of Adrian Kimberly; in a relatively short time, the company just faded away. I've often thought that Donald is harboring a 'gifted' sense of purpose which most people fail to understand. Sometimes, unfortunately, the best swimmers drown.

Their very success even backfired and nearly put them out of business. They had changed the makeup on the face of the music industry. A new era was at hand and they were the ones who kicked it off. The Everly Brothers and the start of rock and roll were synonymous.

Immediately new groups formed and began to copy their style. One of these groups consisted of four very talented young men who at one time reportedly called themselves the "English Everlys" and/or "The Four Everly Brothers," quite a tribute to Donald and Phillip, for this group was none other than the now world famous Beatles.

When the Beatles hit the U.S. mainland, the fickle American public went wild. These kids were talented, they had "cute" English accents, shaggy bowl haircuts, tight pants, great senses of humor; they wrote and performed great music and completely enraptured American teenagers. In doing so, they overwhelmed the American music scene. This phenomenon was called "The British Invasion."

So Donald and Phillip went to England! They did quite well, too, because like the Americans who loved English accents, the English went nuts over American accents! Ironically, there was an article written about that time on the Everly Brothers, calling them "The American Beatles." What a slap in the face!

Felice Bryant once said how tragic it was that when they were attempting to get their popularity back in the '60s, they tried to sing like those they heard on the radio. Sadly, they didn't realize that the people singing on the radio were emulating them! The Everlys were trying to imitate their imitators. They finally wised up to all this, just said the hell with it, and went out and did their own thing.

Their unique way with harmony and precise timing has never been successfully imitated by anyone - not by Simon and Garfunkle or any of the later imitators. Harmony is their bag and it is what has kept them afloat for all these years.

If one listens to music like their 1966 LP, *Two Yanks In England*, it's obvious that Donald and Phillip were trying to sound British and THEY DO! A good example of this is "Somebody Help Me." These guys are so incredibly talented, that when you hear their imitations of others, you realize they can sing any style of music that has ever been written. What talent! It's really quite unbelievable.

Another hard time for all American rock stars was in the 1970s when the awful disco craze hit. Most of those who managed to survive the British influx were unable to survive more years of disco. I mean, most musicians can't dance.

In Session was Phillip's great venture in 1973. This was a thirty minute syndicated rock music television program hosted by Phillip Everly. It followed a show called In Concert and went on the air every two weeks at the unheard of hour of 1:00 a.m.! Phillip's desire was to show musicians, singers and performers at their very best, just sitting around doing their own thing in their own element. He wanted the public to see how talented and human good performers and musicians really are. It was an intriguing idea and it probably would have been successful except that not many people are up at that late hour, except for performers and musicians themselves who know all of that stuff already.

Also in the 1970s, Donald was producing and promoting a group called Starbuck, led by singer Bruce Blackman. This group provided an outlet for Donald to make his contribution to the music world by helping a completely novice group of young people work in the music business. There were seven members of the band all in their early twenties, and they had a happy, young sound which Donald thought the industry would go for. It was a marvelous idea for a "veteran" like Donald to pool his talent, knowledge and expertise with a group of enthusiastic young kids. This group recorded on the Private S. Label, and in May of 1976 they released "Moonlight Feels Right" which made it to Number 3 on the charts and stayed there for fourteen weeks. One year later in May of 1977, they released another single called "Everybody Be Dancin'" which did not do as well.

At any rate, Donald was very excited about these young people at the time, but success never materialized and they just disappeared without a trace. I can't imagine what happened, as I would think that with Donald Everly behind them believing them to be so talented, it would almost follow that they would succeed.

At another time Donald said that Phillip and he wanted to put two other groups out on the road in addition to the Everly Brothers, and that they were trying for a television special as well as a television series. A lot of these pipe dreams went up in smoke, but I love the enthusiasm and positive thoughts that came out of these two men. It's hard to be a famous person and have your hopes and dreams expressed to millions of people. If an ordinary person fails at something, usually only three or four people know about it. It takes real nerve to bare your soul to millions and then fail and come up grinning. The Everly Brothers seem to have that quality, and I admire them tremendously for it.

The solo albums the Everlys did were not terribly successful either, although I can emphatically state that my favorite male album of all time is Donald's *Brother Jukebox*.

(The best female album has to be *Liza With A Z* by Liza Minnelli.) I guess the public wanted them singing together or not at all. What a loss to everyone concerned, because as solo artists they really shine. I don't think people gave the solo stuff a chance. They should have listened harder.

The Everlys also mentioned that some day they might want to record with symphony orchestras. They do like all kinds of music (Donald especially likes Bach) and the Everly sound would surely go with an orchestra. I would love to hear something like that, especially with The Boston Pops, my favorite. I know they could collaborate well with John Williams, and I'm sure it would be beautiful. Why hasn't something like that materialized? How about it, promoters? Isn't that what you're getting paid for?

Donald is an autograph collector. Two that he is quite proud of are those of Roy Rogers and Winston Churchill. He thinks that autographs are important, that "they're part of your memorabilia," and that he had met both Walt Disney and Clark Gable, but he didn't ask for their autographs, and regrets it now that it's too late.

Donald has also stated that he wants success on the charts and just one more gold record, not especially for him, but for Phillip. And, although Phillip says he doesn't have a strong desire to perform indefinitely, Donald admitted that after a while you get to want to see yourself up on stage again.

I suppose another failure would be that Donald and his mother reportedly are not as close as they used to be, especially since Margaret threatened to sue Donald for his (forty percent) portion of the title to the three bedroom, two and a half bath house she is living in near Brentwood. Phillip, incidentally, held sixty percent of the title, which is interesting in itself. Apparently this never did get to court, contrary to press reports, but it took Donald more than a year to finally sign his share over to her. I guess he decided the adverse publicity which would result would not be worth the hassle.

Of course, in marriage they've been great failures, so much so that neither of them has been married for years. This is hardly unique in the music business, however. It just seems that neither of the Everlys can mix a successful career and a successful marriage, although they say they yearn for that simple, homey atmosphere so many other couples take for granted. It doesn't just happen, fellas. You have to be strong and flex more than just phallic muscle. It takes lots of hard work. Marriage isn't just 50-50, it's more like 90-90.

Although Phillip seems to want to be a good father, Donald tends to have trouble in that department, too. Apparently it's because there are such hard feelings between him and his ex-wives. This sours kids towards their fathers, but hopefully now that they are all grown, they'll accept him for what he is. Donald stated one time that the reason for the divorces was that the kids' mothers and he had different ideas on how to bring up children. The mothers believed in boarding schools and lots of help for the children, while Donald probably wanted them to grow up free and loose, as children in Western Kentucky do.

Donald elaborated further. "I don't see my children by my previous marriages too much. I don't get along with their mothers...I just figure sooner or later that my children will show up to my farm, to my place, wherever I'm living, and I will raise them the way that I would like to. 'Cause that mostly was the reason for the breakup was the way that the children were being raised. I'm into a very different kind of an education thing than sending them off to private schools where they have nurses taking them by the hand, taking them to the bathroom, isn't my way that children should be raised. Unfortunately, their mothers seem to think that, so... I figure my best contribution to my family can be to be content and happy with myself, and that's the example I want to set. If there is an example to be set."

Actually, I think the Everlys have a successful little laundry business going. They have plenty of dirty linen to air, and a lot of women have taken them to the cleaners already. Yes, folks, the women took most of it.

In his youth, Phillip had thoughts of becoming a lawyer. Not just a lawyer, but one who deals with music law, which would be right up his alley. Both Donald and Phillip had expressed a desire to go to college, although their vocations made that impossible. When they were youngsters, Donald said he wanted to study art and acting, and Phillip said he wanted to study dramatics. Their mother even said she thought that Phillip had the talent to get along best in life because of his love for dramatics. Neither of the boys even got close to college however, because of their roller coaster careers. They both later said that they wanted their own children to attend college.

Donald has also stated that he might want to be a cartoonist, but that remains to be seen. It's entirely possible that he could do quite well at it, as he possesses artistic abilities, a sense of humor and brains, but I have not seen any evidence of Donald wanting that artistic part of him to be seen. A "Don Everly Original" would be prime stuff, I would think. Apparently it is so private to him he doesn't want to share it. His music is private too, and he shares that, so why not his pictures? His handwriting alone is almost an art form!

I honestly think that the talent God gave Donald and Phillip Everly was given for a purpose. God doesn't just give out incredible talent like theirs without good reason, does He? Yes, some people have a bit of talent for this and a bit of talent for that, but incredible, earth-shattering talent such as the Everlys have been given, should not be kept so buried. Yes, they have performed for years and this gives much joy to those who have witnessed these performances, but most of their recorded music is buried and hidden, difficult to find, if in fact, downright impossible. They don't have many cassettes available in regular stores like so many do, and most major singers have at least one Christmas cassette out! Come on, guys. You could do a Christmas album (by yourselves).

Their approach to their "business" seems entirely too casual but if it suits them, that's their business. Phillip once let us in on how hard they work in the business by saying, "I don't keep my eye on the charts. I use the 'car method' to find out whether we have a hit record; if I hear us on the car radio, I know we're doing alright." He feels that he and Donald lasted as long as they did because they didn't worry too much about surveys, that they just did their thing. Maybe he's right. Maybe not.

Phillip had stated at one point that he would like to win a Grammy, but what he would like most of all is to sing on stage with his son Jason. To my knowledge, this has not taken place yet, with the exception of a few guest appearances at The Palomino Club, and Phillip's wish was made quite a long time ago.

As evidenced by the covers of this book, John Q. Public is only barely aware that the Everly Brothers even exist any more. Their music is kept like some deep, dark secret, shared and listened to by only diehard fans, relatives and acquaintances. There is something very strange here, and I think it stems from the fact that the promotion of these two artists is so bad. But why on earth would they allow such shoddy treatment? It boils down to, again, that they must not care. If they cared more, they would be more public and the promotion of their music would be better. It's as simple as that. Another theory might possibly be that they shy away from that dreaded thing called overexposure. It is a known human fact that we all want what we can't have. Perhaps the Everlys know this.

I read recently about how singer Eddie Fisher promoted an album of his which apparently was not getting off to a good start. In order to sell that record, he travelled across the country talking to every program manager and record librarian he could find. In addition, he saw every deejay and every television talk show host he could find, and appeared on The Tonight Show with Johnny Carson every night for a week. As the LP was on the RCA label, RCA hired ten publicists and Fisher hired ten more on his own. All this hoopla resulted in an article being published in Time Magazine entitled, "How To Make A Hit Record." What an effort!

The lack of interest by the Everlys is carried through even down to their tour buses. Living in North Florida, I see acts going through my town day after day, headed for Ft. Lauderdale, Orlando, Miami and Jacksonville. Almost all of these buses advertise who they are and what they do. Donald's bus usually has an Indian type theme which diehard fans recognize year after year, but the general public would never know whose bus it was. He sometimes has a funny little saying in the front like "SENIOR CITIZEN." Phillip's bus, however, is plain and usually says "PRIVATE," although "BLOODY MARY MORNING" and "HOWIE DOIN" have been used recently. This sort of attitude is pretty hard to take, especially when you expect the public to show up and spend a lot of money for a less than two hour show. I don't know. Maybe I'm a little too sensitive, but frankly I feel I'm not wanted, and the thought has crossed my mind more than once, why on earth should I go see them? Do they really give a hoot? Oh yes, they do. They care so much it hurts.

I also feel a bit for the hard-working fans and the fan clubs. These people work many long, hard hours in Donald and Phillip's behalf without pay, in addition to handling their regular jobs and families. I have been asked to write letters and send information to others, put flyers on cars in the cities where the Everlys are appearing, write TV and radio personalities trying to promote them, etc. I have not done any of these things, because I feel that my efforts in writing this book are more than enough of a contribution to the careers of these two men. Their concerts are usually sold out. The fans work tirelessly, but where is the thanks? Rumor has it that they ignore the head of the American fan club, and when the European fan club president once complained to Phillip that it was a lot of work, Phillip just asked him why he didn't just give the damned thing up. My point is, if the Everly Brothers don't care, why on earth should the fans care? It is hard to drum up enthusiasm when the objects of your enthusiasm are unreachable, unapproachable, uncommunicative and uncooperative.

The bottom line to all this is wrapped up in that old saying, "what goes around, comes around." The people who buy your lunch are called fans.

Their personal relationship was a rocky one, too. One thing that the Everlys couldn't agree on was the choice of venues. Phillip liked the snazzy, elegant clubs of Las Vegas and New York, whereas Donald wanted to do the get-down-get-dirty musician-type smokey rooms of Greenwich Village such as the Fillmore East, and places like the Bitter End, located about a block from Washington Square Park.

After they found out one day in the late 1950s that they had enough money to have their own hotel rooms, from then on it was downhill. They ended up having separate motels, cars, dressing rooms, etc., but on stage they still were together one hundred percent.

Today most of the Grand Ole Opry acts are without record labels. About half of them, as a matter of fact. This is because, like the Everlys, their records aren't selling. Why? Because the deejays only play the "Top 40" or so songs, thus canceling out any hope of radio access for new acts or songs or just plain good music. Actually the radio stations play music that is sent to them on computerized ranking charts which have been chosen by radio consultants. Most of these "consultants" are very young, are living in New York or Los Angeles, and are not close to the heart of the music itself. These merchandised "music lists" are sent to approximately 9,000 radio stations across the country. The stations are monitored by the three performing rights organizations, BMI, ASCAP and SESAC. Only the Independent stations will play an Independent label, which makes it extremely hard for newcomers to break into the business. But the Everlys are hardly newcomers, and their terrific singles of later years have not been played. I guess it all boils down to, again, advertising and good promotion.

Ironically, radio stations won't play records that aren't "on the charts" and the charts seem to be made up of what is listed in the "trades." Where do the trades get their charts? From what is being played by the radio! It's that old, familiar Catch-22 again. The answer, unpleasant as it is, is that a good artist sometimes can purchase about $50,000.00 worth of advertising in the trades and he possibly could be written up as having a hit song. Since he "has a hit song," he will be added to the "music list," played by radio deejays, and the stores will have his single available for purchase by the public. He will have a hit! This constitutes musical talent? No, it is just Big Business rearing its ugly head and it is what Donald and Phillip despise so much. I can only assume that the Everlys don't want to lower themselves to all this sleezy stuff, which, although

94

morally admirable on their part, probably isn't too damned intelligent.

I hear that some of the new "stars" in Nashville today have gotten there through expenditures of $200,000.00 or more. The Everlys, however, do not advertise and/or make public appearances and/or get out and mix with fans and/or promote themselves much in any way except for their bus tours. Again, this won't do.

Quite a while ago Donald stated that he wanted to live somewhere else besides the United States. I sincerely hope he doesn't. By now I guess he realizes that America is the greatest country in the world, but he did say once that he was thinking of moving to a more tropical climate, like Mexico. So far, he is still here, and seems to be quite at home around that cozy, creative community called Nashville.

Phillip as well as Donald has lived in Europe, but he always returns too, thank God. The Los Angeles area and the California lifestyle seems to suit him and he is pretty firmly entrenched there. Of course, his children and nieces and nephew live close by, so that is a big plus.

I hate to say this, but their latest album, *Some Hearts* could be called a failure, although the songs on that album are truly beautiful. There was much hype about the album, including the fact that it was almost all self-penned, and they thought it was their best work.

Unfortunately, it had its share of problems. Number one, it wasn't mixed well, and a lot of the lyrics are difficult to hear. Also again, the promotion of the album really was almost non-existent. Many astute fans couldn't even get a copy for a long, long time! Some of this was the Everlys' fault, though, as they did two years worth of a "Some Hearts Tour," and hardly ever sang songs from the album when they were on stage. I mean, if you don't sing your own songs, who is going to? At any rate it's a shame more wasn't done with what is truly a great album.

The Everly Brothers are "failing" in a public way, even now. They are not heard on the radio except for nostalgia trips of "Cathy's Clown" and songs of that ilk, but the truly wonderful, talented stuff they have written and produced over the years is buried under mountains of less talented ventures. The real point is that the Everlys don't seem to outwardly care. I know that they care inwardly, but they won't give any interviews and they won't appear in public. Their publicist won't answer queries, they don't send out pictures, answer letters, and there is certainly not an overabundance of Everly "stories" around, such as the following:

The late Lucille Ball once received some flowers from a fan, a minister who lived in North Carolina. It was accompanied by a nice note with a phone number at the bottom. Lucy called the man up immediately, and spoke for some time with his astonished wife. Nice gesture.

When Paul McCartney saw an overly ardent fan on his HBO Special, he flew her to a concert and met her backstage.

An acquaintance was driving with her mother to an Elvis Presley concert in Memphis, and had a bad car accident. Elvis saw the newspaper article and came to visit her in the hospital.

Ernest Tubb is known for the way he always treated young talent just starting out (and for that matter, many who were stopping!). If he knew of some newcomers who were broke, he would feed these kids and get them a place to sleep. Many people claim that he helped almost everyone in

Nashville at one time or another. I wouldn't be too surprised at all if he helped the young Everly kids, too. I do know that they appeared several times on his Midnight Jamboree Show.

Roy Acuff is well known for being gracious over the years to newcomers. He would try to be of help to anyone, including giving them his home phone number, in case they had any problems.

Barbara Mandrell adores her fans and goes to great lengths to try to afford them special attention. She answers letters, signs autographs for three or four hours after a show, and hosts a fan club breakfast. These breakfasts are also held by many, many other stars.

Randy Travis also hosts his own fan club breakfast, and has a room in his Nashville gift shop which is devoted to his fans.

I should not fail to mention Willie Nelson, who loves his fans and will stand for hours talking to them and signing autographs.

I personally like actor Jimmy Stewart's attitude. He has said he considers his fans more as partners instead of just customers. What a nice man.

Stories like this abound with many show business people, but not the Everlys. I've never been made aware that they give a lot to charity other than the few Everly scholarships which their names raise in Central City, Kentucky, and I recall once they did a show to benefit an orphanage in California. But they don't participate in any of the "Aid" events such as "Farm

Aid," or "Earth Day." They really could adopt a popular disease or something else noteworthy such as the environment, hunger, save the rain forests, canyon fire victims, tornado and hurricane victims, the homeless, the ozone layer or the protection of a certain animal. Any cause would do, and they could promote themselves and their cause by participating with others of their kind with a celebrity auction or event. Almost all of the performers in the world do something. Of course their most fervent fans have great stories (some real, most imagined), but I see the Everly Brothers as nothing short of being "career recluses." It is very difficult to sustain a career when one is so reclusive in one's life's work.

The Everly Brothers say that they do not want a biography or a movie done about them, but stated in 1989 that in 1990 a TV special was going to come out. It never did. They also say that no matter what else they do, they want to keep singing well into their seventies. I certainly hope they do! As Donald said in the November 22, 1985 edition of The London Times, "We have to see how our voices hold up, and at our age that's something you can't predict. We can't do too many shows at a time. But as far as I'm concerned, it seems to get stronger the more I sing."

So you see, failures are actually a good thing. These two men have expressed wishes and desires. Not all of them have been granted, but if one adds fame, recognition, respect, adoration, children, travel, music, the best bands possible, friendship, good looks, expertise on the guitar, gold records, awards, residuals, touring, modern tour busses, limousines, women, adoring fans and enough money, then these two brothers have achieved a lot more than they have ever failed at. They are truly amazing! And as far as I can see, I think that the greatest of all of God's gifts is the ability to sing well. If you have that, you have been given the very best.

The words of President Theodore Roosevelt still ring true today. He said, "It is not the critic who counts; not the man who points out how the strong man stumbles, or where the doer of deeds could have done them better. The credit belongs to the man who is actually in the arena, whose face is marred by dust and sweat and blood; who strives valiantly; who errs, and comes short again and again, because there is no effort without error and shortcomings; but who does actually strive to do the deeds; who knows the great enthusiasms, the great devotions; who spends himself in a worthy cause; who at the best knows in the end the triumph of high achievement, and who at the worst, if he fails, at least fails while daring greatly, so that his place shall never be with those cold and timid souls who know neither victory or defeat."

Phillip and Jackie's wedding

Little Church Around the Corner

9
THE FEMALE FACTOR

"A hundred men may make an encampment,
but it takes a woman to make a home."
- Chinese Proverb

Donald says that he is still searching for that perfect woman and that house with the white picket fence around it.

Phillip explains his love life by saying that relationships always have to go somewhere but that his usually go out the door - with him.

The Everlys are dreamers, and dreamers hurt. Many dreamers still believe in what the French call *Coup de Foudre*, or love at first sight, but that is very rare. Many people are in love with the idea of "being in love," which doesn't last.

Why don't the women stay? No one really knows except them, but an extremely plausible scenario comes to mind. Men are attracted to smart, knowledgeable women who are independent and capable. They admire them, and marry them.

Then it all changes. The woman is now HIS wife and she is to do what her husband wants, mainly stay by his side and do his bidding. Some women say right off the bat, "Hell, no!" Other women say, "Yes darling, whatever you say, dear." While this second attitude should sit well with the husband, it never does, as he was not attracted to a mamby-pamby "yes" person in the first place. He was attracted to a vibrant, strong, independent woman. So ultimately he gets rid of the nice "yes" person and fights like a tiger with the "no" person, both of which produce problems and divorce.

Another insight into this is that an Everly wife is not married to just one man. Except for the sex part, she is basically married to two men, because almost every move has to be accounted for and approved by both. When on tour, they are usually together for long periods of time. The wife really comes after the act, doesn't she? And no matter what anyone else says, when there is a woman around, men will ask her to do favors - nothing big mind you, just little things like going out to buy something for him or sew on a button or get a beer or a second helping and pretty soon she finds herself waiting on other men, picking up coats (women seem to always be picking up coats!) and literally being mothers to both brothers and probably some of the band members, too. It's all a little *de trop!* Of course, five to six months out of the year the Everlys live on separate coasts, but it is still a bi-coastal arrangement. No real decisions can be made unless the other one is contacted. Lord knows being married to one man is aggravating enough, but two of them? And how much of her time and energy goes into the band members? The Everlys would be dead without one of the best bands in the world. These wonderful guys must be kept happy, healthy and satisfied. Add that to the touring, recording and performing schedules of an entertainer, plus the inevitable "screaming fan" thing, and you have discord where harmony should be. It's really not so strange at all that these two men have such harmony on stage and such discord off stage.

It's hard enough when the women travel with the show (they usually don't) but often they are just left. After all, there are children to be reared. The entertainers themselves are out on the road alone for months at a time, too. It may seem very glamorous, but what you really are left with is a couple of bus-loads full of very bored and lonely men; the stars, the warm-up acts, the crew, the musicians. As Paul McCartney explained it, just about the only free time you have is after the show, and so you have two choices; to go to the hotel room or the bar, and you know what happens after a few drinks in the bar. Many entertainers are provided with "companionship" by their managers and producers. Paul McCartney, however, makes sure he takes his wife Linda, also a band member, with him. Stardom itself is a harsh enough mistress.

Sometimes the loneliness can be debilitating. Everyone has heard of studies done on monkeys where there are two control groups, with opposite familial situations. One test group is raised normally with all the hugging and touching of their mothers and many other monkeys, and the other test group is raised alone, without physical contact at all from another warm being. The results are dramatic. The first group is healthy, happy and playful. The second group is terrified, paranoid, sickly, and self-destructive. They mature slowly and die very early. Human beings are no different. Everyone needs to be touched, loved and hugged - often! When those simple pleasures are denied, loneliness and depression are sure to follow.

There also seems to be a basic primal need in men to have their food served to them by a woman. This need has been an integral part of the male species since before Cro-Magnon Times, when supposedly the women cleaned, cooked and served the kill. "It tastes better," they say, but we all know it is the caring and attention that really is the issue here.

There is a definite conflict when the men come off the road. The poor guy has been eating jungle (junk) food and other bad stuff for a long time and all he wants is some good home cooking and his family around him. Unfortunately, his wife has been home cooking three meals a day for his children, has been working both the mother and the father roles, and now that her husband is home, she wants to celebrate, go out, and paint the town red. This produces a lot of problems.

Many entertainers marry other performers and stars. The Everlys did not. Although their women might have had acting, dancing or modelling backgrounds, they were not stars. Most of them were, however, intelligent, sophisticated women. Phillip's first wife, Jackie, was a business woman. His second wife, Patricia, was a dancer and a working actress who at the time of her divorce was bringing in a fairly good salary. She also sang a bit as evidenced on his album, *Star Spangled Springer*. Donald's first wife was a secretary, his second wife, Venetia, was a smart, sophisticated lady who sang and acted, and Karen, his third, had held a terrific position on the David Frost Show. All of these women had to put a stop to their careers just to be an "Everly wife." Perhaps it's because of their Southern upbringing, but my guess is that both Everlys want their women walking a couple of steps behind them, too.

Throughout their careers, their wives were literally out of the picture and rarely if ever, photographed. They never did the "social scene" or the "charity route"; therefore, the women were never shown off. Perhaps they got tired of being left home, walking behind, and/or shoved off into the green-room backstage. I don't care if the man IS the star. Women like to shine a little, too!

Another theory is that, since we live in a disposable society, many think that if something is wrong with you or your spouse or anything else for that matter, you just get rid of it and find another. Of course, there's lots wrong with everybody, but romantics tend not to believe that. This "disposable" theory, however, does not diminish the pain and suffering of divorce wherein people literally rip each other apart.

Also, television has changed how we view real life. Television is not real, but many people think that those characters they see on the small screen act the way real people do. They should realize that babies do need their diapers changed, husbands yell and snore, wives do not arise from sleep fully made up and coiffed; and families do have bills that at times they cannot pay. People find this hard to accept, as they want the "perfect" TV family.

What do women really want? I have never heard it said better than Elizabeth Taylor's explanation in Kitty Kelley's book, *The Last Star.* "A woman will try and dominate a man. She will try and get away with it. But really, inside herself, she wants to be dominated...she wants the man to take her. And she wants to lean on him - not have him lean on her. If he does lean on her, everything goes slightly off key, like a bad chord. She hopes it will pass, that the guy will come through. When it doesn't, she begins to needle him. If nothing happens, she goes on needling - until he stops listening. At that moment, she becomes bitter and he goes deaf. Finally, there is no more dialogue, they have no rapport."

I have talked at length with a friend of mine named Glenda, who grew up in Kentucky, one hour away from Central City. She married a man from the same town. All of their kin are from Kentucky, and go back generations. She explained the system there as a place where everyone stayed in their own socio-economic niche. In Kentucky there were city people, town people, farm people, mining people and mountain people. None of these people mixed with the other groups and they stayed in their own areas. They didn't mix with people who live one hour away from them, either, but they were aware of the existence of cities such as Louisville, Lexington and Nashville.

Glenda said that they went to Nashville once a year to do Christmas shopping and to view the lights, but normally they just stayed where they were raised and continued their laid back lives. She said mining people were generally distrustful of "city" folks simply because there weren't any cities around mining places.

When Glenda was a child, the women didn't have outside jobs, they just stayed home and cooked three meals a day. Most women are out in the workplace now, and the men begrudge it still. The proportion of women who work outside the home is below the national average, because the men's attitudes are that there really isn't anything to spend money on in a small Kentucky town.

Apparently many Kentucky men still think that women aren't as smart as men are, and the women are not allowed to make many decisions. The men generally control the finances and give the women a "household allowance." This was still in evidence in Donald's household when he was divorced from Venetia. There was a "household" checking account to be disbursed.

The children were brought up strictly, and the woman was expected to be strong and submissive at the same time, a trying combination, at best. Her role consisted of mother, wife, cook and partial confidant. If the wife was not in agreement with her husband, she usually had to abide by his decision whether she liked it or not.

I asked my friend if women are expected to walk two steps behind (in the Everlys' case, they walk in another dimension, it seems) and she said, "Yes. The women walk two steps behind because the men walk so fast. The women stroll. Men are always in a hurry. The men aren't very patient." I guess a lot of men aren't aware that being married means more than being locked together at the lips and the hips. I also have noticed that both Donald and Phillip do indeed walk very fast, and The Donald in particular darts from here to there erratically, with a lot of very nervous energy. His eyes dart, too. Frankly, he makes me nervous.

The Everlys have not been known to have frequented popular or sophisticated watering holes, clubs or restaurants such as The Four Seasons, Sardis, Tavern On The Green or Studio 54 in New York, or Spago on the west coast. Also there is no evidence that in the real old days they frequented The Stork Club or 21, either, but they did say they used to pop into Lindys for some cheesecake once in a while.

The more I think about it, the more I realize that I'd get pretty bored being married to a man who just plays his guitar for hours on end and sits around smoke filled rooms with a bunch of musicians, who stay up all night playing pass the guitar. And does his wife have her house filled with strange men night after night until the wee hours of the morning? Sometimes when an artist is at home, he has an entourage with him, which can consist of managers, musicians, producers, writers, band members, hangers-on, groupies, yes-men, drivers, "techies". Donald has been seen in Nashville restaurants with a retinue. There usually is not much time left to devote to family. If these things are true, God help the marriage! After all, a wife is a man's partner in life and at least once in a while she should be shown off and guided around the room with pride. Perhaps the Everlys were too restrictive in their treatment of their women. Let's face it. Women like and need to feel important, too!

On the other hand, wealth, talent and importance are very strong aphrodisiacs; Elizabeth Taylor insists that "there's no deodorant like success." The Everlys are worldly and experienced and this all adds up to masculine power. Since women love power, they will continue to gravitate towards powerful men.

The saga of megastar producer/director George Lucas comes to mind. This man has produced some of the highest grossing Hollywood films of all time and is a force to be reckoned with. His house is in the middle of a small Lucas town with houses, sound stages and buildings all used in the production of works stemming from his fantastic imagination. Many people live and work there full time and must depend on "King George" for their living. But when asked in an interview what he would like most in life, he hesitated, then quietly admitted that he would like a wife to share all of it with. I will never forget the look on that man's face when he said it, either. So power is not the ultimate. There must be a delicate balance of power, success, talent, and inward contentment. This is a difficult thing to achieve, and most never know the feelings of completeness that it brings.

A couple of the Everly wives were extremely attractive and stylish. But what happened to the Everlys themselves? On stage they are dressed alike in tuxedos and they look fine. They are handsome guys and the tuxes are perfect and add a lot of class to their show. But off stage, they really look like hell. Why don't they care? If they don't have any more respect for themselves than that, then how can they expect a woman to respect them? Of course, they are much better than some other entertainers who look like hell both off stage and on. And I do realize that travelling for months on a bus is hardly conducive to elegant and stylish dress. It is similar to living on a yacht for long periods of time, although on a boat you have salt air, mildew and even less luxuries. In both cases, you're lucky if you can get your underwear washed.

The Everlys remind me somewhat of an actor/director friend of mine with whom I spent two months working in Maine a couple of years ago. This guy was a perfect study in slobbism. His hair was usually a mess; his shirttails hung out; and his shoelaces were always untied. He was so unorganized, rumpled and cute, that the women went wild for him and, when we viewed some of his film rushes and saw him elegantly attired in a tuxedo, we roared with laughter. It was so far from the "real" Barry that it was hilarious. I guess the same goes for the Everlys.

I firmly believe that there can't be a "good" marriage in the true sense of the word until many years have passed. Couples can have good times and bad, but to have a good marriage, you must have weathered all the sadness, joy, births, deaths, financial ups and downs, illnesses, children, pets, emergencies, closeness, apartness, and fears. A couple must grow together, and this process takes years. After all, there is more to marriage than just sex. You must overcome all the little "fighting" things such as money, cooking, drinking, shopping, neatness (or the lack of), dishes, religion, driving together in the car, the raising and disciplining of children, money, friends, enemies, relatives, time spent together and apart, money, how many children you should have, smoking, taste in music, helping around the house, the garbage, choice of entertainment, listening to each other (and hearing), infidelity (shame on you!) money, pets, common consideration, jobs, talking too much or too little, manners, snoring, lack of communication and understanding, gifts, the inability to forgive, failing the other person somehow, taste in clothing, differences in temperament (and temperature), leisure time, jobs, noise, sickness, laundry, travel, sharing a bathroom, and money. People fight about whether the wife should work or be a housewife (personally, I never did want to be married to a house) or perhaps she comes to bed with her hair in curlers or cold cream on her face (shame on you!). Perhaps one is a morning person, the other a night person, but every one of these things can be overcome if you have one thing: respect. Without it, you can't even love, for who can love someone they don't respect? If you both have respect for each other, all the other things in life will soften. All of the Everly marriages ended around the Seven Year Itch stage, when maturity and understanding finally begins to kick into gear. It seems sometimes that they must have had an itch but didn't know exactly where to scratch, and they gave up.

Human beings, however, are meant to exist in pairs, so there is something here that doesn't quite gel. After all, the human being is about the only species on earth that is capable of sexual activity 365 days a year. God must be trying to tell us to couple up! If sex was solely for procreation, God would have made us come into "season" only once or twice a year as most other animals do. But I think God meant for us to have more fun than that! It just seems strange to me that for these two men not to be cozily entrenched with a good woman just seems downright criminal. I suppose it's just a case of their having been burned once too often, and of having lost too much in the fires.

The Everlys have always sung many love songs, but Phillip's comments on this are insightful. "I think we were young and foolish, and hadn't been to divorce courts so many times that we were callused so I think that a lot of that existed. It's a little harder, now. I kind of choke up a little bit when I'm singing about love, now. It's a little harder for me to do it."

There are many people who blame the "other woman" for bad marriages, too. Personally, I don't believe it. I sincerely believe that no woman can take a happily married man away from his wife. Actress Catherine Deneuve recently agreed in a *Parade Magazine* interview, saying, "There is no such thing as a home wrecker, a femme fetale. Some men are available." Thank you, Catherine.

> *"All married women are not wives."*
> *- Japanese Proverb*

WIVES AND GIRLFRIENDS

In about the year 1400, Geoffrey Chaucer wrote The Canterbury Tales. In one of them entitled "The Merchant's Tale," it was said:

"Do not take a wife for economy's sake," he said,
"so as to save expense in your household;
a faithful servant takes more trouble
to watch over your possessions than does your own wife,
for she will make a claim to half of it all her life.
And if you are sick, as God may save me,
your true friends or a faithful servant will
take better care of you than she will,

who continually lies in wait for your possessions,
and has done so for many a day.
And if you take a wife into your keeping,
you may very easily become a cuckold."

Donald and Phillip have been through five marriages and divorces. Both have known the high cost of leaving, and both have reacted in different ways. Phillip in general keeps away from serious relationships with women as if they were the plague, although he does have a girlfriend from time to time. Donald on the other hand, tends to "womanize" which is not necessarily to be confused with liking women. On the contrary. A man who has relationships with many women is often a woman hater. They are under the (false) impression (or they assume) that women are put on this earth solely for their pleasure and manipulation. In general men such as these think women are to be used and then thrown away. There really doesn't seem to be much wrong with this "erotic vagrancy" way of thinking in the minds of such men, as women don't have much value to them as people in the first place. They certainly do not respect them. My father is such a man. I know.

A man who honestly loves women will find a good one and stick with her year after year, through everything that life tosses their way. Their marriage will get better as the years progress. A man like this truly respects and loves women. He is secure in the strength of his own masculinity and doesn't have to run around proving himself to anyone. My husband is such a man. I know.

The type of man who swears off women because he has been hurt is an enigma to me, as I have never known a man such as that. Most of the men I've known are still hound dogging it, so I don't understand Phillip's solution to the female problem at all. Therefore I will not comment on it. Whatever it is he is doing, I hope it suits him and he is happy with his life.

There are those who have "relationships." A relationship is still a trial. You're still on your best behavior most of the time, because neither of you has made that final commitment yet. Both of you are still free to walk out of the house whenever the going gets too tough. Married people have to stand together and face the music. It's tougher to be married. Much tougher! Marriage means total commitment.

Also in today's society, we are obsessed with romantic love. A relationship sometimes provides this. Marriage sometimes does not, although some lucky couples have both. Marriage tends to quickly push all the "romantic notions" aside. Don't get me wrong. What replaces it is infinitely better in the long haul. It is wonderfully sweet and safe and cozy to crawl into bed every night with the same person and to wake up with that same trusted person each and every morning. "Relationships" provide all of the fluff and none of the cement, thus making it a flimsy state at best. A really good marriage means your husband tells you you don't need to go to places like Victoria's Secret or Fredericks of Hollywood to buy sexual trappings, because he thinks you are sexy all the time, any time, every time, without all of that. Marriage means the closeness, the touching, the affection, the freedom to be able to say whatever is on your mind and to tell the truth instead of always being "on." As Joan Rivers bluntly put it after the death of her husband Edgar, "I miss the buddy system."

The lifestyles of many entertainers (and I'm talking about those with a life on the road in particular) often provides a safe cushion which makes it easy not to have to commit to a marriage. For those who do commit, it can be extremely hard for the wife who after a while loses her identity and becomes "His Wife." Touring can be extremely rough on children also, as they tend to grow up whether their dad is there or not, and it is often fatal to a marriage. Eddie Cantor was convinced that when you were in show business, you were already married. After all, show business produces extreme demands, extreme rewards, extreme highs and extreme lows.

Many singers are also busiest at holiday times like Christmas, New Years and weekends, although this doesn't particularly pertain to the Everly Brothers. Marriage on the other hand, means every day, with the garbage, scrubbing the shower tiles, taking the dog to the vet, caring for sick kids and suffering through PTA meetings. It means normalcy. Normalcy begins with a home, and we all know what a home is. It's a house with a husband and wife, kids, a piano, a swimming pool and a couple of dogs. It does not mean life on the road. Although admittedly hard work, that's not real life, and "fan adoration" tends to place a shroud over reality. Life on the road more closely resembles a hard working vacation. But who can take a vacation for seven, eight, or in some cases, eleven months a year? Your feet are not standing in cement, you're rolling in fluff, and marriages fall through when there is too much fluff. Love slowly turns to hatred and war, and divorce is war. Once a love goes, the hatred spreads faster than a California canyon fire. If a man (or a woman) fools around on his or her spouse, it is called adultery. Adultery is doing the right thing with the wrong person.

The Everly Brothers did marry, however, although the longest marriage only lasted about seven or eight years, whereupon The Seven Year Ache must have taken precedence. The following is a short synopsis of the Everly wives, their marriages, divorces, with a couple of girlfriends thrown in for good measure.

MARY SUE INGRAHAM - (Donald's first wife). Mary Sue met Donald Everly when the brothers were in Nashville trying to sell some songs around 1955. Donald and Phillip were practically starving to death, and Mary Sue at least had a job as a secretary. She moved in with Donald and Phillip and the trio managed to keep the wolf from the door. After a while, Donald and Mary Sue decided they had to be married, and so, being under age, the couple eloped. They went to Ringgold, Georgia, a small town just across the Tennessee state line, and on March 25, 1957, they were married. Donald was twenty years old and Mary Sue was nineteen. Phillip served as best man, and took five dollars out of his pocket to pay for the marriage license. When asked about the "loan" later, Phillip emphatically stated that "their" money has always belonged to both of them and whose pocket it emerged from made no difference whatsoever. Many celebrities made The Ringgold Run, including Dolly Parton in 1966.

Sadly, on October 10, 1957, their tiny infant daughter, Mary E. Everly, was born and died. She is buried in Central City, Kentucky in the Everly family plot.

Mary Sue was a small town girl who believed that a wife should stay home and take care of her man. This was fine except that soon thereafter "Bye Bye, Love" became a huge hit and everyone's lives changed as if by magic. In addition, Donald and Phillip immediately left and went on tour throughout the United States and Europe. Life was a whirlwind of activity, and Mary Sue was left out of almost all of it. The only time husband and wife saw each other was when Donald would fly to Nashville to see her for a day or so, and then he was off again. On May 16, 1959, Mary Sue gave birth in Nashville to their second daughter, Venetia Ember Everly.

Although Mary Sue tried desperately to be with Donald, she did not know show business at all, and after the baby was born, she believed her place was in the home taking care of her daughter and waiting for her husband's return. Before the baby's birth she tried to go with him on his performing rounds, but waiting for hours upon hours in hotel rooms all alone made her miserable. After all, at least when she was back in Nashville, she was in her own home and she had friends nearby she could visit and do things with.

Although Donald apparently loved his wife and daughter, he was now being rapidly transposed from a small town country boy to a millionaire who was whisked around the world by jet and limousine. Women screamed and clawed for him and the press was interested in his every move. Clearly he had outgrown what he and Mary Sue had had.

Donald and Phillip, after signing the first million dollar recording contract in the history of music with Warner Brothers, moved to Hollywood to study drama. They attended Mr. Peyton Price's drama classes at Warner Brothers Studios, and made one film which was destroyed at a later date, thank God. Apparently it was pretty badly done, which seemed to be the fault of the script, not Donald or Phillip. When Mary Sue wanted to know why she and Venetia couldn't join them, Donald reportedly dismissed her with the words, "Babe, you just ain't Hollywood."

This feeling was elaborated on by Conway Twitty when he explained in his autobiography, "You find ... a recording artist who's become a front-runner overnight, and the first thing they do is divorce their spouse and get rid of everything around them that is going to keep them anchored or show them up for what they really are. They desperately want people to think that they have moved out of the slow lane and are really going places."

On Wednesday, January 10, 1962, Mary Sue and Donald Everly were finally granted their divorce decree. It was stated that "Isaac Donald Everly was guilty of such cruel and inhuman treatment and conduct towards the cross-complainant, Mary Sue Ingraham Everly, as renders it unsafe and improper for her to further cohabit with him and be under his dominion and control."

Mary Sue was granted custody of Venetia, age three years and Donald had visiting privileges, "... subject to the provision that the cross-defendant, Isaac Donald Everly, will under no circumstances take said minor child in the presence of Venetia Stevenson." Since Donald's second wife's name is Venetia, this statement pretty much sums up what the divorce was all about. This wasn't a love triangle, it was a Devil's Triangle, and as in the Devil's Triangle, there are casualties. Donald's parents were granted the right to take Venetia "to Kentucky on short trips."

Mary Sue did fairly well for herself, but her ex-husband was earning so much money that her settlement seems a piddling amount in retrospect. She got the house plus almost all of the household furnishings. She also got their car, a 1961 Oldsmobile F-85 and he was ordered to pay $10,000.00 to her in cash. In addition, she got $63,000.00 more (in decreasing monthly payments) in return for her promise to never hit him up again for more money in later years. Child support for Venetia was a mere $100.00 per month.

Donald got to keep his guns, gold records and cups, the Hi-Fi and jukebox, and paid both attorneys for their trouble.

VENETIA INVICTA STEVENSON - (Donald's second wife, born March 10, 1938). I don't know if anyone can be naive enough to believe baby Venetia's name was a coincidence, because by the time the divorce from Mary Sue was in the works, Donald was known to be dating the beautiful actress, Venetia Stevenson. Would he really have the balls to name his daughter after his girlfriend? We're talking about Don Everly here. Of course he would!

Donald and Venetia met when they both were appearing on The Ed Sullivan Show, and Venetia was the exact opposite of Mary Sue. She WAS Hollywood! Her mother was the popular English actress, Anna Lee (real name Joan Winnefrigh) and her father was a Hollywood director named Robert Stevenson. Venetia was born in England as were both of her parents, and was very close to her father, but, according to reports at the time, she didn't get along with her mother at all. Of course, at that young age many girls don't get on with their mothers, but these things have a way of changing over the years. Venetia was beautiful, cultured, sophisticated, ambitious, and crazy about Donald Everly.

In 1961 Venetia was quoted in *Photoplay* as saying, "I'm convinced that a woman can never be satisfied being just the woman in the life of the man she loves. I want to help. I want to be important to my husband. I want to know that I can give him the kind of encouragement he needs, not the petty compliments so many wives give their husbands because they really don't understand what their men are all about. I want to share his problems. I want to love him forever." This is a pretty corny statement I suppose, but we're going back to a time when everyone seemed a lot cornier than they are today.

Venetia reportedly had dated other celebrities, namely Anthony Perkins, Elvis Presley, Tab Hunter, David Nelson, and Barry Coe. She had also been married briefly to Twin Peaks star Russ Tamblyn, who she married on Valentines Day and divorced the following year on April Fool's Day. To have her hook up with Donald Everly seems almost as bizarre.

Donald and Phillip may have been quite wealthy by now, but when you travel at great speeds around the world, everything begins to look the same, and all the hotels, cities and airports merge into one great moving picture of sameness. So many entertainers who travel a lot don't actually pick up any culture to speak of, as one has to live in a place and study there to absorb what that country has to offer. Over the years, the Everlys have lived in quite a few countries so they no doubt have learned a lot, but in 1962 when Donald married Venetia, they had not slowed down enough to have (understandably) done much culture absorption.

Donald and Phillip still possessed, however, a lot of their old Southern philosophies, which probably were quite foreign to a cosmopolitan girl like Venetia. After all, she was sophisticated, independent and smart and I don't think she would be willing to take a back seat to anyone. On the other hand, boys in the rural South are taught that women have to be strong on the one hand, but they are still to do what their man says. Sparks must have really flown between these two distinct personalities!

Donald and Venetia both listed their address as 3360 Barham Boulevard in Hollywood. At first glance this would look like they were living together, but don't get too excited, folks. That was the address of Calliope Records and they just happened to list a business address as their home address, for security purposes. I really can't blame them. As a matter of fact, Donald Everly to this day is The Grand Master of Bogus Addresses, leaving a trail of nonexistent addresses wherever he goes, and I still can't blame him.

The couple was married on February 13, 1962 at Camp Pendleton in San Diego in the U.S. Marine Chapel, the same day that Donald and Phillip graduated from boot camp. The ceremony was performed by Roger L. Crabtree, a Methodist United States Navy Chaplain. Once again, Phillip was the best man. Later in the year, the brothers departed on a tour of Europe. A now pregnant Venetia joined them. It was on this tour that Donald became hospitalized and was ill for approximately three years because of his drug addiction. Life must have been hell for poor Venetia. It probably wasn't so hot for Donald, either.

On May 5, 1963, Anastasia Dawn, or "Stacy," Donald's third daughter, was born in Los Angeles.

In August of 1963, Venetia sued Donald for divorce, but he promised to improve, and they reconciled.

On November 8, 1965, Erin Invicta, Donald's fourth daughter was born in Los Angeles, and on August 25, 1968 a son, Edan Donald, was born in Burbank.

On July 6, 1970, Donald and Venetia's Dissolution of Marriage (due to irreconcilable differences), was granted. Their three children were then ages seven, five and two and Donald had visitation rights at any time, although he chose not to exercise this right because, he has stated, he "doesn't get along well" with their mother.

Donald was ordered to pay $750.00 per month child support as well as $500.00 a month alimony to Venetia for five years. The family home in Studio City was to be sold as well as their small cabin in San Bernandino County. In addition to the normal personal holdings, Venetia kept the photographic equipment, which is a little strange since Donald is the one with that particular interest. She also retained their 1966 Cadillac as well as their 1963 Austin Healy. All poor Donald got was a 1938 Ford Coupe, which you can't go far in. Maybe he wanted it.

At the time of the divorce, there were a couple of checking accounts that held about $700.00 in them, and a savings account of approximately $1,500.00 in value. Their normal outstanding bills for doctors, clothes and utilities totalled about $2,500.00. After the divorce, Venetia went to work at the American Film Institute in Los Angeles, but she has not worked there for some time.

JACQUELINE ALICE ERTEL - (Phillip's first wife). Jackie Ertel, hailing from Sheboygan, Wisconsin, was Archie Bleyer's stepdaughter and met the Everlys through Archie. She and Phillip dated for a long time and it was said that the relationship was an on again, off again, rocky one. They finally married on January 12, 1963 at The Little Church Around The Corner in New York City. Phillip was twenty three at the time, and Jackie was twenty two. Donald was best man. Jackie's mother, who was a former Chordette, is now deceased, as is Archie Bleyer.

Phillip wrote "When Will I Be Loved" when he was dating Jackie and once said something to the effect that he should have listened to the lyrics a little better and maybe he wouldn't have married her. Apparently she and Archie were "on" Dr. Max Jacobsen's injections, and they introduced Phillip to them, who in turn introduced Donald to them. We all know the rest of that miserable story.

On September 9, 1966, their first son, Phillip Jason, was born in New York City.

In February of 1970, Jackie and Phillip's marriage was dissolved. The family community home which was bought in October of 1964 for $115,000.00 was listed for $180,000.00 and was ordered sold. It finally sold in March of 1972 for less than the listing price, and this amount was divided in half between them. Jackie also retained half of all the monies Phillip earned from several musical entities, some of which were "A Voice Within," "Bowling Green," "Cuckoo Bird," "Do You," "Lord Of the Manor," "Mary Jane," "Shady Grove," "Talking To The Flowers" and "Texas."

Phillip was forced to pay Jackie $800.00 per month alimony for thirty six months and child support for Jason was set at $400.00 per month. The child was divided between his parents according to a strict schedule, half to one and half to the other, on odd years the first half of the vacation, on even years the second half or visa versa. Each vacation, including minor ones such as Columbus Day and Lincoln's Birthday, were still designated as holidays and the child was ordered picked up by Phillip at 9:00 a.m. to be delivered back at 7:30 p.m. Phillip also got to have the child three weekends a month, two short and one long, as well as Wednesday after school until 7:30 p.m. Jason Everly attended private school.

If you ask me, this passing around of children like a football is horrendous, but I assume this is standard legalese and is done all the time by the courts. Since I have never had to divide a child in half, I never really thought much about it, but realize now that this sort of "child division" goes on daily throughout America. What cruel and inhuman punishment for a little kid. What if he (or she) doesn't want to go that day and wants to play with his friends, but Daddy or Mommy say they want him anyway, and it's their day to have him? What kind of resentment builds up inside a child who is court-ordered to travel from one parent to another? The thought is a terrifying one, at best. Not only do the children get extremely confused, but the adults must also get very "parentnoid."

PATRICIA LOUISE MICKEY - (Phillip's second wife) Patricia was a dancer and a former "Golddigger" from The Dean Martin Show. She was petite, slim, very pretty, and knew exactly how to coyly pose for photographs. She is the "Shy Di" of the Everly family.

Patricia and Phillip were married on July 15, 1972 and on September 25, 1974 in Los Angeles, she presented him with his second son, Christopher Isaac. At one time, commenting on the difference in ages between his two sons Phillip quipped, "It was a long time between activity." At this time the breakup with Donald had occurred and Patricia and Phillip had moved back to Los Angeles.

On December 22, 1978, however, Phillip's and Patricia's marriage was dissolved, and apparently it was an extremely bitter divorce, as it has later become obvious that Phillip has pretty much sworn off women since he was with Patricia. Rumors abound from "fans" about Patricia's escapades, none of which bear repeating. It is said, however, that he still writes songs about her, but keeps most of them to himself. In the settlement, Phillip paid $800.00 per month for twelve consecutive months, then $500.00 per month for three months, and then some other amount to be determined by the courts for the next fifteen months.

This seemed generous, especially since at the time she was earning $1,700.00 per month as an actress. According to Bill Hollingshead, Patricia was a regular on General Hospital as - you guessed it - a nurse! It was also stated in the divorce decree that Phillip's GROSS income for 1978 was only $70,000.00! In addition, it was mentioned that the poor guy owed the IRS $40,000.00 in back taxes. Apparently this was not one of Phillip's best years. In fact for three years after this devastating divorce, he did practically nothing. It must have all been quite a blow and hard to recover from. But recover he did. Good for you, Phillip. Life does go on.

In addition, Phillip had to divide with Patricia all monies, royalties and residuals on every song he had written from 7/15/72 to 10/21/77, which included, "Better Than Now," "Cornbread and Honey," "Feather Bed," "Friends," "God Bless Older Ladies," "Goodbye Line," "Green River," "Invisible Man," "It Pleases Me To Please You," "It's True," "La Divorce," "Lady Anne," "Mabel's Room," "Music Is The Voice Of Love," "New Old Song," "Old Kentucky River," "Our Song," "Poisonberry Pie," "Red, White and Blue," "Snowflake Bombardier,"

"Summershine," "Sweet Grass County Montana," "Sheet Music," "Too Blue," and "You And I Are A Song."

I can see a wife being paid a settlement when a divorce occurs, but to get half of the royalties from the works straight from the heart and from a man's soul, i.e., his song compositions, seems downright immoral to me. I have been thinking very hard about it lately, and since my husband is also a songwriter, I wondered if I would accept money from them. After careful and thoughtful consideration I decided, yes, you bet your sweet bippy I would! I had to suffer when I was exhausted, trying to go to sleep while he was plunking a guitar in my ear in the wee hours of the morning (guitars have since been banned from the bedroom), in addition to not hearing a word I said because he was "composing." Also I was rarely able to sit down anywhere in the house for fear of sitting on a guitar or sheet music and when I was doing something in the kitchen, he would yell at me to "write this down" as if I always do the dishes with a pencil stuck in my teeth. Maybe it's immoral, but I would do it too if I were in Patricia's shoes.

In addition, Phillip was allowed to keep everything at his separate address in North Hollywood as well as a 1949 Cadillac (What IS it with all these old cars?!), various life insurance policies, bank accounts for various corporations and partnerships, shares of common stock and royalties and rights to all of his music that was copyrighted before the marriage and after the date of separation.

Patricia kept all the bank accounts which were in her name as well as a 1973 Buick to drive around in. Strangely enough, she had to agree that she had no interest whatsoever in Margaret Everly's house in Nashville.

KAREN PRETTYMAN - (Donald's third wife) Karen was working as Assistant Producer of The David Frost Show when Donald met her in 1972. They were married in 1975. She was his fiercest fan when he toured with his band, The Dead Cowboys, and they seemed to be close. As a matter of fact, there is a terrific photograph of Karen in The Sutler saloon in Nashville, where she seems to be just beaming up at him. Karen was reportedly of Cherokee and Apache descent, and she was his manager, at least she was up until the time he fired her.

In 1982, Karen sued Donald for divorce. Whatever it was that had been so close, became very distant. It could have had something to do with the fact that Donald had met a new love, a woman by the name of Diane Craig.

In the final divorce decree granted March 8, 1983, Donald was forced to sign over their car, the "VW Thing." Karen in turn was to hand over the key to their safety deposit box and each of them was able to retain any personal property which was in their possession. Donald, however, got to keep the "short wave radio, Minox camera and small oak dresser." (Couldn't you just cry?) Donald was awarded the contents of a storage container held at a moving company, with the exception of a collection of books and patterns which Karen could keep. Karen was awarded alimony of $36,000 which was divided up into decreasing monthly installments.

Karen is now busy at work as editor and publisher of the Nashville Hotline Creative Sourcebook, a reference for the music, film and advertising industries in Nashville. The Hotline is an annual publication.

Donald once again had to pay both attorneys. Donald was said to have been guilty of adultery.

In all of these divorces, Phillip and Donald were required by law to pay all of their children's medical and dental bills as well as to keep approximately $50,000.00 worth of life insurance on themselves, presumably so that even if they died, the women would be sure to collect their alimony. This was particularly hard to swallow for Phillip, who protested loudly by writing a song called "La Divorce" in which he addresses that very issue.

Actress Zsa Zsa Gabor, who has been through a few divorces of her own and knows how all of this works, insists, "You never really know a man until you have divorced him."

GIRLFRIENDS

ANN MARSHALL - This was one of Donald's girlfriends in 1971. She was an English model.

PENNY - Blond and very pretty, Phillip's girl when he was recording solo in England.

DIANE CRAIG - Diane was Donald's girlfriend who he reportedly met in Brown's Diner in Nashville. She supposedly was the one who "broke up" Donald and Karen, as he was still married to Karen when he met Diane. This, I believe cannot be done. I don't think a woman can break up a marriage if it is strong and has good foundations. There has to be extenuating circumstances that have weakened the marriage in the first place for another woman to just come in and take over. I don't know if this is true, however, as Karen flatly refused to give me an interview. But in my opinion, I don't think men will stray if everything is OK at home. Diane and Donald were said to be practically inseparable - until Victoria came on the scene. For a while he freely admitted he was involved with both women at the same time.

ROBIN - Rumored to have been Phillip's wife since 1988 although this is only a rumor. People don't get legally married and then hide their wives away like they did back in the Middle Ages!

VICTORIA - Donald's current main squeeze. Victoria is blond and has a daughter. It is rumored that she had been married previously to singer Larry Ballard, but I was unable to substantiate the facts. Some of the fans have dubbed her "Miss Vickie" and she, her daughter and a friend rode in the convertible in the parade in Shenandoah, Iowa in 1986, as well as in the Central City parade. It did seem rather strange to a lot of people that she and her child had this honor, as she wasn't even married to Donald. I am still trying to figure out why Phillip allowed it, especially since his own young son, Christopher, was there also and rode in a car all by himself at the end of the parade. He was not photographed much, and seemed to have been shoved into the crowd with everyone else instead of having a place of honor beside his famous father. None of Donald's four children were present, either. It all seemed to be an uncomfortable situation at best. Victoria, however, is still in evidence.

There is something very strange about all this, especially since it's generally thought that Phillip is hardly ever seen with a woman, and Donald terms his own relationships "adventures," a word which in itself has the connotation of something that will end after a while. He admits that he is a constant dreamer who wants to find true love but he also states (somewhat self-defeatedly) that his loves always end up "wrong."

> "If there's one thing better than marrying a millionaire, it's divorcing him."
>
> - Anonymous

Jackie, Phillip, Donald, Venetia and baby Stacy

New York

10
CHILDREN

*"Familiarity breeds contempt -
and children."
- Mark Twain*

It is generally believed that there were six Everly children born, four to Donald and two to Phillip. However, in Rose Hill Cemetery in Central City, lies the first Everly child who died the day she was born. According to the cemetery personnel, this was Donald's and Mary Sue's first child, Mary, and she is buried in the family plot next to Ike Everly.

The next oldest living "child" (they are all grown up, now) is Venetia who was a model for the Wilhemina Agency in New York. Her professional name was "Penelope" and she is quite exotic looking - very lovely and unusual. Donald and Mary Sue, Venetia's parents, were divorced when she was only three, so she was not around all that music her whole life. As a result, even though it is in her blood, she apparently had no particular interest in music, just in being a fantastic model in New York. I wish her luck. Venetia was born in 1959.

The next "child" to be born in 1963, was Donald and Venetia's daughter, Anastasia Dawn, or Stacy. Stacy now lives in Nashville.

The fourth girl born is also Donald and Venetia's daughter. They named her Erin Invicta. Erin was born in 1965, and she had joined her Uncle Phillip quite a few times on stage in California. She seemed to enjoy it. Calling herself a model by profession, she is a very pretty girl with a healthy head of long, dark brown hair, and has been famous in her own right to the younger generation as the girlfriend of W. Axl Rose of the rock band, Guns N' Roses. Axl reportedly wrote the song "Sweet Child O' Mine" for Erin, and on April 29, 1990, they were married. According to Axl's publicist, Bryn Brydenthall, the couple dashed across the state line by limo, in the pre-dawn darkness. After two or three indecisive moments, they were married at Cupid's Chapel in Las Vegas. It was all quite unplanned, but certainly not unexpected, as they had been together for a long time. It is pretty upsetting, however, when one reads an interview describing Axl's many women and sexual appetites, which are considerable, if he is to be believed. How could anyone marry a man like that, I thought? Perhaps in some way he reminded her of her father.

It was also not surprising that on May 30, 1990, just one month later, that Axl filed for divorce from Erin due to "irreconcilable differences." They apparently tried to make a go of it though, although breakups were quite frequent, and with all that money what should be a bed of roses, seems more like the War of the Roses. Not only that, the reputation of the Guns N' Roses Band follows them.

According to *Spin* in the summer of 1990, in response to a song called "One In A Million" which was not highly flattering to policemen, fourteen officers stormed their apartment, explaining that they were there because of an alleged complaint about loud music. The only thing that had been going on, Axl said, was that he, Erin and a friend, Sebastian Bach, were having dinner on their patio.

In October of 1990, Axl was arrested for hitting his female neighbor over the head with a wine bottle. Charges were later dropped. This event followed poor Erin's miscarriage, and so it goes, on and on. Life must be anything but dull at the Rose House. They stated, however, that they wanted to have children (!) and if they did, they would name them Shiloh Blue if a boy, or Willow Amelia if a girl. What, no Isaac? Later in the same year however, the very rocky marriage was finally terminated.

The next Everly baby to be born was Phillip's first son, Phillip Jason, who was born in 1966. He was named after Jason Robards because his father had seen Mr. Robards once in a play and he really liked him. Jason is the result of the marriage between Phillip and Jackie and he seems to enjoy singing. Although his voice is closer to his Uncle Don's than his father's, he enjoys singing the harmony part. Sounds like the best of two worlds. Tall, blond and handsome, Jason attended Chapman College in Orange, California, and at one time was considering pursuing a political science career at Santa Monica College. He is smart enough to know there are too many pitfalls in the music business to do that full time. Although sometimes he writes music, he stays away from collaborating with his dad because he thinks his dad is too famous and too talented. His home is in the Toluca Lake section of Los Angeles.

The next child born into the Everly clan was Donald and Venetia's long awaited bundle of boy, Edan Donald, born in 1968. Here we are again, two boys two years apart, except in this case they are cousins instead of brothers. Yet could there be a third generation of Everly Brothers? Although everyone would love it, I guess the two main people concerned do not think so. Edan, however, is apparently the most musical of all the children and he had his own band in Los Angeles for several years. It was called The Jive Spiders and Edan (naturally) played lead guitar. He is the only one of the six who has said he wants a career in music. He has joined his cousins on stage at The Palomino Club and joined a couple of the Everly tours in California, where he played guitar once or twice. In 1989 he showed up on stage with long, blond hair. In 1990, at the DNA Lounge in San Francisco, he played an Everly Brothers Tribute Concert with Bill Spooner of The Tubes. The band is under contract with Geffen Records.

Edan is the first to admit that it would be hard to be an Everly and not play the guitar, and he has been playing it around the house for years. He seems to just want to play guitar and not sing very much, but that could change. His father and uncle give him advice if he wants it, but they do not tell him what music to play and what to do. For that he is thankful. His music has more rock to it than that of Donald's and Phillip's, but he enjoys all music, including that of his famous dad and uncle. He thinks they're great as they are so very knowledge-able about music.

When Donald was interviewed once by Dolf Ruesink in London, the subject of raising his son cropped up. When asked if Edan ever criticized his father, Donald replied, "Oh, no. My son wouldn't." The interviewer said, "I mean in a positive way." Donald quickly replied: "No, he don't. Sons don't criticize in our family. I think that fathers and sons should have more respect for each other. I've always taught the thing about criticizing is, I think it's Michelangelo or Leonardo DaVinci, one of them said, 'I criticize by creation.' If you want to criticize somebody, create something that shows 'em. No, he doesn't do that. He doesn't pass judgments on our music. Neither (do) I pass judgements on his. I'm a believer every man's music is his own, and should be that, you know. Critique is made by the public, not individuals. In my life, anyhow."

Unbelievably, it was reported by The San Francisco Chronicle that Edan didn't even meet his own father until he was fifteen years old, even though he lived near his Uncle Phillip and became quite close to him!

Christopher Isaac, the youngest Everly offspring, was born in 1974 in Los Angeles, and was the result of the union between Phillip and Patricia. He is a great looking blond who, when just a little boy, was happy to bring his father's guitars out to him after the strings had been replaced. He would sit on a stool backstage and watch the shows from there. Sometimes he sings with his brother, Jason, and spends as much time as he can with his famous dad.

Jason teamed up with his little brother Christopher when Phillip was performing at The Palomino Club, and they often sang also with Donald's two daughters, Stacy and Erin.

Apparently Jason and Edan play guitars well together. Imagine such an Everly night!

When Donald was asked by *People Weekly* in 1984 why he doesn't spend much time with his children, he intimated that that's just how it is. He said, "When you have nothing, nil, with their mothers but a lot of strain, it's better to stay away." He also once stated that he didn't think his children really would miss him when he divorced their mothers, because he was never around that much anyway. How very tragic.

Phillip was once asked if he was going to make his young son a singer, or if he was going to tell him to keep well away from the business. Phillip answered quickly that he was going to make him a man first and then he can do anything that he chooses to do.

11
THE REUNION

"A man whose errors take ten years to correct is quite a man."
- J. Robert Oppenheimer

In late 1982, Donald picked up the telephone and called his brother in Los Angeles. Since he had left with the impression, "don't call me, I'll call you," he figured at long last to just do it. I guess he finally yielded under the daily pressure from family members and friends who kept asking when they were going to get back together again. Phillip later commented, "At least we don't have to listen to that question any more."

Basically, they wanted to settle things between themselves. They had that strong desire to see themselves up on stage again, and as Donald put it, "We had a lot of people that wanted to see it happen. I think probably all in all there was one thing, I didn't spend one day without somebody saying, 'why don't you get back together?'"

Donald had tried to call Phillip on his fortieth birthday, but sadly his brother wasn't home, and he never tried again until 1982. He said, "Hi, how you doin'?" Phillip answered, "Fine. How you doin'?" and they decided right then to get together.

Phillip stopped in Nashville on his way home from Luxembourg, and once together, they couldn't not sing. First, they had lunch and as Phillip later revealed, "We managed to get drunk and sick." (Donald's version was that they got "drunker than skunks and had a wonderful time.") Phillip said that it was a really fun lunch though, because Donald is so very funny and most of the lunch was spent laughing. That special lunch did the trick, and they were off.

Donald said that their reunion was a once in a lifetime thing, as music is what they are made up of, so it felt natural, once the wheels were in motion. Phillip added that it was the 'rightest' thing they could have done, because who knows - something bad could happen like one of them could die and "we fought before we made records, but we're going to be brothers for the rest of our lives."

In 1984, in London, England, on September 22 and September 23, at the ages of forty four and forty six, the Everly Brothers staged the comeback of the century.

After their much needed ten year hiatus, the Everlys decided to hold their Reunion Concert at the 6,000 seat Royal Albert Hall in London. They had both independently decided on this venue because they had sung there with their father before he died, and he had received a standing ovation. Therefore, they wanted their reunion concert to be held there. It was almost as if they were letting Ike see that his sons were one unit once again.

Phillip said, "When we decided that we were going to do something, we had to pick a place and we talked about the various places in the world that we would want to play in. The Royal Albert Hall is a special musical memory for us. We played here with our father one time and it was a chance for us to see him on stage and the people here gave him a standing ovation and it's just one of the fondest memories we've ever had and it just has always been a good place in my heart and I'm glad we chose here because it was just delightful last night. It was fun."

Many of their friends and families pleaded with them to do a couple of warm-up concerts to see how well they could sing together after all those years, but Donald and Phillip felt that that would be living a lie, that a Reunion Concert should be just that: a reunion, honest and real, and that's exactly what they did. They didn't think it would be fair to do anything they had tried out in secret; they just walked out on that stage that first night, cold.

Phillip later mused, "Without tooting our horn, we both sing very well separately. Before we went out on the stage at Albert Hall for our reunion concert, I guess it felt like two

parachutists fixing to jump off a plane. We didn't really say anything to each other. What can you say?"

It was also a personal reunion. Phillip said, "We decided to do this because we wanted to just settle the family thing
and we ended on stage and we thought we would start up on
stage again, although we had to be brothers first to make this
work."

Since they had to relax and be themselves first, of
course brothers can do that easier than most. They don't have
to try to be someone they are not. Also, if you've ever watched
the Everlys lately, it seems that over the years they have adjust-
ed to each other's stride, and seem to be comfortable with each
other's outbursts and silences. They just seem to fit.

Donald further explained it, "Phil and I have been
together musically since basically I was seven years old and Phil
was five. We were a family act with mom and dad and music
and it's just an extension of what we are. And it's always been
that way and we're now, I think we've really got the brothers
in front, the personal relationship in front of the act. I think the
act took over the personal relationship. I think that was the
problem. We sang off of one microphone for twenty five years."

Before the show, Donald reportedly told *People
Weekly* he was so nervous he couldn't eat. To help him calm
the butterflies, he "walked around Knightsbridge, thinking, 'Oh
my God, what if I forget this or that?' But once we got out
there, we got into it. It was an amazing sensation, a wonderful
high."

Although nervous as never before, they entered from
opposite sides of the stage down long staircases, in similar fash-
ion to the personalities of the men themselves; Donald fast, nervous and edgy, Phillip slower and more cautious. They were
amazed at the audience reaction and happy to know that it was
a sold out show. 'Sold out', Phillip's two favorite words, may be

putting it mildly. People flew over from the United States and from all parts of the world for this concert, but there were many people who were unable to purchase tickets. (Phillip's information was that 60,000 or 70,000 applications were sent in for tickets.) The crowd that was there went wild and gave them standing ovations time and time again. The crowd roared, and the music soared. It was a once in a lifetime experience, and to each of them, it was the culmination of a lifetime of ups and downs. It proved to the world that nothing could finish off the Everly Brothers. This was what they were born to do and that's exactly what they went out and did. They wowed 'em!

They looked at each other practically the whole time and one could see the connection in their eyes. The bonding and the love were there, and it was then we realized that it never had gone away in the first place. They opened the show with the rocker, "Claudette" and went through song after Everly familiar song. This concert formula has been used ever since, and the Everlys do sing the "oldies" when on stage. The reasoning behind it is simple: it works. They have decided, I suppose, not to get off the merry-go-round while it is still turning. Donald once explained it, saying that if they didn't sing the oldies, they don't think people would be very pleased. I know if I went to a concert to see one of my favorite artists, the reason I would go would be to hear them sing the songs that have made them famous, and the Everlys try to do the most requested tunes. Although it gets pretty boring for those who attend a lot of their concerts, it seems to tickle the memories of newcomers who rapidly become avid fans.

The variety of this Reunion evening, however, was endless and there definitely was something there for everyone from age ten to one hundred and ten. These guys were limitless in their universal appeal. It should also be noted that it was the first time that they performed "Ebony Eyes" live. They had omitted that song in the past because of the depressing subject matter of a man's fiancee whose plane crashes while he is at the airport waiting for her to arrive so they can be married. I agree that's pretty depressing, but now they place it in a medley of songs as a normal part of their concert routine. As Donald recalled, "It made a better record than a performance."

They were dressed in their familiar tuxedos with the high winged collars and worked their black topped Everly guitars precisely and beautifully. Phillip entered and exited with exquisite timing, while Donald knowingly and strongly moved the show through its paces. It was as though they had never been apart. One could have easily been fooled if they didn't know about the years of personal crises and the horrible separation the brothers had gone through. But the Everly Brothers are survivors and they staged a triumphant return. Indeed, they were victorious warriors returning from their own personal wars.

Phillip explained that it was quite scary at first and even though they had rehearsed together beforehand, it was still a little bit like learning how to swim. Sometimes you just have to jump in the water to find out what it's really like.

Afterwards Donald said, "Phil was like the Rock of Gibraltar out there. He has the high harmonies, which means he lays back until the last minute, so you never know with him until he cuts in. But when he did, he was really strong. I looked at him, and thought, 'He's doing great!' I was struggling."

Phillip countered with, "Donald just says that. When I'm not being a rock, he is, and I'm looking at him. Really, we're pretty stable. When we get on stage, we're on stage."

The day after, Donald said that they had heard a little from the night before and he enjoyed it and thought that they sounded pretty good. Of course, a performer always thinks he can do just a little bit better, but he thought that under the circumstances, they sounded mature, confident, musically sound, and they went over extremely well with their audience.

It was a Public Personal Performance and Phillip fairly bubbled about the experience afterwards. "It was as exciting as it could possibly get. Probably the most unique experience I've had in a long, long time. Probably never will in my entire life. It was a special, special night. It lived up to what we thought it would be like here in London, and I don't know. It's beyond words, it really is. Last night I described it like being in the twilight zone. I thought I was in some wild place." And wild it was - to go out there cold the way they did with a minimum of rehearsal time. You've got to really hand it to them.

Phillip remembered that during the song "Love Hurts," even he got chills, and they both stopped playing their guitars and just looked at each other and sang their hearts out during that one. It was beautiful. Donald likened the night to that of an out-of-body experience, where he could see everything happening there on stage as if he was a fly on the wall, and at the same time, he was prodding himself to remember lyrics, notes and just to do everything correctly. This fly on the wall feeling is common with many stage actors and entertainers.

The great thing about the Reunion Concerts was the fact that the Everlys became brothers and friends first and then they sang. Previously they put their shows before themselves as people, and of course that produced a great amount of deterioration in their relationship.

The story of the last song of the show is typical of their amazing abilities. The introduction to their scheduled song, entitled "Blues (Stay Away From Me)" is similar to another song, so by mistake Donald started singing, "Baby What You Want Me To Do," a song by Jimmy Reed that he and Phillip had not sung for eighteen years. Phillip jumped right in and they sang it in the best Everly tradition: perfectly.

After the concert they flew to Paris for dinner.

The night they began the concerts, the brothers were staying at different hotels, which they do quite often. Apparently some newspaper reporters were going around asking everyone why they weren't speaking, and if they were fighting. One spokesman, completely exasperated by all this, answered with, "What do you think they do, room together? They're grown men!"

Phillip remembered the ten years apart, and the differences they face in performing today. He thinks that they are definitely older, but "wiser is debatable." Of course things are more fun now, and people accept their music more readily than they did in the 1950s. The travelling is easier, due to the fact that the busses are so modern and comfortable, and the audiences are glad that rock and roll has lasted. They are proud that they have contributed to all that music.

Donald likes life more now than he did when they were just starting out. He said, "I'm enjoying it a lot more than I did, all in all. We're more mature and enjoy it... We had some time to ourselves which we had never had in our whole life. We had been working since I was about eight and Phil was six and so we had never had any stretch of time that we could call our own and I think that that was important...I think the Everly Brothers superseded everything else over Don and Phil." He also believes that the Everly Brothers are completely capable of singing almost anything together. He's right. They are.

Phillip brought up an interesting point about being an "oldies" recording star when he said, "There's another interesting fact that, when people say, 'back in the old days,' it was like if you did a song it was only as good as your current record. After you read a good book you don't necessarily throw it away. And I think that people are finally coming around to realizing that about music, you know, if they like it, they keep it. And they play it year after year."

To which Donald added, "We've been in the music business so long it's a lifestyle. It's a life with us. We don't think of it as old. We think of it as just what we do."

In a release from his publicist he had this to say: "Phil and I are tighter than before. As long as it continues to be as much fun as it's been, we'll go on. Our reunion has been a gift...you can call it manna from heaven." We hope so.

The reunion concert was recorded by Home Box Office into a fabulous LP, a video, and it is also on compact disc. All of these are definitely worth having (and keeping forever) by anyone who just loves a terrific show.

Doing What They Do Best

1964

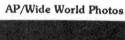

Doing What They Do Best

1983

12
PERFORMING

"After silence that which comes nearest to
expressing the inexpressible is music."
- Aldous Huxley

It is my guess that the Everly Brothers do not listen a whole lot to their own records, because many of their compositions and recordings relate so closely to their own life experiences. I tend to think, in fact, that it would be extremely painful to be struck over and over again with numerous bits of nostalgic shrapnel. Just a woman's name might conjure up months of feelings, situations and personal circumstances which would best be forgotten. A time or place could also evoke feelings which had been buried for years and which would be better off not brought to the surface again. Feelings, people, events, places and situations, even if joyous, become painful if they are no longer with us. I wonder how many songs are not re-sung and LPs not listened to for these reasons.

It is also almost impossible to truly enjoy one's own work because the performer remembers specific situations such as the musician who was off, a mike that didn't work or a sound engineer whose ideas clashed with his own. The session problems are remembered, and the music is barely heard. It is true that once an artist knows too much, all he can do is criticize and his enjoyment vacillates.

This might provide some explanation of why when on tour, the duo sticks basically to old, safe, non-personal tunes, and the really deep stuff is omitted. Even though they try, however, ninety-nine percent of their songs still have to have much personal meaning, as evidenced by the looks, glances, smirks, and other emotions which cross their faces when on stage. It really is a study in human behavior. Their eyes, which are at most times glued to each other, speak volumes. Their reactions to each other emit many emotions and they are as visibly affected by the music as are their vast audiences. This is why an Everly concert is such an emotional and exhausting experience, both for the performers as well as for the viewers.

As lead singer, Donald's work is constant. He starts and stops the songs with the band, sings all the solos, does all the talking, tells most of the jokes, and is "on" one hundred percent of the time. In contrast, Phillip's job is to be "on" when harmonizing, though he must bow out for portions of some of the numbers. His problem, therefore, is akin to an actor who makes numerous stage entrances and exits during a show. Although he gets several "breaks," he must bring his energy level up to snuff at each "entrance." This "on" and "off" scenario is just as exhausting and demanding as Donald's work, though not obvious and appreciated as much by an audience. Tired or not, they revel in it and are the ultimate pros in their performing milieu. Of course, Phillip has more physical freedom of movement than Donald does, due to the fact that his guitar is free, whereas Donald's guitar has a hook-up, thus limiting his movement on stage. One senses, however, profound movement in this man's very immobility.

Their unique talent, aside from blending perfectly, is that each one accurately anticipates what the other is going to do. They've done it this way since they were kids, and they don't even have to think about it, it is so natural. According to Donald, "We just open our mouths and we sing. That's how we do." And as is usual with brothers, one seems to call most of the shots. Donald seems to have taken on this role.

When one watches and studies these two men in action, some interesting things happen. Phillip is the more mysterious of the two, and he changes the most. Sometimes he seems nothing more than an older man with circles under his eyes and a boy's haircut; at other times he is like a rumbling volcano just before it erupts. A third time he will seem young, happy and carefree. Donald, on the other hand, is all business. Sometimes he is relatively jovial; other times he is dark, brooding and yes - angry. This man lately seems to have the weight of the world on his shoulders; he seems haunted by his own private demons. But at all times, Donald wears his emotions on his sleeve for all to see.

Terrific guitar work and their unique harmonious interpretations of the lyrics wields a certain magic that only the Everlys are capable of. Back in the 1950s, bandleader Mitch Miller, host of Sing Along With Mitch, stated that the Everlys' voices sounded like "two mice in a barrel," which Donald thought was pretty funny. Most, however, say that the Everlys' harmonization sounds like one voice with an echo. It's that close. Even though on their earlier recordings it seems as though Phillip sings a micro-second behind Donald, that slight variance disappeared as they matured.

The freshness of their live music stems from the freedom and talent that Donald has to improvise on the spot. He often changes the melody and sometimes even the words! He would never allow himself that freedom without having the express confidence in Phillip's uncanny talent to kick in and follow right along with whatever he can come up with.

Although they are famous for this ultimate closeness, at the same time because they are so famous, most audiences only want to hear the same songs the exact same way they have done them for years, thus halting any real creative processes. This very unwillingness of audiences to accept new material has been a thorn in their sides for years. I sincerely believe the Everlys have always been far ahead of their time; as a result much of their musical creativity has been wasted. Perhaps they could write a musical - a country musical if you will - as musical theatre audiences seem to be more flexible in their thinking.

No live performance is perfect, however, and things do go wrong. If by chance something strikes them funny and they start laughing in the middle of a song, barely a beat is missed and they come back strong with that Everly-perfect intertwined phrasing, intonation and harmony.

Lake Tahoe was a good example of a staging problem. One concert was not going well and it ended early when the Everlys walked off the stage. Apparently the management had complained that the music was too loud, which infuriated Donald and Phillip. The result was that, in subsequent concerts Donald kept angrily yelling at the sound engineer to "turn it up!" He also mentioned that they were not the Dorsey Brothers but the Everly Brothers. When the engineer finally got the sound to where the Everlys wanted it, the crowd couldn't get enough and went crazy. Incidents like this are fairly common in the business, but anyone working "tech" on one of their shows should be smart enough to realize that after thirty plus years of performing, the Everly Brothers should (and do) know precisely what they are doing. In short, you don't have to be a fucking genius to know they know what works with their music and no one should try to change it "for the better."

At rare times, one microphone will go out so they must finish up sharing a single microphone like in the old days, which is a special treat for their fans. One time in Florida, the entire sound system went out and they finished up the concert by singing "Kentucky" without any mike at all. Beautiful moments like this are so very special.

Phillip tried to explain how he feels: "I have no idea what really motivates me, because I've never had to be motivated, other than before we had a hit, I was trying to get some money - we were starving, so I know what I was doing - I suppose I could have gotten a shovel instead of a guitar, but outside of that I've always been motivated by working and you get a reward for it. But I think that if I weren't being paid, I think I probably still would do it. There are good parts and bad parts in it while you are doing it. You like parts and you don't like parts. So you can't walk off and say, 'Oh, that was a bore.' You just can't do that. I think you're too scared to do that. To be bored. Some things don't work the same as when you recorded them, and they have to be ... most songs are faster on stage and the ballads are slower and over the years we've found that that seems to work the best."

As brothers everywhere do, they sometimes get into backstage fights, but I think that's entirely normal. Number one, they are brothers and number two, they are creative, artistic, volatile, musically brilliant and perfectionists. It must be terribly frustrating to put one hundred and ten percent into something and then have just fifty percent say in what will be done with your brilliant ideas. As Donald stated in The Los Angeles Times: "You couldn't sing like that together if you didn't like each other. It's not like we're joined at the waist and spend all our time together ... but we do enjoy each other." That seems to be true, because if there weren't deep feelings there, there wouldn't be any fighting. It's just when the feelings run so deep that every-thing becomes meaningful and larger than life. As Donald's friend Tommy Smothers of the Smothers Brothers explained, "It's a lot like a bad marriage - lots of fighting and no sex!"

The Everly Brothers' band is one of the best in the world. It consists of Albert Lee on lead guitar, Larrie Londin on drums, Buddy Gene Emmonds on pedal steel guitar, and Phil Cranham on bass. The keyboard player changes. John Earl is back there also, making sure that all the guitars are strung, per-fectly tuned, and in good working order.

The brothers sing to near perfection and correctly assume that the music backing them will be perfect also. But no matter who is behind them, they will always sound like the Everly Brothers. Who on earth could copy the natural gift that they possess? Many have tried but none have succeeded. The closest I have heard is the Beatles, but there were four of them.

Phillip's harmonic perfection seems to enable them to sound like four! Their sound is unique.

On stage, the Everlys perform so intensely that there is a lot of sweat, (more on Phillip than on Donald for some odd reason), and they break a lot of guitar strings (Phillip again more than Donald). When Phillip's guitar string breaks, he hurls his guitar over the band, through the air to their equipment manager John Earl, who usually catches it perfectly. This has happened literally hundreds of times during their career, and I must say, it really adds to the show. And showmen they are. Even though sometimes in the press they are called things like "two hillbilly boys from Kentucky," they really have complete control of their audiences. It is the only life they have ever known.

It irks me, however, that they are STILL being called "boys!" But they are from the south and the south tends to call its men "boys" and its women "women." In contrast, for some weird reason northerners generally call their men "men" and their women "girls." Northerners also tend to think southerners run around saying things like, "Well, shut my mouth." In all the years I have lived in the south, I have never heard anyone say that, although I have heard a lot of people say "shut your mouth."

The Everlys perform in tuxedos, sometimes with high-wing collars and they look very dapper indeed. Though they joke about those tuxes with statements about feeling as though they look like two grooms on top of a wedding cake, the image they present is that of absolute professionalism. I love it! Personally I am sick and tired of seeing performers jumping around on stage in torn jeans and sneakers, a style that was probably started by the Rolling Stones. I just can't take them as seriously, somehow. Performers should look like performers.

Let's face it. The Everly Brothers are The Cry Kings, and have cried rivers of tears in their music, in some form or another. Every one of the following songs mentions it: "Crying In The Rain," "Don't Forget To Cry," "Be My Love Again," "I'm So Lonesome I Could Cry," "Have You Ever Loved Somebody," "Somebody Nobody Knows," "Sweet Grass County," "So Sad (To Watch Good Love Go Bad)," "Sigh, Cry, Almost Die," "Always It's You," "Kiss Your Man Goodbye," "Summershine," "She Means Nothing To Me," "I Wonder If I Care As Much," "You Make It Seem So Easy," "Since You Broke My Heart," "Yesterday Just Passed My Way Again," "I've Been Wrong Before," "Some Hearts," "A Nickel For The Fiddler," "I'll Mend Your Broken Heart," "The Sun Keeps Shining," "Bye Bye, Love," "Maybe Tomorrow," "Devoted To You," "Long Time Gone," "Oh, So Many Years," "The Ferris Wheel," "That'll Be The Day," "The Price Of Love," "It's All Over," "I Don't Want To Love You," "Talking To The Flowers," "Love Of The Common People," "She Never Smiles Any More," "It's My Time," "You Done Me Wrong," "Woman Don't You Tie Me Down," "The Facts Of Life," and they shed a tear in "Cathy's Clown."

For years the Everly Brothers appeared to be all but identical twins, but as they have matured, the differences between them have become much more apparent. When they were young kids, people could hardly tell them apart, but now they are physically very different and Donald in particular seems to be the one who makes the most of the changes. These two "moppets" have hair that won't quit. Phillip's hair is straight and basically manageable, but Donald's is an unruly mop. I wonder how he can get a comb through it. I guess I'm just jealous because I don't have all that curly hair. Donald also has rawhide hanging from his guitar, he sometimes wears cowboy boots on stage (which I detest) and he has an earring in his right ear (which I don't understand). In 1990 he sported a five inch long ponytail, which made him look a lot like Paul Revere with a perm. Even after the show, with his hair just washed and towel dried, some people think he looks a lot like a caveman. What's he going to do next? Put a tattoo on his forehead?

Comedian Rita Rudner says she thinks earrings make men feel big and knowledgeable, because after they have pierced their ears, "they think they have experienced pain and bought some jewelry." Who knows.

Both men have their own habits on stage, too. Phillip whips his guitar off and on a lot, whereas Donald keeps his on until he is ready to exit the stage. On the other hand, Donald's guitar is often held at an angle, classical style, and he moves it up and down a lot while singing. Phillip keeps his guitar more horizontal and stationary. Donald plays guitar harder and more often than his brother does, but Phillip is the one who concentrates on the harmonies that produce that unique Everly Sound. In addition, he darts all over the stage and on numerous occasions I would have bet a beer that he wouldn't make it back to the microphone in time to sing. Knowing when he is to come in, one sits there and panics, thinking "Where's Phillip?!!" He always makes it.

At the concerts I've been to, there seem to be two basic types of fans. There are "Donald people," and there are "Phillip people." I have seen a few who love both of them equally, but species such as these are rare. At times a fan might put flowers on the stage. Since Phillip is free to move he might pick them up, but sometimes they are for Donald. He then asks his brother why he has to be his flower delivery boy.

They make it look so easy, but both of them literally work their tails off up there. They both seem to cling to their guitars for moral support even when they are not playing, and Donald will play a riff or two for no reason in the middle of nowhere. Donald stays by his mike when singing, and during close-ups he seems not to move much. But from the waist down, he really is an active guy, often resorting to his little "bee dance" that he does when he sings. He improvises and hoots and hollers a lot, and yells at the band whenever he wants to. He plays all the time. Phillip will sometimes stop playing and just sing. Another thing of interest is that, although they are both left handed and play right handed guitar, when they grab a microphone for adjustment or whatever, the left-handedness resurfaces.

I think that the Everlys should hire someone to do a "ties and flies" inspection before walking out on that stage. I saw one show from the second row, where they really could have used some help in that direction.

The music of the Everlys is sometimes ultra simple, sometimes utterly romantic, sometimes sad and lonely, sometimes quite sensual. Of course their lyrics do not come close, sensually, to those of Conway Twitty, who sings the most sensual stuff of all. I used to adore him until I noticed in his autobiography that he implied that his songs were not sexy, they were completely innocent and if people think anything else, then their thinking is wrong. Oh, now really! Does this man think we just got off the turnip truck? Does he think we are all (as the Kentucky HeadHunters say) "dumber than rocks"? Conway Twitty sells sexy songs for money, and there is nothing wrong with that at all. What is wrong is for him to deny it. At least with the Everlys, you get honesty.

I might mention also that singer Don Williams ("The Gentle Giant") in my estimation, sings the most romantic songs on this earth. I could listen to that man all day long. What a superb, sensitive talent!

The two most important things that the Everlys seem to have wrong with them, however, is that Donald is overweight (which could kill him) and Phillip chain smokes (which could kill him).

When singing, Donald has a frequent twinkle in his eye. Both of the brothers, however, are basically serious and quite nervous as individuals. Donald's nervous habit of rubbing his fingers together in circles even makes ME nervous, and Phillip is all over the place, which is kind of cute. Donald stays right on top of his twin microphone, mostly looking at Phillip or the audience. He moves back to the band to play with them and/or talk and/or yell. He begins and ends the songs with either a hand signal or a downstroke of the neck of his guitar, and does the talking in between numbers. Of course his sense of humor, as well as Phillip's, is top notch and one wishes he would joke more, but the jokes he does come up with are downright hysterical. His humor is very subtle and dry.

Phillip, on the other hand, is Donald's rock. He comes and goes as the harmonizing requires, entering and exiting with smoothness and grace, almost always searching Donald's face for clues as to what he is up to next. Phillip is fluid and smiling on stage, easy and carefree, although he sings so hard into that microphone one wonders how his voice has held up all these years, especially with the number of cigarettes he smokes! It also amazes me that he never hits his microphone, even though he turns by moving his guitar neck either over or under the mike. It looks so damned easy! He usually says little on stage, and he laughs at Donald's jokes even though he must have heard many of them a million times before, but there is a love there that is unmistakable. In the final analysis, no one can deny that his older brother is very special to him, indeed.

These two individuals (and they are that) make up a third sound called the Everly Brothers. Both are certainly capable of holding their own as solo artists, but the public wants them to be pressed together like a wheel of cheese. In fact, when I listen to their solo works, I am truly amazed at their individual talents.

If anyone ever begins to think these two are washed up, the following review is typical of what they receive time and time again, city after city. Joel Selvin wrote in 1984 in The San Francisco Chronicle, they were "dressed in matching black tuxedos and playing identical blacktop guitars, their voices flowed together like water, Phil floating around on top, nimbly threading his way through his brother's singing. Lead vocalist Don Everly sang so hard, his sinuses must have hurt. There is a big difference between nostalgia and classic. A classic is something whose elegance time cannot disturb and The Everly Brothers are definitely that: the supple grace and shimmering beauty of the sound these two singers make together has only grown more lustrous over the years. They have a level of intuition others couldn't hope to match. Their voices are like shifting shadows of one another, rolling together in song, spinning, dodging and darting in and out like strands of string. They etched a spellbinding reverie out of old rock and roll songs and, for true believers, it was like going to church to hear the Everly Brothers sing again." Wow.

Their music is definitely God given, and it is a wonderful thing that - in turn - they give it back to others. It must make God proud that a talent can be given not just once, but twice. Their voices are astonishing. I think Donald's voice is one of the finest in the world and Phillip's voice is unique in the world as well as being so sentimental and sweet that there is no one who can come close to it. These two voices blended together are incomparable. These two men are music personified.

I find it hard to understand, however, why these men do not have a hit record, as they certainly have the talent and expertise to produce one. Perhaps it is because of the tendency of today's industry to concentrate on the "young stars" and leave most of the older but very talented artists in the lurch. Sometimes I think that if one of those "young favorites" sang "Three Blind Mice," it would be promoted ad nauseam into a hit song.

In addition, it seems that today's concerts in general have deteriorated to a new low. The excuse is that the kids who attend concerts now want instant gratification, big production numbers, and they do not necessarily require talent. Many performers have shows that include laser beams, fireworks, hoards of dancers (some of which seem to insist on at least one episode of mock sexual intercourse), giant movie screens, scanty costumes (which change with each song), innovative lighting designs, and worst of all, canned music! Yes, many of the entertainers of today lip sync their routines, and with all the other things going on in the show, their output is limited to eight or ten songs. They seem to be caught in a definite lip sync/dancing ego trip, and I cannot possibly imagine paying high concert ticket prices to see someone dance to a tape. It's utterly ridiculous. If I want to see a performance of that caliber, I might just as well stay in the comfort of my own home and watch it on television.

Of course the lowest of the low was in 1990 when Milli Vanilli won a Grammy for a record that they didn't sing a note on! Actually, someone should have presented those two with an Oscar. They surrendered the Grammy when the news hit the press, but that doesn't excuse such blatant dishonesty. I think the entire worldwide industry needs to take a long, hard look at itself.

I also think that the whole video scene has more or less ruined good music. Personally, I think most videos stink. The acting is bad (most singers are not good actors -why should they be?), there is no story line, method or reason for the video in the first place, and worst of all the camera work on most videos makes me seasick. For some unknown reason, the constant, rapid jumping from one scene to another is perpetrated upon the public as good video. It is not. Also people tend to place the video before the song, and that, too is backwards. Music is to be listened to. The song must be the foundation.

I really must give the Everly Brothers credit for not succumbing to this latest non-talented lip syncing craze. At a live Everly performance, what you see is what you get. If their voices are strained because of one night stands, then you hear them strained or hoarse, but they don't cop out and rely on technical voodoo. They sing all of their songs themselves, and do one after another like the true professionals that they are.

13
CREATIVE
EFFORTS

*"One machine can do the work
of fifty ordinary men.
No machine can do the work
of one extraordinary man."*
- Elbert Hubbard

ACTING

In 1961, armed with their new million dollar Warner Brothers contract, Donald and Phillip decided to travel to Hollywood to become actors. They enrolled in Mr. Peyton Price's class at Warner Brothers Studios. Although a screen test was reportedly done on them by a major film studio at a cost of $25,000.00, and they were photographed with a copy of Constantin Stanislovsky's *An Actor Prepares* and other Method reading material on acting, someone forgot to tell them that acting takes years to learn and just because you can sing doesn't mean you can act. They both were smart enough to admit that this was true. As a matter of fact, Donald thought it would probably be easier to make an actor a singer than the other way around (which is not true!).

After they saw the rushes from their screen test, they thought they were terrible. Over the years they have wisely turned down numerous other film offers because they felt the film people were just exploiting their singing talents, which was probably exactly what was happening.

In their one and only movie, Donald and Phillip were cast in a B-grade western where they would say some lines and then sing something like "Take A Message To Mary." This all progressed along quite well until Donald had to say a line which read as follows: "And bravely dare the danger that nature shrinks from." This sentence has no place in the English language, much less in a western! It was such a ludicrous line that Donald understandably could not remember it and finally had to read it off of a piece of paper taped to the table. When they left the studio that day, Donald said to Phillip, "See you" to which Phillip replied, "Yes, but not in the movies." Thus, their careers as actors ended and they returned to what they did best. The footage was later destroyed.

ART

"Art is the most intense mode of
individualism that the world has known."
- Oscar Wilde

Although extremely talented in many areas, when it comes to using the brush and easel, Phillip is not particularly artistic. Donald happens to be though, and, in fact is quite gifted. He has many ideas of his own about art, which he discusses from time to time. "I got very interested in art and I am very interested in how music connects with the art world, and that to me should be ... the artists are aware of the music, but the music's not aware of the art - the artists. That should be together. All of the writers and all of the singers and all of the musicians and all of the artists, all that should have more in communication. Because the art world will not be governed by the business world which is such a drag."

When questioned on his hobbies, Donald answered that he has collected many things, including cars, horses, antique guns and pop art. He also paints. Apparently Donald inherited his artistic bent from his father, Ike.

IN THE RECORDING STUDIO

"It is wise to learn; it is God-like
to create."
-John Saxe

There have been quite a few stories about the Everly Brothers in the recording studio. According to production people who have worked with them, it was an experience unlike any other. In some ways it was terrifying. To begin with, the brothers would write their own songs and then go into the studio without any arrangements whatsoever. Most of the time when they were young, they would just sit together on the floor and work out what was going to be done, go into the studio, and then record the song. This was very unconventional behavior, but luckily some of the studio executives were intelligent enough to realize that these kids were turning out hit records all the time, and they didn't want to rock the gravy boat. So even though no one else worked that way, they were allowed to, though with a great amount of trepidation on the part of management. We know now that they were geniuses at work, but at the time I am sure the older executives were not too convinced.

In the '50s Phillip explained, "Usually if we were preparing to record, we would come into Nashville and we would just start looking, just go through all the songs that they had. If we'd been writing, we wouldn't always use it. We would just go through everything that they had and sometimes we would find something immediately, sometimes it would take a long time and we did "Wake Up, Little Susie" the second record. We went through everything we had and Boudleaux wrote that on the way to show us some other songs, and we finally wound up with that. And "Problems" he had specifically written for us with the holes in it for the guitar and things like that. So once we got the song settled and a sort of basic guitar arrangement and what would work harmonically, we just called ... Chet Atkins and Hank Garland and Buddy Harmon and Ray Eddington and 'Lightening' Chance on bass. And Floyd Cramer on piano. And we would just all go in and show them the song at the session once it's started, and go with it."

He also remembered Archie Bleyer's basic recording principles. Archie wanted a great song sung by people that the song fits and it needed to have something interesting in the beginning to arouse interest and then he just let the song do its thing. Donald and Phillip basically have followed along those general lines.

When they got older their style changed somewhat, but it was still very strange. Donald and Phillip would usually arrive at the studio in separate cars and Donald would go into the booth and strum his guitar and sing a few different versions of the song. He'd bang around in there for quite some time while Phillip sat in the control booth quietly studying him. He didn't say anything, he just watched Donald start and stop and try this and that. When he was good and ready, and not a moment before, he would join Donald and they would proceed to try out the song. They would not talk to each other, but would just look at the other one and sing. At first it would sound terrible, and studio executives would give horrified looks to each other and become very worried. But they kept working and working and all of a sudden the incomparable sounds of the Everly Brothers' harmony filled the air. Then they would leave. Separately.

Some of the time, however, Phillip would talk with the band and go over the rhythm and instrumentals that he wanted, and Donald would go sing the choral part with the backup singers so they were sure of what he wanted. Then both of the brothers would explain to the sound engineer exactly what they wanted for the whole production. Then they would record it.

Looking back on the old days Phillip remembers, "We might run over it for two days and you might do it for like an hour, you know, fooling around with it, trying to get a formulation for the direction you're going to take on the arrangement. And then you'd go in and cut it and it usually would take you know, seven or eight takes at the most. You know, a dream might be like four takes and those kind of things, you know, when you were cutting live. And it just, it's a nice thing about cutting live that I still, it's a question whether you, with all the technology today whether you're better off. I don't know."

On their early two track recordings, the brothers were expected to play guitar on the instrumental track, and then do the vocals on the second one. As the technology improved, however they stopped playing guitar on their recordings.

Nowadays, some of the records in Nashville are being made with computerized sound systems like the MIDI System. If it is mixed correctly, it can be made to sound as if one has an entire orchestra backing the singer. It is a fine system for beginners or for someone who can't really pay for a lot of session musicians, but it is not for the Everly Brothers. They use real musicians and live music is heard. And who can blame them! Perfectionists? Professionals? Nothing but the best? "Yes" to all three.

While Donald writes much of their material, he claims he doesn't really finish the song until he gets into the recording studio. But, whatever it is they do, it works. The magic has never left.

COOKING

"All sensuality is one, though it takes many forms, as all purity is one. It is the same whether a man eat, or drink, or cohabit, or sleep sensually. They are but one appetite, and we only need to see a person do any one of these things to know how great a sensualist he is."
- Henry David Thoreau

Donald considers himself to be a great chef, a great "Mediterranean Chef." Maybe so, but the following does not exactly fall into that category. It more closely resembles Heart

Attack Heaven. It is, however, one of his "roots" recipes, and is real Southern cooking in its most basic form.

DON EVERLY'S FRIED CHICKEN AND CREAM GRAVY

1 fryer
Salt and pepper
2 cups milk, or more
Shortening
Flour
2 tablespoons bacon drippings

Rinse chicken in cold running water. Cut into serving pieces. Salt and pepper lightly and place in large bowl. Cover with milk and refrigerate at least two hours or overnight. Remove from refrigerator and allow to return to room temperature. In a large skillet, melt shortening to measure 1/2 inch. Drain chicken pieces, reserving 1-3/4 cups of milk for gravy. Dust with flour, salt and pepper by shaking pieces in a paper bag. Add bacon drippings to skillet; when small bubbles appear on surface, reduce heat and place chicken pieces in pan. Brown evenly on both sides. Cover and fry for 15 minutes; turn pieces and fry for 15 minutes uncovered. Drain on paper towels. Pour grease from skillet, reserving brown drippings and about one table-spoon of fat. Place over high heat, add 2 tablespoons flour and stir constantly to make a brown roux. Gradually pour in the reserved milk and continue stirring until the gravy comes to a boil. Reduce heat and simmer for 2 minutes. Season to taste. Serve with fried chicken and buttermilk biscuits. Serves 4.

At one point Donald and an attorney friend of his founded a little group called Les Amis du Vin, and no doubt toasted many times to the glories of the grape. Phillip also is a wine drinker as are most Californians.

Donald likes pasta and Italian dishes better than any other food, whereas Phillip's favorite food is meatloaf! It probably has to be made like "mama" made it though, as meatloaf is one of those foods like stuffing. Many people make it differently but you always like it the way your mother made it.

Another thing that is very personal is what you eat when you are sick. It has to be what your own mother gave you as a child, such as chicken noodle soup or cinnamon toast and tea, or you honestly don't feel you will ever survive the illness.

Do you suppose that Margaret made them spaghetti and meatloaf?

JOHNNY CASH PRESENTS THE EVERLY BROTHERS SUMMER REPLACEMENT SHOW

In the summer of 1970 the Everly Brothers were hosts of Johnny Cash's show while Mr. Cash took the summer off. There were ten shows in all, and they gave the Everlys a chance to do something different than they usually did, as well as shine as individual performers. The shows were excellent.

The format used was simple and effective. The Everlys began each show with their theme song which was "Bye Bye, Love" and ended it with "Let It Be Me." (Surprised?) Because it was the year 1970 however, they always ended the song with a final phrase, "Give peace a chance" which was a real sign of the times.

As guest stars, the Everlys hosted Mac Davis, Rick Nelson, Linda Ronstadt, Johnny Cash, Ike Everly, Marty Robbins, Arlo Guthrie, the Statler Brothers, Neil Diamond, Dennis Weaver, Stevie Wonder, the Lennon Sisters, the Carter Family, Jimmie Rodgers, Brenda Lee, and the Ike and Tina Turner Revue.

In addition they had some little known entertainers, including a fellow called Tony Joe White who was billed as the "King of Swamp Music." Now, I have heard just about every kind of music in the world, but swamp music was a real surprise. These people sing of 'gators in swamps and swamp cabbage and other disgusting things. Even though I live in North Florida, I have a hard time forming any kinship with such weird stuff. Perhaps that's why the Everlys had this on their show. Was it yet another rebellion?

There were two comedy sketches on every show that were very good. The most popular with the audience seemed to be when the ABC parking lot guard by the name of Joe Higgins appeared on every show and gave the Everlys a hard time. Guard Higgins' character was a "You in a heap o' trouble now, boy" kind of person. He called them "summer replacement boys" and "two singing boys who wear funny clothes." He also labelled their music "that narcotic music" and was endlessly towing their car away unless they did what he wanted. Guard Joe Higgins was very funny and immensely popular with the audience.

The next popular segment was a weekly visit from Aunt Hattie, "The Everly Family Historian" who would tell stories about relatives and ancestors of the Everly family. This bit was played by actress Ruth McDivitt and the names of the Everly uncles used were actual names of Donald and Phillip's real uncles. In addition, there really is an Aunt Hattie in the Everly family. This sketch was also tremendously popular.

167

The music that Donald and Phillip sang was so varied it took your breath away. They sang "their" songs, new songs, patriotic songs, religious songs, Beatles songs, medleys, solos, accompaniments, duets, and they even sang a barbershop quartet song with just the two of them. Amazingly enough, it sounded like there were four men singing. Only the Everlys could have pulled this one off!

My favorite part of each show, however, was in the very beginning when Donald and Phillip answered live questions from the audience. In the first place, it takes a lot of guts to stand in front of millions of people and answer questions right then and there. In the second place, the answers have to be amusing or interesting in some way and it's not easy to come up with something very good at the drop of a hat. The Everly Brothers did it, however, and did it well. So well in fact, that the thought did cross my mind that the questions might have been staged. Their quick wit and good humor, however, endeared them forever to their audiences who appreciated some closeness with the performers. The following is a sample of some of their wonderful answers.

Q: Do you like sports? (from a girl)
D: Indoor sports
P: Are you a sport?

Q: For a hobby, I'm a part-time brain surgeon. What are your hobbies? (also from a girl)
P: Well, I've got a little bit of brain damage...

Q: What kind of girls do you like?
P: Soft girls.

Q: Do you two ever fight?

D: Do we ever fight!

P: We've only had one fight. It's been lasting 25 years now.

Q: Do you have any animals? Pets?

P: Yeah. He has me.

D: He's not housebroken, though.

Q: Why don't you grow beards?

D: Phil's been shaving for 10 years and he's cut himself both times. That's one reason.

Q: How long have you been singing together?

P: About 20 minutes.

D: About 25 years. This is our 25th year.

Q: Do you find that girls are always chasing you?

P: They're always chasing him.

D: I'm pretty easy to catch, too, by the way.

Q: Do you carry your complete sound system with you when you travel on the road?

P: Just our vocal chords.

Q: What is the age difference between you two?

P: Six months.

Q: Do you ever get nervous when you have to perform?

P: No, only when I'm not performing.

Q: What embarrasses you?

D: Questions! I don't get embarrassed too much any more. I wonder if that's good? I think so.

Q: Are you eligible?
P: What? To be read about? Or for anything else?
D: I'm eligible!
P: What've you got in mind?

Q: Are you twins?
P: Mama said we weren't, but you know how women lie.
D: I'm the oldest, he's the youngest. Has been ever since I can remember.

Q: Do you answer any controversial questions?
P: No, we don't.

Q: Of all your hits, which is your favorite?
P: "Let It Be Me" is my favorite.
D: The next one.

Q: What kind of woman do you find most attractive?
P: A woman woman.

Q: How long does it take for you to rehearse for the show?
D: Oh, I don't know. We've been rehearsing now for about 25 years.
P: And we're gonna' keep at it until we get it right.

Q: Do you ever read about yourselves in fan magazines?
P: Not lately. I wonder why.

Q: Do you wear the same clothes on the street as you're wearing now?

P: No. I go naked on the street.

Q: Is there a song that you've done or haven't done since you started that you wish you would have done?

D: Every hit I ever hear I wish I'd sung.

Q: When did you learn how to sing?

D: We're still learning!

Q: What makes a person sexy?

D: Pardon?!!!

Q: What makes a person sexy?

D: I guess, sex!!!

During their last show, good friend Tommy Smothers was in the audience, and he asked the Everlys how one stays on television. To which Phillip replied that he was asking the wrong people, as this was their last show! It was a perfect ending to the audience's questions.

Unfortunately their TV show was not renewed, but I feel that the Everly Brothers showed a marvelous innate ability to communicate and endear themselves to a television audience. They should have been given more shows, as talent like this is almost impossible to come by nowadays.

Photo by Jerry Spie

14
ROCK AND ROLL
HALL OF FAME
AND
MUSEUM, INC.

"Fame is a fickle food upon a
shifting plate."
- Emily Dickinson

On January 23, 1986, the First Annual Rock And Roll Hall of Fame Induction Ceremony was broadcast live from the Waldorf Astoria in New York by "Mr. Music," Norm N. Nite. It was a black tie affair hosted by Radio Station WCBC-FM. The Everlys became Charter Members. With thirty four charted singles, they were one of the first ten inductees, along with James Brown ("The Godfather of Soul"), Fats Domino, who had over seventy charted singles, Chuck Berry, Jerry Lee Lewis ("The Killer"), Little Richard, Ray Charles ("The Genius of Soul") and posthumously Elvis Presley ("The King," with one hundred and forty three charted singles), Sam Cooke and Buddy Holly. Disc jockey Alan Freed was also awarded a special place in the non-performance category as was Sam Phillips, founder of Sun Records. In addition, a precedent was set to honor three pre-rock pioneers each year and call them "early influences." The first year they included Jimmy Yancey, Jimmy Rodgers, John Hammond and Robert Johnson.

The evening was attended by approximately one thousand people who paid between $300.00 and $1,000.00 a plate to be included in this event, and the night ended with an all-star jam. Most exciting was the caliber of both the attendees and the presenters, all of whom were enthusiastic about helping to make this an annual event.

Chuck Berry's award was presented to him by Keith Richards, Steve Winwood presented James Brown with his, and Quincy Jones gave Ray Charles his award. Herb Alpert presented Sam Cooke's award to Sam's father, and Billy Joel gave Fats Domino his trophy. Neil Young, who insisted that the Everly Brothers were the inspiration for Buffalo Springfield, presented the Everlys with theirs, (Neil Young, interestingly enough, has a pet buffalo named Mammouth!) and John Fogarty gave Buddy Holly's award to his widow, Maria Elena. Hank Williams, Jr. made the presentation to Jerry Lee Lewis,

Roberta Flack presented Little Richard with his, although he was not in attendance due to an automobile accident. He had made a videotape, however, for all to enjoy. Julian and Sean Lennon gave Elvis Presley's award to the Executive Director of Graceland and a telegram was read from Elvis' daughter, Lisa Marie. This event marked her first public announcement.

As of this writing, many of these people, both inductees and presenters alike, are still in the news. Neil Young has had hit albums, and in 1990 he claimed the dubious distinction of releasing the first LP to have the new lyric "warning" on it; Hank Williams, Jr. is very big in country music; Lisa Marie Presley is married and gave birth to Elvis' first grandchild; Billy Joel continues strong; and Jerry Lee Lewis' autobiographical book and film entitled *Great Balls of Fire* was an enormous success.

On the other side of the coin, John Lennon was murdered; Little Richard came and went on the news; James Brown was in jail for a long time and is now in a release program, and Chuck Berry was accused of secretly videotaping women using the rest room, and has since brought suit against *High Society Magazine* which published pictures of the sixty three year old Berry in nude photos with several different women. He claims that the photos were stolen. But what a great talent he is!

The regulations for induction into the Rock and Roll Hall of Fame are as follows: It must have been twenty five years since his/her first recording release. The selection system is relatively simple. Ballots are sent all over the country and around the world with a list of thirty or forty artists who had had charted hits from 1950 - 1959, inclusively. Approximately three hundred industry professionals are invited to vote for as many as ten acts. The ten with the most votes were inducted into the Hall of Fame. Each year another year is added, so 1987 included the years through 1960. In subsequent years such as 1989, sometimes there were as few as five members inducted. In 1990 there were only eight. The selected inductees are usually announced in October.

Fortunately, although the Everly Brothers were counted as one inductee, they were both awarded a trophy. Donald later remarked, "This award we won't have to saw in half."

The Hall of Fame was the brainchild of Ahmet Ertegun, who had worked at many record companies and had been president of Atlantic Records at one time. The Hall of Fame building is scheduled to be built in Cleveland, Ohio. It was designed by world-renowned architect I. M. Pei at a 1984 cost of approximately twenty million dollars. By 1989 the cost had more than doubled to forty eight million dollars, and in 1991, sixty five million dollars was quoted. Much of the financing is to made possible through taxation of the Tower City Project which will consist of a hotel, an aquarium, The Great Lakes Museum of Science, Technology and Environment, retail shops, a radio broadcasting studio, a recording studio, a rock 'n roll sound and video system, and the world's most extensive rock 'n roll library and archives. The entryway to this Tower City will be eighteen stories high and encompass 85,000 square feet of space. This will be The Hall of Fame. Apparently the City of Cleveland is responsible for financing this huge project. The city requested $6.9 million from HUD to help finance the project, but was turned down. HUD stated that it was up to Cleveland, private citizens, rock and roll musicians and the music establishment to raise the money.

Why the City of Cleveland? It just so happens to be the city in which disc jockey Alan Freed coined the term "rock and roll." It is also where the first rock and roll concert was held in 1952. In addition, the people of Cleveland wanted the museum in their city. Over 650,000 people signed a petition and an additional 110,000 telephoned their support in a poll conducted by USA Today. It is hoped that the museum will attract over 700,000 visitors a year, the amount needed to make the project pay for itself.

By the November 15, 1989 deadline, it was announced that $40.2 million had been raised and that a groundbreaking ceremony will be taking place in late 1992, although its location has been moved to North Coast Harbor on the shores of Lake Erie in the heart of downtown Cleveland. Many people contributed to the fundraising efforts and it seems that the museum will be a reality after all.

In 1987 The Second Annual Hall of Fame Ceremonies were successful also, although there were more inductees than ever. Honored that evening were the Coasters, Eddie Cochran, Bo Diddley, Aretha Franklin, Marvin Gaye, Bill Haley, B. B. King, Clyde McPhatter, Rick Nelson, Roy Orbison, Carl Perkins, Smokey Robinson, Joe Turner, Muddy Waters, and Jackie Wilson. In the non-performance category were the songwriting team of Jerry Leiber and Mike Stoller, as well as Leonard Chess, Ahmet Ertegun, and Jerry Wexler. The three "pre-rock pioneers" that second year included singer/songwriter Hank Williams, rhythm and blues singer and composer Louis Jordan, and bluesman T-Bone Walker. Somehow I think that the selection committee is straying from the name "rock 'n roll" when such diverse artists are lumped into one category.

Interestingly enough, the "backstage dinner" that night was typical fare and included meatloaf, mashed potatoes and gravy, and Oreo cookies. How elegant!

Very few artists were inducted in 1988, but they included some powerful names. They were the Beach Boys, the Beatles, the Drifters, Bob Dylan and the Supremes. In the non-performance spot was Berry Gordy, Jr. and, for early influences, Woody Guthrie, Leadbelly, and Les Paul.

In 1989, Dion, Otis Redding, the Rolling Stones, the Temptations, and Stevie Wonder were inducted. Phil Spector was included in the non-performance category, and the Ink Spots, Bessie Smith and the Soul Stirrers were honored for their early influences. The ceremony was dedicated to Roy Orbison, the first Hall of Famer to die since being inducted.

As the years pass, the distinction of being chosen seems to become more dubious each year. The 1990 inductees included Hank Ballard, Bobby Darin, the Four Seasons, the Four Tops, the Kinks, the Platters, Simon and Garfunkle and the Who. In the non-performance category were brothers Brian and Eddie Holland and Lamont Dozier, and Carole King and Gerry Goffin. As early influences of rock 'n roll, Louis Armstrong, Charlie Christian and Ma Rainey were honored.

At the 1990 induction ceremony, Paul Simon stated that he felt at home in the Rock and Roll Hall of Fame, because his relationship with Art Garfunkel had been so rocky. He said, "We can join those other happy couples, Ike and Tina Turner, the Everly Brothers, Mick (Jagger) and Keith (Richards), Paul (McCartney) and all of the other Beatles. Maybe they'll have a separate wing for all of us, probably completed in time for the Eagles to be in."

Apparently even associates who have known the Everlys for years still believe they are at odds a lot of the time.

15
MUSIC
FESTIVALS

*"You must look into people,
as well as at them."*
Lord Chesterfield

THE EVERLY BROTHERS
MUSIC FESTIVAL
CENTRAL CITY, KENTUCKY

In 1988 a phenomenon called The First Annual Everly Brothers Central City, Kentucky Music Festival took place.

In addition to the Everlys, many other performers appeared, including John Prine, Lisa Childress and Dennis Payne. It was a one day festival and approximately 8,000 people attended. The Everlys were billed as "new legends" which sounds something akin to "fresh raisins" or "free agents." These terms are oxymorons in the purest sense.

There was a parade, the Everly Brothers Monument was unveiled in front of City Hall, (I thought monuments were only for dead people!) Donald and Phillip pressed their hands into cement for posterity, and speeches were made. The entire city boasted it was the "Home of the Legends" and many out of towners flocked into Central City, in Muhlenberg County, Kentucky.

In 1989 The Second Annual Everly Brothers Music Festival took place. This gala had by now mushroomed into a three day festival, so my husband and I ventured to Kentucky to see what all the hoopla was about. I told my mother we were travelling through the coal mining region of Kentucky, and her retort was, "But Dear - no one in our family has ever been to Kentucky!" My brother, who lives in Greenwich, Connecticut, had a different reaction. All he said was, "I hope you had your shots." After being there for about an hour, however, I fell in love with both the region and its people. The only complaint I had was that Muhlenberg County is a "dry territory" (meaning

180

no liquor allowed, darn it!) which tends to put a damper on one's vacation.

On the first day, there was an Everly Brothers Luncheon and Golf Tournament. Not one celebrity participated, including the Everly Brothers. The Central City Times-Argus reported that the tournament would include some celebrities in the future.

At 6:30 p.m., The Muhlenberg County Everly Brothers Fan Club Picnic took place. Local musician Royce Morgan of Beechmont, and others, entertained. About two hundred fans reportedly attended, fifty of whom were from out of state.

The second day a Fan Fair was held where souvenirs and T-shirts were sold, and a Celebrity Auction was held. About twenty five items were sold and a little over $2,000.00 was raised. Various items were donated by artists such as Willie Nelson, the Statler Brothers, Hank Williams, Jr., Alabama, and John Prine.

At 8:00 p.m. a massive talent search was held. Sixty people auditioned, and eleven were chosen to compete. The winner of that contest was Debra Tuggle of Louisville, who won $250 in cash and five hours of studio time at the local Central City Recording Studio which is located on Ash Street. In subsequent years, auditions were conducted via tapes sent through the mail.

On the last day of the Second Annual Music Festival, a Thumbpicking Contest was held. "Thumbpicking" is a term used for the unique guitar playing method for which Muhlenberg County is famous. The entrants were all unbelievably good, and I would think that this contest must have had a special meaning to Donald and Phillip, because their dad had been one of the first to use that method of guitar playing. Mose Rager and Merle Travis were also thumbpickers and those gentlemen's wives, Mrs. Mose Rager and Dorothy Travis were present. Mrs. Ike Everly was, well - conspicuous by her absence. At lunch that day Donald said that he wanted to go see the show, but of course he couldn't. He said it was too bad he couldn't just go sit and listen without being the "belle of the ball."

The "colors" of the festival in 1989 were yellow and black. The drinking cups were all yellow and black, and Everly fans around Central City were all wearing yellow T-shirts with black photos of the Everlys on them. At lunch, the Everlys (Donald in particular) said they did not like them at all and kidded with his cousin Ted about his part in designing them. Donald then said he thought all the people around town looked like a bunch of bumble bees. He then held a T-shirt up to his chest and proclaimed himself to be a "Killer Bee."

At a press conference that afternoon, the Everlys urged industry to come to Muhlenberg County so people would have more jobs. Katy Moffat arrived late, but John Prine was there as well as Duane Eddy. The Everlys STILL expressed a wish to be on the top of the music charts.

At 6:00 that night, the Concert Pre-Show started. We sat in the second row. We were required to bring our own chairs, and luckily we had very comfortable directors chairs which were lifesavers. I couldn't believe how many people attended. There were people everywhere! Estimates ranged from 12,000 to 15,000 people, and about $40,000.00 was raised. When I got back home to Florida, I told my daughter that I had indeed attended "Kentucky Woodstock." I think that's almost as good as the fact that my husband actually did attend the real "Woodstock."

Amazingly enough, the show started EARLY, at 5:20, which must have been a first in the history of show business. It seemed everyone connected with music was there, and it was damned impressive, I must say. One disappointment was that Chet Atkins had been scheduled to appear but had to cancel out at the last minute due to scheduling conflicts. What a shame, as my husband is a die-hard Chet Atkins fan! He did, however, perform at the 1990 Festival.

Katy Moffat, who was the Everly Brothers' opening act that year, performed. She has a lovely, clear country voice and plays guitar with expertise. She is friendly, talented, cute as anything, and usually manages to sing at least one song that her brother Hugh Moffat has written. Another singer, a local resident of Central City, Molly Helton, sang "C.C.'s Ready To Go," a song about the Everly Brothers returning to Central City. Also appearing were Capitol recording artists New Grass Revival, an Italian singer named Ricardo Biano (who didn't fit in with the scheme of things at all), and instrumentalist Duane Eddy who was accompanied by his fabulous saxophone player, Dennis Solely. Mr. Eddy, a Grammy Award winner who recorded such songs as "Pepe" and "Peter Gunn," also performed his famous "Rebel Rouser." Sonny Curtis was there from the original Crickets, singing his self-penned hit, "I Fought The Law And The Law Won," and another local, John Prine along with his wife, sang several tunes and ended with "Paradise" which Donald said had become "the national anthem of this festival." This extraordinary song describes in detail the town of Paradise, down the Green River from Central City, which is now nothing but a bunch of smokestacks due to the "rape" of the land by the coal companies. Donald referred to John Prine as "the best kept secret in the music business." All of these entertainers played and sang a lot of songs.

In addition to all these relatively known entertainers was Debbie Tuggle of Louisville, winner of the Amateur Talent Contest who played and sang a few songs, along with Dr. Larry Kilgore of Birmingham, Alabama, winner of the Thumb-Picking Contest of 1989, and the world-champion thumb-picking winner for the last two years, Eddie Pennington. Two recipients of

$1,000.00 scholarships, Melissa Turner and Matt Bell, went up on stage to be introduced. I think the crowd considered Melissa the real winner of the day as she got a kiss from both Donald and Phillip!

The concert was opened by none other than the city's own Mayor Hugh Sweatt who is a jolly chap and Central City's answer to Billy Carter. Mayor Sweatt is a character, and a nice one at that. As a matter of fact, there were so many people playing (this was, after all, a Music Festival), that by the time the Everlys got on stage to sing, I was exhausted and wanted to leave. Of course the Everlys are the best and I quickly changed my mind, but by the time I did, they were gone and the whole thing was over. Many fans were disappointed by their short appearance, but fortunately for me, I was to view one of their best shows ever two days later.

As my husband had a Press Pass, he was permitted to stand right in front of the stage and snap pictures. He quickly took two rolls of film of the Everlys singing, one right after another, with his most expensive camera equipment. How lucky we were to be able to stand right there in front of the Everly Brothers and take photo after photo!

We took our film to a professional studio so it could not be lost in transit. Here is the result of our once-in-a-lifetime photo session: Due to a technical error, your film was damaged during processing. We have enclose a replacement roll of film and your prints at our expense.

Please accept these and our apologies

If you have never seen a woman go into shock and complete hysteria before, you really missed the show I put on in the store that day! Thank God I am not the proud owner of a gun, or I might be finishing this book from Death Row at Florida State Prison.

Donald and Phillip had discussed the show that day at lunch and Donald wanted it to be an easy, "hometown" show, sort of like singing on their back porch, and said that he just wanted to have fun and not do their "act," that they will take their "act" to Vegas. Tempers began to flare as they also argued over whether to wear their trademark tuxedos. It was almost decided to appear for ten minutes or so in them and then change into something more comfortable, but eventually they changed that to doing the whole show wearing them, after which Phillip said to Donald who was becoming quite agitated, "Don, OK, OK - don't get your blood pressure up. Someone decide what we're going to do and I'll go along with it!" Apparently he did just that.

Donald's present girlfriend, Victoria, was much in evidence and was accompanied by her daughter and a little friend of hers named Francesca. It's smart to have a friend along, as the kids have someone to be with when Mom is busy doing other things, such as making The Great One happy.

One thing I must say about the people of Muhlenberg County is that I was charmed by them. In the first place there was no booze there, and as far as I could see, no drugs. I usually am fairly reluctant to attend events with thousands of people present, but this was a joy. The people of this Kentucky community were soft spoken, "country nice," friendly and quietly behaved. I would enjoy going anywhere in Kentucky to be with such beautiful people. According to newspaper reports, the event raised $40,000 for the Everly Brothers Foundation, and in 1990 seven $1,000 scholarships will be awarded to students from various Muhlenberg County schools.

There are approximately 400 volunteers who work all year to stage this music festival, and I think it is a fabulous thing if it accomplishes all that it sets out to do. The work that was put into the festival by everyday people clearly showed. The handling of that many concert goers was smooth and friendly, and went without a hitch. Later in the year, all the volunteers are invited to a "thank you" potluck dinner, which I think is a nice way to show appreciation.

After the concert while walking back to our car, there were a lot of people yelling at us to walk the other way because of the mud. They kept warning us about the mud as if it was quicksand. My husband finally mumbled to one woman something intelligent like, "Mud's mud." She replied, "But this is Muhlenberg County Mud." We thought she was more than a little strange, but I am sure that anyone who has ever been to Muhlenberg County understands what she was trying to tell us. Where I come from, mud dries and you just brush it off. Right? Wrong! Muhlenberg County Mud hardens and stays there. Back in the hotel we tried to get the stuff off our pants legs and shoes. I know we ruined almost every towel in the room and actually it did look like something pretty awful had taken place in there, like an ax murder or something. I was relieved that I probably won't have to fight with Muhlenberg County Mud again for a long time. It would be difficult to be the mother of little boys in Muhlenberg County! I give Margaret and all the other mothers a lot of credit in this department.

The nice thing about these festivals is that the proceeds go to the Everly Brothers Foundation which helps provide some other worthwhile things besides scholarships. The Everlys themselves initially donated $7,500 to Central City so the city could buy new police radio units. Apparently they had had antiquated systems and the city did not feel as though it was able to adequately protect its citizens. With the new money, they installed a high-band frequency with a new base station, as well as new radios in all the police cars. The Everly Brothers were rewarded in 1982 when local Highway 62 (also called Chestnut Street) was rededicated and became Everly Brothers Boulevard.

In 1988, the Everly Brothers Concert cleared about $20,000 and in 1989, it cleared almost $40,000, not including about $15,000 worth of souvenirs. Gate receipts counted for a lot of that money, but there was also a lot of food sold. In particular, 5,000 hamburgers, 1,200 hot dogs, 1,000 polish sausages, 250 pounds of barbecued pork and 800 gallons of RC Cola. It clearly proved to be an event worth remembering. The scholarships themselves are awarded from the interest generated by the money which is deposited in a trust fund. A student in Muhlenberg County has a pretty good chance of getting some of that, because in 1989 there were only 5,844 students enrolled in school in the entire county.

The Third Annual Everly Brothers Music Festival in 1990 was extended to cover four days! Chet Atkins joined them; the Kentucky HeadHunters generated a stampede; John Prine played again, as well as singer/songwriter Lane Brody, son of the legendary Merle Travis, who died in 1983. The Everly Brothers were present more as hosts than as entertainers, and they dedicated the concert to the soldiers in Saudi Arabia. The concert reportedly cleared close to $100,000.00.

The activities included a couple of golf tournaments, a local fan club picnic, an EBI fan club luncheon organized by Jeanette Blackstone, gospel singing, a celebrity auction, a talent search, a couple of track meets, a thumbpicking contest and then finally the concert, which is the first thing that the Everly Brothers attended. The 1990 event, Homecoming III, was attended by approximately 20,000 people.

SHENANDOAH, IOWA

Shenandoah, Iowa is located in Page County and it has a population of 6,274, less than it had in 1960. It has a 44 bed hospital, 20 Protestant churches, 1 Catholic church, and no Synagogues. It is commonly known as the "Seed and Nursery Capitol of the World," and it is the childhood town of the Everly Brothers.

The May Seed & Nursery employs approximately 108 men and 84 women, and the Henry Field Seed Company now has its own unique Trial Ground and Show Garden where thousands of varieties of flower and vegetable seed, grasses, farm seed and nursery stock are tested. Thousands of visitors from all over the world come to see it. The favorite display is an American flag made up of 5,000 red, white and blue petunias. It "sits" on an 83 foot "flagpole" made up of 950 marigolds. The trial ground covers 25 acres and definitely should be seen if you are ever in the area during the summer months.

After perusing all of the brochures and pamphlets sent to me by the Chamber of Commerce, I noticed that there was no mention of Shenandoah's most famous "sons." I guess someone did not want to acknowledge all the brouhaha of July 5, 1986.

On that date, Phillip and Donald Everly rolled into Shenandoah, Iowa to be honored guests of the day. They participated in a parade down Main Street. Then, after stopping at the Depot Deli for hot dogs and beer, they held a press conference in the library, and signed autographs all day. The Depot Deli has an "Everly Wall" with lots of photographs, and now it has been scrawled on by the Everlys themselves, thus authenticating it. Fremont Street was renamed Everly Brothers Avenue, and both were presented with honorary Shenandoah High School diplomas. In addition, there was a dedication for an Everly Brothers Memorial, and they both managed to pose in front of one of their old childhood homes. They stopped at the local drug store to get a cherry coke (for Phillip) and a cherry phosphate (for Donald). At 7:00 that night, dressed in their standard tuxedos, sweat pouring off of them, they put on a fantastic outdoor concert in front of approximately 8,500 fans. Unfortunately, the concert was cut short because of a very strong thunderstorm which drenched everybody. The Everlys hurried to their class reunions of 1955 and 1957, and then boarded the busses for the trip to North Dakota, their next stop. No wonder they look tired!

A large amount of the Everlys' pay went to establish an Everly Family Scholarship for students, which assists children from Shenandoah's Middle and High Schools as well as those wanting to go on to college. The scholarship is based on need, not on academics, although I believe both surely should be taken into consideration. It has been set up as a self-perpetuating trust with the interest from that trust to be used for the scholarships. Only local children are eligible, which is as it should be. Apparently the Everlys have expressed a wish that all students, regardless of income, should be able to attend school if they so desire.

What is perplexing to me is that this Shenandoah Festival was a one time thing. Granted, the Everly family "roots" and "kin" live in Kentucky, but Donald and Phillip themselves went through all of grade school, junior high and part of high school in Iowa. These were their formative years, so Iowa holds a very special place in their hearts.

According to a report in Newsday, the Everlys were sponsored by Iowa Homecoming '86, the same group that sponsored bringing twin sisters Ann Landers and Abigail Van Buren to Sioux City, Iowa, for their high school reunions. With backing such as this, I don't know what went wrong.

Reportedly the concert organizer, Bill Hillman, lost money on this venture, but hopefully he will be able to recoup some dollars on souvenirs and other paraphernalia that the Everly Brothers Committee has to offer. This was the dream of one ordinary man, to bring the Everlys back home, and I hate to have dreamers squelched. I am very big on dreamers. Good luck, Bill!

16
THE PRESS

"Modern business and persons and organizations that seek publicity must recognize their obligations to the public and to the press."
- Henry F. Woods, Jr.

Donald and Phillip are extremely cool towards journalists and the press. Aawwwww. What has the press ever done to them? Almost everything I have read has been absolutely glowing. They have been referred to as the Terrific Twosome, the Woosome Twosome, the Dream Team, the Dandy Duo, the Dazzling Duo and the Dynamic Duo, as well as the Brothers in Charms, the American Nightingales, and of course the Foreverly Brothers. There has been an occasional reference to the Neverlys or the Elderlys, but titles such as these are usually used to make the writer seem clever and cute. Phillip humorously dismisses such drivel with comments like, "at least they're talking about you." I am glad they have such self-confidence. After all, they know their kind of talent will always survive.

Basically, there is hardly anything bad ever said about the Everlys, and if anything derogatory has been said in the past, a little of that is to be expected. They are public figures and it goes with the territory. The Everlys talk of so many bad experiences with the press, but I have yet to see much evidence of this at all. I have notebooks filled with articles vowing that these guys are the innovators of harmony, the heroes and role models that past and present singers emulate and singers in generations to come will continue to try to copy and will idolize. If you see an Everly article, you know it will be almost boring before you even read it because it is so cheerful and glowing. You know what I mean? It's a bit like their concerts - same old stuff.

I have read only a couple of bad reviews on these two, and know of only one or two writers who do not hold them in high esteem. That's quite a track record for two men who have lived over fifty years each and who have met literally hundreds and thousands of people all over the globe. They should be pretty happy with their reputations both in the business and outside of it. Most artists can't come close to being so loved and respected by their peers. In 1989 there was some bad British press, but then the British press says bad things about lots of people. Apparently someone asked a question that Donald didn't exactly appreciate, and as reported in the May 10, 1989 issue of The Daily Mirror, Big Bad Don blew up and let loose with a string of obscenities "you'd never find in an Everly ode." After several more steamy oaths, he reportedly marched off in frantic search of the bar. So what? Why isn't the man allowed to swear when he flies off the handle if that's where his proclivities lie? Maybe he was just having a bad day and was at the end of his rope.

In contrast, once when Donald was being interviewed on radio, the deejay thanked him and accidentally called him Phil. The man realized his mistake almost immediately and started frantically apologizing. Donald very good naturedly came back with, "That's OK. We answer to either one."

Let's look at the men themselves. They have been hounded by the press for over thirty years, and for the most part have been asked the same questions over and over again. That in itself could bore one silly. If a reporter asks how old you are, it's simply because he didn't do his homework. Prince Phillip sometimes will snap back with, "How old do I have to be?" Let's also not forget that the Everlys are geniuses, both musically and in the area of comedy, so they should be expected to be a bit erratic in their behavior. And lastly, I think swearing is good for one's health. It makes one feel good to sound off, as it releases a lot of pressure. Some people say that those who swear can't speak English, or are too dumb to think of something to say. Baloney. I think I am quite intelligent, and both Everlys are very smart as well as being quite verbose. No, the men have every right to swear if they so desire.

It should also be realized that some members of the press deliberately goad personalities not to get information, but they are trying to get the most interesting interview possible in order to further their own careers. To do that they try to trick the artist and/or ask "cutesy" questions that will baffle, shock and/or enrage the person being interviewed. The Everlys know this.

Entertainers should remember also that those who giveth applause can also taketh it away, and bad press is only a vehicle. Sometimes it helps more than it hurts. If, however, an entertainer treats interviewers badly, then the ink can really hit the fan.

Donald insists, "We had bad press until the late '60s or early '70s." In the '50s, he recalled, "Rock got terrible press then. Many adults thought we were all stealing hubcaps when we weren't on stage. Either that or we were doing something else evil. There were a few people who would treat you good, and of course the audience that came to see you was great, but there was a lot of junk in between that you had to contend with."

We need the press. The press keeps tabs on what is going on and it can actually change the world. For instance, just try to imagine where we would be if it were not for Carl Bernstein and Bob Woodward, the two Washington Post reporters who broke the Watergate Scandal.

Not that the Everlys have been angels, of course. After all, they are men and have done all those men things, but never with malice and sometimes certain things happen to people which are beyond their control. Their lives have been filled with long, lonely nights, weeks and months out on the road. That can encourage any performer to seek solace whenever and wherever it can be found. Of course this does not bolster up one's marriage, but it is the same tale told throughout the entertainment industry, especially when on tour. The Everlys are no different, and as they grow older, one can see that their faces have taken on that haunted, world-weary look.

Touring must be very exciting for the first three or four years but after that, it has to become extremely boring. Your only reward (and the most sought after) is that wonderful sound of crowds cheering and giving you night after night of standing ovations. This is the food and drink of the performing Gods. For they are just that: performers, and that is what they do - open their mouths and sing. They don't know any other way to do it; they don't know any other life. The Everly Brothers have been on tour (with the exception of the ten solo years) since 1957. That's a lot of tours and a lot of songs and a lot of travelling. Obviously they must sing "Bye Bye, Love" at every performance. One fan told me they made a joke of how many times they performed it in the past when she saw them at a concert in Atlantic City, which signaled the end of one of their long tours. Donald said, "This is the eighty second time we've sung 'Bye Bye, Love' on this tour." To which Phillip added, "On a career basis that's one million, seven hundred thousand times!" But the amazing thing is that they sing it a little bit differently every time, yet it is still the same song, by the same guys, and it seems fresh every time. What troupers. What madness. What joy.

As Phillip stated in 1984, "The travelling is harder than when we were younger. We have three times as many people as we had in the old days. The venues are better, but there's a lot of difference. You can still tell when you're doing it right and when you're not. But it's so technical now that you can hardly keep up with it." Their singing still comes naturally to them, but it comes with a lot more sweat.

Speaking of touring, a newspaper article in The Boston Globe comes to mind of an interview with Nanci Griffith, who had been their opening act that year.

Nanci toured for almost five months with the Everly Brothers, and she raved about the experience, especially of her relationship with Phillip. She told the press, "I think watching their show every night was a massive influence. They were influences in my youth anyway. But just watching how they sing harmony and work the stage was a very good experience. Plus meeting Phil was great. He's a wonderful friend. A pal." Strangely, she never mentioned Donald, and I wanted to know why. Nanci Griffith would not grant me an interview.

Phillip was once asked if he was anti-press. He answered, "No, but I try to avoid them. It's not worth the time." Gosh. I was under the impression that all people in this public game need the press. As George M. Cohen once said, "I don't care what they call me as long as they mention my name." I really don't know how the Everlys got to be so different. Perhaps they think it adds to their charm, but they should try to remember that old saying by Rafio, "Never argue with people who buy ink by the gallon."

On the other hand, referring to his composition entitled "Safari," Donald said, "I didn't get good reviews ... from *Rolling Stone* I thought it was a very bad review. Yeah. They also said, they said in there that "Safari" was an excuse for me having gone to Africa, and I don't need excuses. I can travel wherever my passport lets me and even places that it won't if I take a notion. *Rolling Stone* doesn't give me permission to go to Africa. That's what I mean. When I set down to write a song, I don't write a song for the money ... a song like "Safari" was not directed at all towards the top ten records. It's about my problems. I write about what I do, what I think. It's like a picture of a place in my mind, and I just describe it. I don't just sit down and write a song because I think it'll make a good song. I just don't do it that way. It's just a feeling about a place and I try to put those feelings in my music and it comes out that way." So there.

In 1989 after the British press lambasted the Everlys, the brothers said that they will never give another interview to anyone. It's a shame that they feel that way. It's also a shame that some reporter sitting in his cozy den can write untruthful things about entertainers. It is similar to the air traffic controller in a control tower telling the pilot that he is cleared to fly through those cumulonimbus thunderheads. He is sitting safely on the ground, whereas the pilot is being bounced around in the middle of a dangerous storm. What does the controller know - really? The same is true for the touring entertainer. He is out there barely surviving long, arduous nights on the road, singing with many problems some nights, lacking many of the luxuries we all come to expect, and sweating like a pig. What does the press know of what is really going on in their minds and bodies?

That's precisely why entertainers should grant honest interviews to defend themselves against hard core journalists who are determined to make them look like losers. Sometimes they lose out no matter what they do.

Phillip and Donald

COMMONWEALTH OF KENTUCKY

•DEPARTMENT OF HEALTH
Bureau of Vital Statistics

CERTIFICATE OF BIRTH

12004

1. **PLACE OF BIRTH**

County of _Muhlenburg_

Vot. Pct. of _____

Inc. Town of _Browni_
or
City of _____

No. _____ St.
_____ Ward.

Registration District No. _1087_

Primary Registration District No. _685_

File No. _____

Registered No. _15_

If birth occurs in a hospital or other institution give name of same, instead of street and number.

2. FULL NAME OF CHILD _Isvac Donald Enerly_

| 3. Sex _Male_ | 4. Legitimate? _yes_ | 5. Twin, triplet, or other _____ 6. Number in order of birth _____ | 7. Premature _____ full term _____ | 8. Date of birth _Feb 4_, 19_37_ (month, day, year) |

FATHER	**MOTHER**
9. Full name _Ike Enerly_	18. Full maiden name _Margarett Enerly_
10. POST OFFICE _Central City_	19. POST OFFICE _Central City_
11. Color or race _W_ 12. Age at last birthday _28_ (Years)	20. Color or race _W_ 21. Age at last birthday _17_ (Years)
13. Birthplace _Ky_	22. Birthplace _Ky_

OCCUPATION
14. Trade, profession, or particular kind of work done, as spinner, sawyer, bookkeeper, etc. _Coal miner_
15. Industry or business in which work was done, as silk mill, sawmill, bank, etc.
16. Date (month and year) last engaged in this work _____, 19____
17. Total time (years) spent in this work _____

OCCUPATION
23. Trade, profession, or particular kind of work done, as housekeeper, typist, nurse, clerk, etc. _housewife_
24. Industry or business in which work was done, as own home, lawyer's office, silk mill, etc.
25. Date (month and year) last engaged in this work _____, 19____
26. Total time (years) spent in this work _____

27. Number of children of this mother (At time of this birth and including this child) (a) Born alive and now living _1_ (b) Born alive but now dead _____ (c) Stillborn _____

28. If stillborn, period of gestation _____ { months { or weeks

29. Cause of Stillbirth _____ { Before labor _____ { During labor _____

CERTIFICATE OF ATTENDING PHYSICIAN OR MIDWIFE

I hereby certify that I attended the birth of this child, who was _Feb - 27_ at _2_ _8_ m. on the date above stated.
(Born alive or stillborn)

{When there was no attending physician or midwife, then the father, householder, etc., should make this return.

(Signed) _____, M. D.

Given name added from a supplemental report _____ (Date of)

or _____, Midwife

Address _Central City Ky_

Filed _7-11_, 19_37_ _A L Bradfll_

Registrar.

Mayfair Auditorium, Shenandoah, Iowa

Georgia Department of Human Resources

VITAL RECORDS UNIT

CERTIFIED COPY

STATE FILE NO. _____

COUNTY NO. 1 - 732

Marriage License

To any Judge, Justice of the Peace, Minister of the Gospel, or any other person authorized to solemnize: You are hereby authorized and permitted to join in the Holy State of Matrimony

Don Everly 20 and Sue Ingraham 19

according to The Constitution and Laws of this State, and for doing so this shall be your sufficient license.

Given Under My Hand and Seal, this 25 day of March , 19 57

Harold G. Yates, Ordinary Ordinary
Probate Judge

I Hereby Certify, That

Don Everly and Sue Ingraham

were joined together in the Holy State of Matrimony on this 25th day of March , 19 57 by me in the City of

Ringgold, GEorgia , County of Catoosa , Georgia.

Recorded April 1st 19 57 Signature of Official Alfred L. Pullen

Book No. 5 Page 197 Title M. G.

Harold C. Yates, Ordinary Address Ringgold, Georgia
Judge of the Probate Court

I hereby certify that the above is a true and correct copy of Marriage Record as it appears in my office.

Witness my hand and seal this 10 day of August , 19 89

L. Queen, Clerk

IKE EVERLY
APR. 29. 1908
OCT. 22. 1975

Rose Hill Cemetery

MARY E. EVERLY
OCT. 10. 1957
OCT. 10. 1957

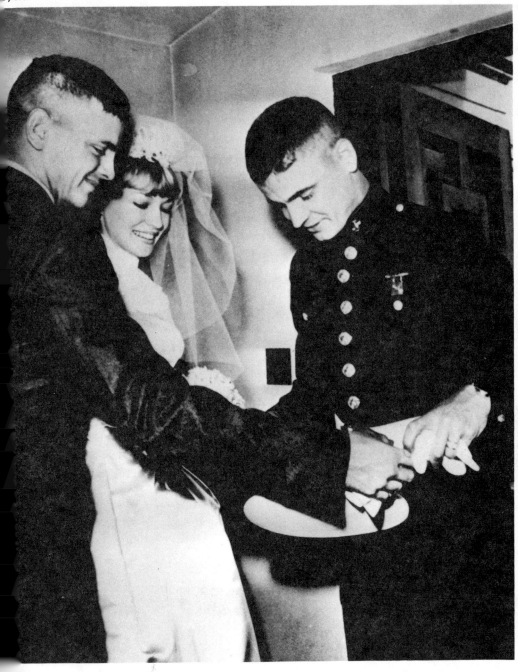

**Donald marries Venetia Stevenson with
Phillip serving as best man**

Donald walks with Venetia to waiting ambulance as he leaves Idlewild Airport, after drug overdose

Donald and Venetia's House
Studio City, California

Donald's House
Nashville, Tennessee

Brown's Diner

Brown's Diner
Dining Room Entrance

The Dead Cowboys
The Sutler

Photo by David L. Dodge

Karen Everly

Phillip, Albert Lee and Donald
Milwaukee, Wisconsin 1988

Janesville, Wisconsin

Waiting in the Wings

Hands cemented for all time
Central City, Kentucky

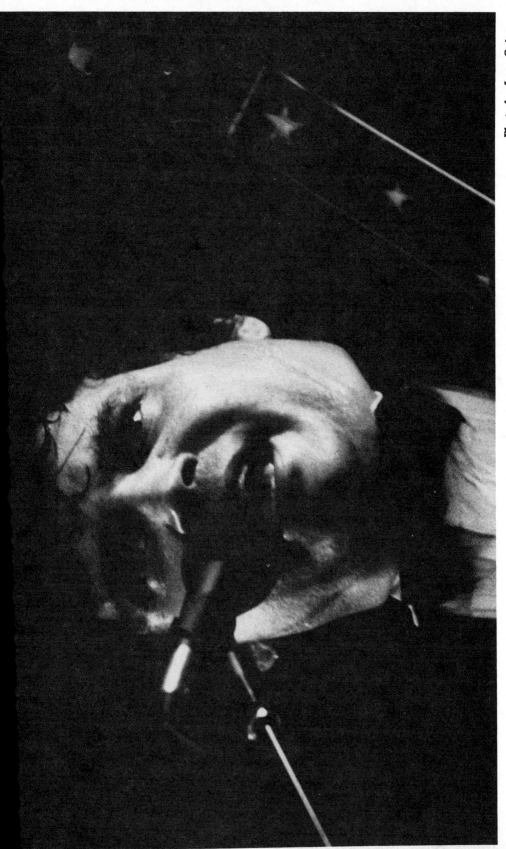

First Annual Everly Brothers
Music Festival in Central City 1988

17
SONGS

"The crowning fortune of a man is to be born to some pursuit which finds him employment and happiness, whether it be to make baskets, or broadswords, or canals, or statues, or songs."
- Ralph Waldo Emerson

The Everly Brothers' song catalog is interesting as hell. Since everyone knows all the juvenile recordings such as "Bird Dog," I am not going to dwell on these, although these young, simple songs earned them the most fame and fortune. One thing is certain; the Everlys can sing any type of music on earth extremely well.

For example, Phillip won BMI's (Broadcast Music, Inc.) award for his composition, "When Will I Be Loved," which was awarded to him for its having been performed more than two million times. Donald's song, "(Til) I Kissed You" was given an award for one million airings. In October of 1990 Donald was honored at BMI's 50th Anniversary Show with an award for "Cathy's Clown." Even though both brothers had written the song, Phillip had apparently signed his rights over to Donald at one point.

Congratulations are due to any composer who attains these levels, as BMI has listed only 99 two million level songs, and 653 one million level songs in recording history, up until the year 1989. These statistics are from a list that BMI gave me when I was in their Nashville headquarters.

One of the recurrent Everly Brothers song character-istics is the plethora of girls' names used. Sometimes it seems as though these men have little else on their minds as they have sung of Amanda Ruth, Mary, Mary Jane and Mary Ann, Jeannette Isabella and Jezebel, Carol Jane, Caroline, Anne, Louise, Rosie, Nancy, Jenny, Susie and Susie Q, Judy, Cathy, Ruby, Amy, Diane, Evelyn, Claudette, Chloe, Julianne, Suzanne, Mabel, Mabeline, Barbara Allen, Molly, Sally, Sal, June, Judy, Thelma, Rosie, Linda, Lucille, Bessie, Jessi and of course Donna who tortured them so by saying no.

Sometimes when introducing "Crying in the Rain," they mention that Carole King wrote it. Donald cries, "We should have married her!" Phillip replies, "And ruined her life, too!"

I have listed some of the following better known songs with a bit of prattle about them, which explains some whys and wherefores of the songs' makeup. I think it is interesting and adds a great deal to the songs themselves when the listener knows a bit of background.

> "Laughter is the tonic, the relief,
> the surcease for pain."
> - Charlie Chaplin

TUNE TRIVIA

"Amanda Ruth" - Donald really likes this song as it contains his favorite sound, similar to "Lucille." These two songs really set Donald into orbit. As a matter of fact, he thought for sure that it would be picked to be a single in the pop field, but it wasn't.

"Asleep" - This song is Donald's favorite that he wrote for the Everlys, and he admitted that it was written specifically to be sung by Phillip and himself. He started writing it at the time they broke up. It was a song of hope, a cry for forgiveness.

"Bird Dog" - Donald said this was "one of the songs that helped get us off the Grand Ole Opry." But on radio station KOA, Phillip mused over the recording of this strange song as follows: "You know, when you think about it, I liked it at the time. I kind of thought it was, you know, kind of cute, and then when Donald put in the chord changes, you know (he sings a little example), it just had something, you know? We almost, the producer of the record, Archie Bleyer, wanted to get ... there used to be an act on television that had a dog named 'Farfel' and he used to say, 'Choockooolllate' you know, it was kind of a commercial and he wanted get Farfel to come in and do 'he's a bird' and 'he's a dog' and we thought that that was the corniest thing we'd ever heard. We were fighting tooth and nail with him about that." At one of their later concerts, Donald admitted that they felt a little bit silly singing this song dressed in tuxedos. Of course, a female fan screamed at them to "take them off, then," which both brothers got a big kick out of.

"Born Yesterday" - This song took years for Donald to write. As he vaguely explains it, "It's a song about relationships that people sometimes, I think they aren't quite as sympathetic when they see a relationship breaking up you know, as they could be. They gossip, you know. I think it's a normal human thing to do but sometimes I think that they don't give the sympathy that is necessary to their friends and people, and it's a terrible thing for a relationship to break up. If anyone's ever gone through a divorce or a relationship that just isn't working and they need sympathy, instead of criticism, you know? And also people mess up their relationships. It sort of puts the blame in both places, actually. Relationships, I think, are important. That's basically what I think it is." Sadly, the man rarely mentions the finality of marriage, just the temporary term, "relationship."

A video of "Born Yesterday" was also made. Most of the song was "born" in Brown's Diner in Nashville.

"Bye Bye, Love" - Written by Boudleaux and Felice Bryant, this song was recorded in 1956 and was the Everlys' first hit in 1957. It was considered a 'fusion' record as it covered both rock 'n roll and western. It had been rejected by a great many artists (some estimates are as high as thirty) before the Everlys recorded it. Phillip remembers, "There's a famous story about Gordon Terry who was also signed to the company at the same time and Gordon felt they were sort of pushing the song on him so he was, he just resisted, and he tells the story on himself. I guess it had been turned down before, too. Mind you, Donald and I would have sung anything for the $64.00 session fee. So it wasn't like we were so bright that we knew it was a hit." The unique introduction was done right in the studio by Donald as he was just fooling around with his guitar. Boudleaux Bryant picked up on it and told him to play the intro at the beginning of the song. This guitar riff was the same one Donald had written and arranged for a song called "Give Me A Future."

Once on stage at the Palomino Club in North Hollywood, Phillip admitted that this song had paid a lot of alimony for him, and admitted softly, that he had indeed paid a LOT of alimony.

"Buy Me A Beer" - Was recorded for Phillip's friend Snuff Garrett. As Phillip thought of it, "It's about a guy down to no money and he needs somebody to buy him a beer. In fact, he needs an entire case (referring to the line 'slide me a case down here'). I must have been nuts when I wrote that. (But) it's a fun thing. I've lived it more times than I'd care to reiterate. It's a divorcing man's lament at a beer parlor which I'd been through a couple of times, so I knew the song real well."

"Cathy's Clown" - Their biggest all time seller, which was also their first record for Warner Brothers. Donald said, "I felt it was an awfully good sound. Very, very big sound for, considering we were still on two-track. I thought it was a good sound, a good idea. I was very happy with the way it turned out." He also said that he had re-arranged it a bit himself. Phillip remembered it, also. "That was our last year under contract with Cadence and we moved on to Warner Brothers and it was very important because there was much wondering I guess around us of what we can do by ourselves. It was an important record. We did a complete album before we did this. Donald called me one evening and he had written the chorus to "Cathy's Clown" and asked me what I thought. It sounded real good to me, and we were in the midst of cutting an album and we finished it off together. I felt very confident about it when we walked out. It had a brand new drum sound to it that in fact, hasn't been fooled with over the years. I was intrigued with it over the years and in fact just recently they had spun a couple of covers of it, but they still don't mess with the drum sound which is interesting ... we cut it in Nashville with the same musicians, the same everything, the same studio, the same everything, except without Archie. The drumming was done by Buddy Harmon. Buddy has done all the drumming out of Nashville for whoever cut in Nashville, Buddy Harmon was the drummer. The reason that rock and roll has that basic kind of raw, raunchy sound, is that Buddy, when he wasn't getting sessions, he was playing in a place called Printer's Alley which was a stripper's place, kind of an illegal stripper's place and well I've gone down to see not the girls, mind you, just to hear the drumming." Sure, Phillip.

In a May 8, 1986 interview for *Rolling Stone*, Donald remembered, "Part of the inspiration for "Cathy's Clown" was The Grand Canyon Suite: domp-de-domp-de-da-da-da, boom-chacka-boom. And then I had this girlfriend called Catherine. That was the formula for that one." Since that statement, several women have insisted that they are that very Catherine.

Donald also said he remembered his father telling him about a girlfriend he had named Mary. All the kids used to tease him saying, "Mary had a little lamb." That kind of attitude is also reflected in "Cathy's Clown."

This song was named by Donald in 1989 as his favorite song, but I think it was a tongue-in-cheek comment because at the time the money was rolling in due to Reba McIntyre's unusual hit cover. As a matter of fact, in October of 1990 Donald was presented with the Robert J. Burton Award at BMI's 50th Anniversary Celebration for The Most Performed Song Of The Year. Although they admittedly wrote this song together and both names are printed on record labels as writers, Nancy Moore of BMI confirmed that Donald is credited with being sole author.

"Claudette" - This Roy Orbison song was written for Roy's first wife, Claudette. Phillip once observed, "Donald's hands were really fast." It was given to them backstage by Roy, who wrote down the chords and lyrics on a shoe box top.

"Crying In The Rain" - This came out of New York, and was written by Carole King and Howard (Howie) Greenfield. It is one of the Everlys' favorite ballads.

"Dream" - The second most requested song they've ever recorded. At one point Phillip also mused, "I guess it's mankind's downfall. A dream is what he does, and that's why that song has lasted. I think it was probably the most important record in that series of first initial hits that we had. I think without "Dream" we could have, I think it turned a difference in our career ... I think it helped cause us to last. I think it turned a key. Because we'd had an up-tempo until that one. And that was a big record during the summer. It was a bad record sales in '58 and (it was a bad year recession-wise) and that record did quite well. I think it helped kind of stir everything up again. We feel quite good about that. It's the kind of song that you only come across in your life maybe once or twice. "Let It Be Me" and "All

I Have To Do Is Dream" are still two songs that will probably last with us. Somebody will be singing them because they're always ... "Dream" has been in the charts five different times with five different acts since we've recorded it. And it shows the song is really good." It has been said that the song was written by the Bryants in about fifteen minutes, and it has also been recorded by Richard Chamberlain, Glen Campbell, Bobbie Gentry, Andy Gibb and Victoria Principal.

"Devoted To You" - Phillip commented, "There's a strange thing about this song. Again in general it's a Boudleaux Bryant song designed like an English Madrigal. We just utilized the harmonies that we had ... I think a lot of that is that physically that we're brothers, plus we were trained exactly the same way by our father."

"Ebony Eyes" - Phillip said, "We never performed that song live. We just made the record and left it alone. It was so depressing." Recently, however, they have added the partial song to a medley of tunes in their live stage act. Once when reminiscing about this song and the fact that Donald always sang the solos (which was the one thing they never did argue about), Phillip said that while doing "Ebony Eyes," "you know there's a recitation in the middle and the lines are the plane is way overdue. And Donald sings the lead so much that I came up with the suggestion that I might do the recitation, right? So I went out there and did it and (imitating himself), I came back and I couldn't believe it. I said that's the worst damned thing I ever heard in my life. I will not have it. And that's the only time. There's still a copy of that around." Donald added, "Well, the recitation of that has never been done since." They thought the sound was similar to either a chipmunk or a mouse.

"Let It Be Me" - Was originally an instrumental on an album by Chet Atkins. When the Everlys found out that it had lyrics, and the lyrics turned out to be as good as they were, they got really excited about the song. It's a French song. They left Nashville and cut the record in New York City with strings, which is the first time they had done that and the song is terrific. Phillip said, "It's a great song." It is Phillip's favorite, and is one of Donald's favorites, also. Phillip has often said that he won't leave the stage until he sings it.

"Love Is Strange" - Strangely enough, another Everly favorite. According to one of Donald's interviews, "We weren't the first ones to record it, of course. Mickey and Sylvia recorded it. I remember when I first heard it. I remember it well because I was at that age; I was in the back seat of a '57 Chevy at the time. Mickey and Sylvia came on the radio singing "Love Is Strange." I thought it was wonderful. I learned it could be all kinds of things. You learn things as you get older. I found out also that love is just about the best thing there is in the world. Maybe the only thing. Feels good trying to find out. The middle of this song is about getting your baby back. And I guess that's because you've done something wrong. You've sort of messed things up and you have to call up and say, 'Sweetheart, I'm sorry. It's my fault. I want you back.' That's really difficult to do. Of course, it's never happened to me, but ... when you do it in the middle of a rock 'n roll song, this is what it sounds like when you're begging."

Sometimes he will refer to it as the kind of song where a man has to ask to be forgiven and hope that his lover will be sweet and welcome him back into her arms. He quickly adds that this, however, has never happened to him.

"Lucille" - One of their all time favorite rockers, written by Little Richard. Phillip said, "What a dream that was! When you first heard that coming over somebody's car radio, it would just scare you to death!"

"On The Wings Of A Nightingale" - Dave Edmonds called Paul McCartney and asked him if he would write a song for Donald and Phillip, and surprisingly, he answered, "OK." A week later he brought the song in and according to Phillip, "It was a perfect fit." When sung live, it is usually sung well, although Donald sometimes isn't willing to hit the high notes and has changed it a bit. It is definitely a song extolling the marvels of sexual intercourse. No doubt about that. And it is heavenly. Paul McCartney really outdid himself on this one.

Pass The Chicken And Listen - An album title, one of my favorites. Phillip translated it as "a Southern expression that means, like, get around with home cooking and family singing and good times." He also had the idea to change its title to "Pass The Chips And Listen" for the British release, but he was apparently outvoted.

"Poor Jenny" - Phillip said, "We were looking for an up tempo song and this is the one we sort of settled on. It's a very peculiar thing about "Poor Jenny". If you don't catch the first three or four lines, the story gets confusing. It's a strange song. I've listened to it for years and I wonder why we did it, sometimes." This song tells the story of a girl on her very first date. There is a fight, and everyone else manages to run away except Jenny who winds up getting thrown into jail.

"Problems" - Phillip told *People Weekly* in 1984, "The song was a problem, too. We had a terrible time getting it recorded.

It was, it really was. We just kept saying, well, we can get it better kind of a thing. We just went around and around in kind of a circle, and we finally said, we got it, and we went with it." It was also "the first record we put out that I didn't like 'cause it was the first that didn't sell a million. Only sold nine hundred forty something thousand."

"Take A Message To Mary" - According to Phillip, "This was an effort where instead of it being sort of a flowing Nashville arrangement with just musicians and Don and I, Archie Bleyer, the producer, sort of applied some New York techniques to it because ... this one wasn't quite coming off. And it sort of got a little stiffer, I thought. It's more of a polished, more of a contrived, instead of a flow." The "New York Techniques" included the background sound of a screwdriver being tapped on a Coke bottle. These were all innovative people, struggling with innovative methods of making music and new sounds.

"Temptation" - At the time this was done, recording artists had two-track technology. So Donald and Phillip hired every guitar player they could find (about eight of them) who tuned their guitars a little bit off from each other, and although they were all playing the same melody at the same time, it gave it an eight-track sound. If you really want to get down to it, you could say the Everly Brothers invented eight track.

This song was the straw that broke the camel's back in the Everlys' relationship with Wesley Rose. He tried to have veto power over their song selections, and vetoed this one but the brothers insisted on releasing it and it was a hit. They thought (and rightly so) that they should be the sole decision makers on their recorded material.

"That's Old Fashioned" - Was another New York song. The year was 1962, they were having publisher troubles, and had to find material elsewhere.

"('Til) I Kissed You" - Was done in 1959 with Jerry Allison on drums. Phillip says, "Donald wrote this song. We were in Australia on tour. And when we came back to record it, Jerry Allison added this bram, broom, bram brooms, which became sort of the first time that somebody had taken a rock 'n roll drummer and made sort of an idea about it. Unusual."

Donald told *Playboy,* "I wrote "('Til) I Kissed You" about a girl I met in Australia. Her name was Lillian, and she was very, very inspirational. I was married, but ... I wrote the song about her on the way home."

"Wake Up, Little Susie" - Donald really liked the beat and the arrangement. This song was the best seller of all their records, "Bye Bye, Love" included, and Phillip thought that a great number of copies were bought by people who bought the record for their daughters named Susie and played it to wake them up in the morning.

It was a very controversial song as Donald remembered, "Well, it was for the times, I guess. The song lyric was because of the falling asleep at the drive-in movie, it was banned in Boston. I think it (the banning) helped it." In another interview Donald said that it was banned because it had the word "sleep" in it and we'd better watch those five letter words. Sometimes Phillip will offer that it's one of their "dirty" songs.

The recording of the song itself was difficult however, as they had only two days to do it and the first day they did twenty eight takes, all of which were rejected. The second day they finally got it right, but only after fourteen more takes, totalling forty two takes in all. Whatever the problems were, it was well worth it.

"Walk Right Back" - Was recorded in 1961, and was written by Sonny Curtis. The drums were by Jerry Allison, the guitar parts were done by Sonny, some session men and of course, Donald. Phillip's high part was excellent and even though he admits he can't reach those high parts now, whenever he sings that song live in a club the audience reacts favorably, because it is so different that it stands out from all the rest. Phillip also contends that the Cricket's drummer, Jerry Allison, was just about the best rock 'n roll drummer that has ever been. He was innovative and exciting and Phillip especially gives him a lot of credit for the success of this song.

"When Will I Be Loved" - Was written quickly by Phillip while he was sitting in a car outside an A&W Root Beer stand. Thanks to Linda Ronstadt, this won Phillip The Robert J. Burton Award in 1975 as The Most Performed Song Of The Year.

"Be not forgetful to entertain strangers: for thereby some have entertained angels unawares."
- The Bible: Hebrews

THE ABSOLUTE BEST OF THE BEST

The following are, I think, the best from the Everly song catalog. They are all unique and I have pulled them out from the rest because of that certain something each of them possess-

es. I hope you will get to hear some of these during your lifetimes, as they are an experience unto themselves!

ALWAYS DRIVE A CADILLAC
By Larrie Raspberry III

Recorded on their *Born Yesterday* LP, this song is
unique, especially for the Everly Brothers. Donald once stated
that he was surprised that this one was not picked to be used
as a single, but was told that it was too long.

Like many of their recordings, Donald at first claims this
as his by soloing in the beginning and then Phillip joins in. That
is where the similarity ends, as this song has three totally separate parts. In part one, Donald sings solo; in part two, Phillip
joins in and they harmonize beautifully together; then in part
three Phillip soars on high, claims it, and it becomes his song.
It is an exciting and thrilling rendition with somewhat strange
music, but put together and sung by the Everlys, it works!

I really have never heard anything quite like it, and I
doubt that any others could give this piece anything close to
what Donald and Phillip contribute to this song.

ANGEL OF THE DARKNESS
By Phil Everly and John Durrill

This song is depressing and scary. It touches on madness
and the fear of a man who was left alone for "another fool." I
guess it is the male version of how a woman feels when she is
deserted for another woman. It is terribly sad and frightening,
and whatever this woman did to him, she devastated him and he
is paying with his very soul. This song is deep, dark and ugly and
if that is how Phillip felt when he composed it, I, too, am very
frightened for him. The word "scream" screams out, as does he.

ANY SINGLE SOLITARY HEART
By John Hiatt and Mike Porter

Although this song was not written by an Everly, you would have a hard time convincing me, as it is on the same wave length and the lyrics are almost more than one can take at one sitting.

Unfortunately they are a bit unclear on the LP but once you understand what this song says, it can devastate you, as you hear "only the lonely know the pain of letting go" and it gets sadder from there, referring to first love

"When you had confidence
In love's sweet innocence
And now you have evidence
That love can be unkind"

Just couple those sad sentiments with the title, and you have a lonely, embittered situation on your hands, sung by two lonely, very single, solitary men.

BETTER THAN NOW
By Phil Everly and Terry Slater

This song is fantastic. Not only is it spirited and varied, but it shows Phillip off as a versatile solo performer. It also shows some insight into Phillip himself and hints that perhaps his love life has not been all that bad. It is a happy, joyful experience, and the more one listens to this song, the more one appreciates Phillip's basic sweetness and his unique musical expertise. Oh, sweet mama!

BORN YESTERDAY
By Don Everly

This song reportedly took Donald about three years to write, and I can believe it. It is varied and moving; in addition, it flashes ugly pictures across the walls of the conscience. Is it true that divorcing couples are so childish and cruel? Alas, it must be true. The things people do to each other are so outlandish - both trying to inflict pain on the other, like small children will do. The frustration voiced in this song is a scream from the darkness of his very soul.

BRAND NEW ROCK AND ROLL BAND
By Tony Colton and Ray Smith

This is another unique song with surprises in the middle. Although it does not have the stuff of which great hits are made, it seems as though Donald (minus his brother) is just having a wonderful time singing. The tune varies throughout, so it does not get boring. His backup singers do a great job also, and it sounds an awful lot like party time. Nothing deep, nothing complicated, just good, clean fun. Some songs should be just that.

BROTHER JUKEBOX
By Paul Craft

This title song recaptures some heavy drinking days filled loneliness and despair. Whether Donald has actually been there or not, I can only surmise. My guess is a definite "yes," as he reportedly likes his booze, has probably been kicked out of more relationships (or has done the kicking) than one can imagine, and seems to have a desire to drown his sorrows in a song. He says the jukebox is the only family he has left, so there sits the poor lonely guy in the bar, hoping against hope for better times (or a better woman). Drunk and lonely, he wails his lament.

You almost feel sorry for this man until you think past his story and wonder what he did to her, although the possibility always remains that she could have done the doing. Of course, unless there is something very definite, no one ever really knows what takes place between a man and a woman except the parties concerned.

In 1990 Mark Chesnutt covered this song and parlayed it into a big hit. Although Mr. Chesnutt is a very fine singer, in my humble opinion his rendition cannot hold a candle to Donald Everly's recording.

BROWN EYES
By Phil Everly and John Durrill

This is just about the only "new" song the Everlys now sing on stage. Wishful thinking perhaps, of someone returning to be with Phillip again? Or is it just a simple song? It is effortless and pretty, but if penned with a certain woman in mind, she should listen with her heart. WHY on earth can't men and women work their differences out and stay married? What's the MATTER with everybody? If there were such good "old times," why don't people keep "loving away the night?" Times change and the "old times" keep changing as people age, but other things replace them. Frankly, I think someone should sing about the "bad old times," because in the end those are the times that bind people together in a marriage. How about it, fellas?

BUY ME A BEER
By Phil Everly and John Durrill

This ditty was written by Phillip during his solo years and was presented to the public on his LP entitled, *Living Alone*, (which he insists no one bought) in 1979. By then he was divorced from his second wife Patricia, and was indeed alone, hence this tongue-in-cheek rendition of drinking with the boys and not caring about much. Perhaps at that time of his life, he didn't. The rhythm of the song is terrific, though, and Phillip does an amazing job with this one.

On the record his girl was so hot she couldn't be satisfied with just one bed. She left the poor guy with a stack of bills, dirty sheets and an unfamiliar pair of socks. When sung live, Phillip sometimes substitutes "socks" with "shorts," making it even funnier and yet bluer at the same time. A kind of hurt laugh escapes, because a situation like this is nothing short of rotten. Sometimes women get tired of being left alone. Sometimes things just happen.

CAN'T GET OVER IT
By Don Everly

This is pure Donald Everly again, with melodic surprises in the middle. He sings of the eyes as being windows to the soul (an often used phrase in poetry) yet I think he is saying that these lyrics are the pathways from his own soul, and he allows us to sashay musically along those paths. Although all the "doing" doesn't need any explanation, I surmise only Donald knows what all that getting under it and over it means. He does, however, mention empty days and nights, which seems a bit exaggerated. I mean, how can this guy ever be alone? Could it be that he is alone even when he is surrounded by hordes of people?

DEEP WATER
By Fred Rose

Expounding on the dangers of falling in love, especially for sensitive, artistic people, is the theme for this song and one must tread carefully. This precise song about deep water is not particularly deep, but once again it seems as though the woman is the heavy, not the "sensitive" man. What is it with these men? Do they not know that women cry, too? Or are women really affected less by lost love?

DONNA, DONNA
By Boudleaux Bryant and Felice Bryant

This song was done when the Everlys were quite young, and I am still wondering why it was allowed to be performed in that innocent, censored period of time.

It deals with a centuries-old problem, that of a young man on a date with a girl, getting all worked up and then being turned down "flat." Listening to it as an older person, I can hear and feel the pain of rejection and the frustration in their young voices as they wonder why she is torturing them this way. Looking back, I wonder how on earth they made it seem so real.

You see? Times never really change; that's why the Everly Brothers' music will always be in demand. Girls still say no and young boys still suffer because of it. I just dunno, Donna.

DON'T DRINK THE WATER
By Don Everly

"Don't Drink The Water (Drink The Wine)" has my vote for being the worst Everly song ever recorded. Although the premise is good and addresses the very important issue of water pollution, surely Donald could have come up with a more tuneful environmental rendition. Before the song begins, there is an outtake that sounds like those in the studio have probably been taking the song's advice literally for several hours.

DON'T WORRY BABY
By Brian Wilson and Roger Christian

Written and originally recorded by the Beach Boys, now sung by a combination of the Everly Brothers backed by the Beach Boys (coined "the Beach Brothers" by Donald), this song has the swing of the '60s along with the subject matter of macho car racing and young love. What impresses me most about this song is the fact that you have to be pretty important in the music field to have a terrific group like the Beach Boys as your backup singers!

It seems a bit weird for men in their fifties to be singing about drag racing and bragging about their cars, but when Donald sings about being made love to, all is certainly forgiven, and we are transported back to that time when love was such a simple thing and cars were "the most."

Although the refrain "Don't worry, baby" seems overdone, the beat is terrific. I only wonder why the Beach Boys didn't re-record it themselves.

FOLLOWING THE SUN
By Don Everly

Does this really say how he feels? Is he really so disgusted with his life? How terribly sad. This gets into the long argument of how fame tears entertainers apart. They want it, they need it, they have to have it and thrive on it, but after they have it, what is there? Where does one go? It should be remembered that the Everly Brothers peaked at the tender ages of about eighteen and twenty. What does this do to a young man's ambition?

As Donald stated after they had been the number one act in the country for several years, "there's nowhere to go but down," and this takes its toll. As he sings of needing love and leaving, one aches for him.

HAVE YOU EVER LOVED SOMEBODY
By L. Ransford

This is an English song that rocks hard, stays strong and lures the listener to England once again. The Everlys seem to do these so very easily, it makes one wonder if they aren't part English themselves and were swapped at birth with two little Kentucky boys! Simplicity, strength, and a mind photo of loving all night makes for a listening experience to be remembered.

ICH BIN DEIN (I AM YOURS)
By Phil Everly

Although this song is not on my list of favorites, nevertheless it is extremely beautiful due to its simplicity and the sheer movement of the music. As a matter of fact, the rhythm itself reminds one of a luscious, indolent sex act of interminable duration.

"Ich Bin Dein" was penned by Phillip when he was doing an East German television show for a friend in 1979. What confuses me is how on earth someone can radiate such beauty from that drab place? East Berliners, however, were very aware of all of the Everly Brothers' hits, and since 1989 they are now free to not only listen to various artists, but to see them too, thanks to the recent demise of the Berlin Wall.

I'M MOVING ON
By Don Gibson

This is an old rock 'n roll standard that many, many people have covered. As a matter of fact, it is listed in BMI's "Million Aires" as having been performed over one million times. I have heard it sung before, but absolutely no one has sung it like the Everly Brothers.

The primitive drum beat used on their rendition is reminiscent of Bo Diddley's sound, and their energy really grabs your attention. Coupled with their singing "at" each other and echoing the other, it makes for a unique listening experience. Aaahhhhhh!

JANUARY BUTTERFLY
By Phil Everly and Warren Zevon

Mr. Phillip Everly really outdoes himself on this song. His voice is so special and there is such warmth and tenderness flowing out that the listener just melts. Surely a cruel word could never emerge from these lips. This is an extraordinary love song sung with such wonder and longing that one wonders how this man could ever long for anything for long.

KISS YOUR MAN GOODBYE
By Don Everly and Phil Everly

English throughout, and very male chauvinist pig in lyric, nevertheless it is excellent, both in its content and especially in its young, free treatment by the Everlys. Frankly with songs like this, I think the brothers prove themselves to be almost better than the Beatles, if that is possible. Oh yes, girls. You had better treat your man right if you know what's good for you.

LADIES LOVE OUTLAWS
By Lee Clayton

This song I feel exemplifies the Everly Brothers, even though it was written by Lee Clayton in 1972. I have subtitled this book in its honor.

From all past and present publicity, these two men seem to be outlaws indeed, but not in the sense of the Nashville Outlaws themselves, which consisted of such persons as Willie Nelson, Waylon Jennings, Michael Murphy, David Allan Coe ("Mysterious Rhinestone Cowboy"), Rusty Weir, B.W. Stephenson, Tompall Glazer and ("Cowboy") Jack Clement. I guess the real "father" of the outlaw movement had to be Hank Williams himself. The Everlys, however, seem to stand apart. There can be no imitations. This song is just the yee-haw vehicle which is tailor made for them (when in a Nashville mood) and Donald's personal addition shows the "bad boy" part of them vying for attention.

Donald and Phillip Everly have been "outlaws" in another sense since grade school when they wore their hair and clothes different form the rest of the kids, and they worked on radio which no one else did.

221

Their further rebellion from that organization included refusing to make the required appearances on the Opry stage. As a result of all this, when one visits The Country Music Hall of Fame in Nashville, the Everly Brothers are practically nonexistent, even though they still retain and annually renew their original Country Music Association membership cards; Number 11 for Donald and Number 12 for Phillip.

In their later years the Everlys still refused to fit the mold, whether in their personal or their public lives. Their hair was always longer, their clothes stranger, (Donald is still a leather aficionado), their touring, personal interviews, radio and TV appearances were fast and furious and came in from all parts of the world. Their marriages, children's births and divorces were also accumulating at a formidable pace. Their brotherly discord hit the news media, and after their celebrated reunion, they emerged victorious but with Phillip still chain smoking and Donald sporting a shaggy mop of hair, cowboy boots, and an earring in his right ear.

Who cares? They still sing better than anyone, they compose beautiful, heart wrenching songs, they are witty, sexy, clever, and their audiences adore them.

LETTIN' GO
By D. Sanger and Darlene Shafer

This song spells out D-I-V-O-R-C-E, loud and clear, complete with too many "misty conversations." The singer admits they tried to hang on, but now the time has come to part company.

The irreparable damage that has been caused by these two people is there in all its ugliness, yet the feelings of resignation to the marriage's demise are also there which is, in its own way, a blessed relief.

What I am unable to understand is the pain this man feels, as well as his mate, so why can't they iron things out? Why do people who really love each other do such horrible things to each other? As the saying goes, "we only hurt the one we love." It shouldn't be that way, but as Donald once mused in *Disc and Music Echo*, "Marriage is silly in the first place ... the first time, much less the third! I don't recommend it for everybody, but that's my way of thinking." With thinking like that, who can expect anything more?

LIKE EVERY TIME BEFORE
By L. Ransford

This solo is Phillip Everly's finest hour. It seems to be a difficult song to sing; it is concentrated and has no accompaniment to speak of but a guitar. Phillip's voice is versatile, melodic, raspy, strong, and definitely shows how very talented this man can be when he wants to and he has the right vehicle to let it fly. I could listen to this one forever.

The sad thing about Phillip's records is that he sometimes needs the services of a great harmonizer, and he needs the best. That unfortunately leaves him out in left field, because no one can harmonize as well as he himself can.

LOVE AT LAST SIGHT
By D. Sanger and Darlene Schafer

Just the title of this is intriguing, and when one listens to the words, a picture of a young girl drinking alone in a dingy bar forms. It then becomes a horrible scenario indeed.

Donald refers to the last remaining customers (termed losers) who leave together at closing time because neither one has anyone else. These two cling to each other, thus giving definition to "love at last sight." This is a truly sick situation which somehow allows a certain sweetness to creep in. Is there, at least for that one night, a hope of love for the two of them? Nevertheless, it is one of the saddest situations I have ever been exposed to musically, and it is right there, ringing out in glorious stereophonic sound. Throughout, Donald's voice pours out like a mellow blend of smooth Kentucky whisky, which fits in perfectly with the song's surroundings. I feel as though I am almost going through it with them, and herein lies the absolute power of Mr. Everly's euphonic skills.

OH, I'D LIKE TO GO AWAY
By Don Everly

This song, written by Donald and recorded on his solo *Brother Jukebox* LP smacks so hard of autobiography that one can visualize his packed suitcase by the door. Donald sang this one in his solo days while living in Nashville, and one imagines that he has to get away from the area because of a bad relationship. This is entirely possible, since by now he had been through a great many similar situations.

At the onset, this sounds like a simple wish to travel, but it has a fabulous Latin beat which astounded me and caught me up in its sophisticated tempo. The underlying humor of the lyrics is so dry that whenever I hear "fly to China or drive to North Carolina" I fall off my chair in fits of laughter. I don't know why I continue to go into hysterics over this particular part of the song, but I guess it is similar to when my large part-husky dog Max belches. I never stop screaming with laughter even though it is really not that funny. But Donald Everly is. The man has a sense of humor that completely throws me unto the edge of insanity. I sometimes wonder if he knows how funny he actually is. As a matter of fact, Phillip, who is extremely funny also, has stated in print that he also thinks Donald is very funny, so I must be right.

<u>OH, WHAT A FEELING</u>
By Don Everly

This is a quiet, sad, lonely song which hints at long periods of depression over a woman who left. I find it hard to think of Donald Everly feeling that way for months and months, as there is probably a sizeable gaggle of women waiting to replace whoever does decide to jump ship.

The picture of a dejected Donald sitting by the phone waiting for it to ring is a ludicrous one at best, and it really does bestow a flair for the melodramatic, which Donald can hit us with quite well. I feel it goes a bit overboard.

One interesting twist to this song, however, is that he sings of keeping letters from her, but they are letters she didn't even write, which adds a strange taste of causticity to this now defunct relationship. Oh, what a feeling.

<u>RIDE THE WIND</u>
By Phil Everly

This song has been improved over the years since its inception by Phillip during his Palomino Club days, but the melody is not the best that he can do. Also, on the LP it is hard to hear the composer singing and most of what we hear is Donald. What Donald sings is sometimes garbled, but his voice is gruff, strong and soaring, all at one time.

What is miraculous about this song is its lyrics, which really put it where it's at and flow straight from Phillip's very soul. Perhaps at times he is afraid, as we all are. What separates the winners from the losers, though, is keeping at it and leaving the shelters we erect around ourselves until we emerge victorious (at least some of us do). Most people don't have the strength of their own convictions and are afraid to persist even though they are faced with many barriers, but Phillip's advice rings strong and true. Yes, these guys are dreamers, but having dreams is certainly not enough and they apply the courage and hard work it takes to realize those dreams. It certainly sounds like the Everly Brothers, who indeed have faced a great many storms but through them all they do touch the stars. Hell, they ARE the stars!

ROCKY TOP
By Boudleaux Bryant and Felice Bryant

This song was reportedly written in a mere ten minutes by the Bryants, but has since become the State Song of Tennessee. I have heard it performed by many, many artists but I honestly believe no one gives it the excitement and clarity that the Everlys give to it. It just makes one want to pull up stakes and move to Tennessee, doesn't it?

SIGNS THAT WILL NEVER CHANGE
By L. Ransford

This composition gets my vote for being some of the best harmony singing I have ever heard, and it is tailor-made for the Everlys. The simplicity and beauty of it cannot be described. Unfortunately, unless one owns a recording of this song, it won't be heard. As far as I know they only recorded it in 1966 on their LP entitled, *Two Yanks In England,* which is now out of print. It is a shame that vocal beauty such as this has to be lost to the world. Harmony singing just doesn't get any better than this, folks.

SINCE YOU BROKE MY HEART
By Don Everly

This seems to be a rocking blues number with a Latin beat; a difficult thing to describe, as it defies categorization. I will admit that Donald Everly knows exactly what he is doing with things like this, however.

Again, this seems to be autobiographical. The song is about a man trying to recover from (yet another) woman who left him and do-gooders trying to tell him to read more or try a little painting, which of course is no remedy for his heartache. It is probably the first time that Donald's artistic abilities are touched upon, and he did it all by himself! And yes, so he should. The man has so many talents, it's hard to single one or two out and think you are seeing the whole person. Now if he could just write a song about photography, art, cooking, fishing, wine tasting, horses, old cars and antique guns, he might have himself just about covered. This man is an extremely complex individual!

SOME HEARTS
By Don Everly

In this song, one wonders if the couple is together or apart, friend or foe, or if anything at all is even remotely settled. It is so garbled that the listener is confused as to what the hell the man is even singing about. Perhaps she is fictitious and this great romance is merely wishful dreaming.

There are mouthfuls of lyrics, some practically unin-
telligible; the refrain also is difficult to understand; and the tune
changes so much that it is like five songs all blended together.
What it really ends up being, though, is an exciting song which
could never be a hit as it is too complicated and sophisticated
for the average listening public. After all, we must remember
that most people love to hear the Everlys singing "Bye Bye,
Love" and sadly, that's the complexity they seem to request. It's
unfortunate, for there is so much talent in this song that it spills
over and flows along like a churning, bubbling river that finally slows in a peaceful pool of still water. The review in *People
Weekly* stated, "Instead of being overwhelming, it's only a total
success."

SOMEBODY HELP ME
By C. Edwards

This is pure Beatles fare. As a matter of fact, one could
swear it was the Fab Four singing, not the Dynamic Duo. It is
done in excellent English style, and is thoroughly enjoyable to
listen to. The ironic thing here is that many will say the Everlys
sound just like the Beatles, when in fact the Beatles sounded like
the Everlys (the Everly Brothers were here first, remember?) and
tried their hardest to imitate them. They were once called "The
Everly Brothers of England" when they were starting out. The
fact cannot be stressed often enough. As Donald simply
explained it, "We exported Rock 'n Roll to England and they
exported it back. That's about what happened."

SWEET GRASS COUNTY
By Phil Everly and Terry Slater

This song can be found on Phillip's solo album, *Star Spangled Springer*, if the album can be found. Right now it is as scarce as a Baptist at a Bar Mitzvah. One of the interesting things about it though, is that Phillip, in need of a harmony singer, would settle for only the best, which is, of course, himself. His harmonization with his own voice contains sweetness beyond belief.

I think that Phillip Everly may be the only man in the world who can sing a song about hitchhiking in the pouring rain and make it sound like he's dancing and falling in love in a field of Kentucky wildflowers.

This song is presented with such warmth, sweetness and yearning, that it's hard not to look around for a hitchhiker to pick up! Mr. Everly certainly outdoes himself on this one. It is one of the most beautiful songs ever.

THE LAST THING ON MY MIND
Author Unknown

I do not believe this song has ever been recorded, but when the Everly Brothers were hosting The Johnny Cash Presents The Everly Brothers Summer Replacement Show" in 1970, Phillip demonstrated his unique solo style with this song. It was done virtually without backing instrumentation and it was so simple and lovely the way it was sung by Phillip, that it was overpowering. I don't think any other artist could have sung that song the way Phillip did. Something must have affected him deeply also, for he broke down crying at the end, right in front of millions of people, and was almost unable to finish the song.

It was an emotional experience for anyone listening to this very sensitive man.

THREE BANDS OF STEEL
By Don Everly

This is one of my favorites on the *Some Hearts* LP as it provides a (yet another) glimpse into the sensitive parts of Donald, who has admittedly survived a lot of heartache over his love affairs. He lets us in on his loneliness, professing that he has given everything and that just isn't enough for some women. Maybe.

Something here doesn't ring true, and I would like to get the other side of the story about all this giving business, because I have a sneaking suspicion that probably most of the women (as most women do throughout the world) gave everything they had in the beginning, until there was nothing left to give.

I will not belittle his feelings though, as when a man is left and his heart breaks, he really does feel "incomplete" but I can't help thinking that if a little while later some gorgeous young thing availed herself to him, his heartache might mend like magic.

Speaking of magic, Donald took this idea for the song, he says, from a Grimms Fairy Tale. What's he doing reading fairy tales?

TURN THE MEMORIES LOOSE AGAIN
By Don Everly

There is almost nothing that sums up Donald Everly's existence like this song. Although it is Donald's solo, it also sums up his and Phillip's entire lives and spits it out at the listener with great resolution. He sings of feeling old, not looking or sounding the same as he once did, of having seen the world through all types of windows, of being simply handed a new car when he became a new millionaire. After all that, even though he is far different now, he has his memories, with no regrets, for all he ever really did was sing. As for money, it was just "there," which paints a picture of complete dependency, particularly when an artist is so young, and you know that The Music Machine will control these two boys' lives, and many others will take on the characteristics of jackals, eating away at them piece by piece until there is nothing left for them to give.

Such depth, simplicity and honesty all at once, makes for a memorable experience for anyone who hears this story of a man who remembers, and who remembers it well. I sense a feeling of sadness and wonder at his life and all that has gone before. It reeks of finality which fortunately was not to be, as the memories are still being made and Donald's singing is more talented than ever before. God, what a song!

Young Stars

18
THE FAN CLUBS

"Wickedness is a myth invented by good people to account for the curious attraction of others."
- Henry Wadsworth Longfellow

EVERLY BROTHERS INTERNATIONAL

The Beatles probably have more fan clubs than the Everly Brothers have fans. Also, the doomed TV series, Beauty And The Beast, which has been canceled twice in three short seasons, retains fifty fan clubs in the United States alone. The Everly Brothers have three. I wondered why this was true. Now I think I know.

The Everly Brothers International Fan Club with headquarters in Gouda, Holland states that it is the "only official, world wide" fan club, and the only one that Donald and Phillip endorse. This isn't true, but if it makes them happy, let them say it. The total fan club membership for some reason is real "Top Secret." Perhaps Presidential candidate Al Smith was right when he stated, "Nothing un-American can live in the sunlight." I have been told it is as low as 200 members and as high as 3,000 members. At any rate, this is a grand title for such a small organization. I understand also that the Everlys really don't give a hoot if they have a fan club or not, which seems strange to me as most other artists seem to love their fan clubs.

The earliest Everly Brothers Fan Club was organized in the 1960s and had a president by the name of "Susan Rose" (The name Rose does seem to crop up again and again in their lives, doesn't it?!) who was actually Donald and Phillip's mother, Margaret Everly. A fan I know who was a member at that time remembers "Susan" saying things like how much the boys enjoyed being home eating Mom's fried chicken, that they were still in school but loved making records, and statements like that.

There used to be a club in England which put out a publication called Stories We Could Tell but the two clubs, which should have been olive branches of peace for Donald and Phillip, became nations at war. I don't know what it was all about, but I think greed, control and self importance headed the list. In the end, the English branch disbanded because of intense pressure from the Dutch branch who views other fan clubs as competitors (?!), and now only the one in Holland remains active. Their slick magazine entitled *Kentucky*, is attractive, but some of it is written in Dutch (naturally) and it has stated that it will be less geared to Americans than before. What a shame. The Everlys are Americans, and should be proud of the fact. This fan club, in my opinion, is a little too full of itself. Maybe if you're from Gouda, you start thinking you're a big cheese! An Indiana fan wrote me once, "It's really pretty impressive to have a fan club publish a quarterly magazine about you when you peaked thirty years before." That sums it up fairly well, I think.

The fans really should be doing everything in their power to generate more interest and to keep the fans that they do have, for Donald and Phillip's sake, if for no other reason. I have heard from several people who say that they are no longer interested in remaining in the European club because of the leaders' overbearing attitudes, which is a damn shame. I do not know how many fan clubs the Everlys had in their prime, but I do know there is always room for more. After all, singer Eddie Fisher stated in his autobiography that in his heyday he had 65,000 fan clubs!!!

The Dutch fan club is also not a member of IFCO, The International Fan Club Organization which monitors its member fan clubs and appears to be an excellent organization. Membership in EBI is $19.00 annually.

SHARING & CARING

There is another fan club in the United States called Sharing & Caring. Although it does not have a pretty, slick magazine, their newsletters are varied and informative. Not only that, the comments and writings are complimentary to the

Everlys, as well as sprinkled with the kind of constructive criticism that every performer worth his salt should welcome. Anyone who belongs to a fan club obviously has admiration and respect for the performer, but in the American tradition, should also feel free to criticize if something needs improvement. We Americans do not accept things blindly.

I object strongly to the label "fan club" because it has the connotation of one being a "fanatic" if one becomes a member. This should not be, but I am hard pressed to figure out another name for an organization such as this. Should it be an "admiration society"? An "audience membership"? I don't know. What it should NOT be is a bunch of people who are so in love (or in lust) with the celebrity that they do him no good at all, and they idolize every fiber of his being to the point of mass hysteria. This idolization of a performer, I think, confuses him and does him more harm than good. If he is not careful he thinks he need not improve or try any more, or even be friendly to those very fans that gave him that sense of self-importance, and a very good living for many, many years. The worst thing that happens, and has happened I think in the case of these performers, is that the fans "protect" the stars right into oblivion. I mean, who are they to protect anyone? A fan is a fan, nothing more. A fan is on a completely different plane than a friend and/or business associate.

Incidentally, this American fan club is also operating with Donald and Phillip's full knowledge and written consent according to its president, and is a member of IFCO, which specifies having artist approval before joining. During its membership, it has consistently maintained a Gold Star Rating. You can reach them by writing Sharing & Caring, 1501 N. 15th Street, Reading, PA 19604-1851. Vicky Sokoloff is the president and editor of their newsletter. A membership costs $9.00 per year.

Another wonderful thing about this fan club is that its proceeds are used to further the cause of gifted children, who should be given everything they can get. These gifted kids are the future leaders of America and, yes, the world. As the saying goes, a mind is a horrible thing to waste.

MUHLENBERG COUNTY
EVERLY BROTHERS FAN CLUB

This is a small, local fan club in Central City, Kentucky, hosted by some very nice people who seem to have a lot of fun just being themselves and remembering the Everlys every few months. They host things like picnics, sock hops, Don and Phil Everly Look-A-Like Contests and other activities. Anyone who is interested in the Everly Brothers is welcome to just stop by and/or join. Although I have never honored my invitations due to scheduling conflicts, this is the way it should be. This is how a couple of country boys should be represented. The annual cost is $5.00 and they can be reached at P.O. Box 894, Central City, Kentucky 42330.

TODAY'S FANS

The Everly Brothers have ardent fans today, many of whom have stuck by them through thick and thin. This is a great thing, and it makes an artist feel good to know that he is loved through the years. Loyalty is an honorable trait and fans are capable of incredible loyalty, which should be treasured.

Loyalty however, does not mean hysterical hero worship, and many of the fans do go a bit overboard. In the first place, they follow their heroes across the country, attending concert after concert. What about jobs? Family? How can some people just leave life and follow the Everly Brothers around? I certainly do not have that kind of time to waste and I am sure the Everlys don't really notice, care that much, or particularly want people to go so ape over them. It's scary, really. As Mel Tillis stated in his book entitled *Stutterin` Boy,* "They build up these huge fantasies, thinking the entertainer is nine feet tall with a twelve inch dong. They go through some crazy things to get at him."

Many fans give the Everlys flowers when they perform. Flowers are lovely. I adore flowers, but after thirty years of flowers night after night, I would think one might get sick of them. Anything to excess becomes trite, and too many flowers unfortunately could mar the very message these fans are trying to convey. Why don't they give them something they can really use? Somehow booze comes to mind.

There are a couple of fans who even try to LOOK like Donald or Phillip. This is really going overboard. I mean, why wouldn't you want to look like yourself? Everybody is unique and has something beautiful about them, whether it's inwardly directed or outwardly obvious. That's what is so terrific about being a human being instead of a baboon. We all can be our own person. Why someone would like to look like someone else is beyond me. After all, Donald Everly is not just a look, he is an entire person with an incredible amount of talent. Without that supreme talent and the unique personality that only Donald has, the imitator becomes just a frivolous shell of a person, trying but ever failing to be what he/she knows he/she can never be.

Some fans even try to buy the Everlys' friendship which, of course, will never work.

There is occasionally a fan who goes to almost all of the Everly concerts. In 1989 there was one gal who went to all thirty three of the Everlys' Las Vegas concerts, as well as sending flowers every night for their lapels. When people do this, the

Everlys sometimes make a joke of it by saying that the fan has been to more concerts than they have.

A research assistant friend of mine recently conducted a survey of fan clubs of various artists and I was delighted by the honesty, warmth, willingness to provide information and pride these other fan clubs exhibited. They were really a delight, and most of them provided even more information than was asked for. A few of my nicest responses were from the presidents of fan clubs for T.G. Sheppard, Johnny Cash and June Carter Cash, Vicki Bird, Ricky Skaggs, Kathy Mattea, Mel Tillis, Hank Williams, Jr., Kris Kristofferson, the Forester Sisters, David Allan Coe, K.T. Oslin, Ricky Van Shelton, Vern Gosdin, Tammy Wynette, and Dolly Parton's Dollywood Ambassadors. The list goes on and on, and includes generous, friendly people who gave out such information as the number of members in the club, the cost of membership, the personal relationship between the artist and the president, advantages to joining the club, nice personal notes to me and many times a note from the artist himself.

There was, however, NO ANSWER FROM EITHER OF THE EVERLY BROTHERS` FAN CLUBS! This shroud of secrecy that the fan clubs exhibit with regards to the Everlys is a very strange and macabre type of thing, sending waves of hostile feelings across the miles. Why? This only hurts the two artists they are trying to promote, although I really hesitate to use such a word, as demote is closer to the truth.

In addition to all this baloney, there seems to be a Rule of Everly Management that fans are not allowed (?!) to gather together for lunch or dinner in any hotel that the Everlys are staying in!!! (I will eat where I choose, thank you!) Other than the fact that in larger hotels there are often private entrances and quarters set aside for entertainers, how could a simple luncheon in a dining room hurt anyone? Really, now. The Everly fans are a different breed, anyway. They are older, established, and fewer in number than those some "hot rockers" have. Most stars would welcome the opportunity to briefly meet their fans, some of whom have been supporting them for close to thirty years. Apparently the Everlys do not feel this way, but if they are unaware of this rule, they had better get the whip out.

My advice to the fan clubs and management is to lighten up! You really could be very important but if you act hostile all of the time, one of these days there will be no one out there cheering your beloved Everlys on and/or paying their bills.

19
THE FUTURE

*"Those who bring sunshine to the lives of
others cannot keep it from themselves."*
- James Matthew Barrie

What seems to be in the future for these brothers? They have spent six months or more a year on tour just about all of their lives. I would think it would be a terrible strain. For instance, when one of them needs a dentist or a doctor, he has to take his chances in a strange town and the possibility is there that this guy might not be very good at his profession. Always remember that half of today's doctors and dentists graduated in the bottom half of their class! Maybe that particular doctor flunked his flu and arthritis tests, but passed medical school anyway. Still, a performer must perform. He must perform when he has a headache, when he has a toothache and when he is very, very tired or sick. The Everlys rarely cancel a show, and when they do, it is because of loss of voice, which is about the only excuse they have ever given their fans. I admire Donald and Phillip for this fortitude. They are amazingly natural about it, though, as evidenced when Phillip was asked what he was going to do when he gets old and his voice starts cracking. He quickly shot back with, "Continue to get older and let it crack."

As a matter of fact, many people in and around Nashville are of the opinion that a male singer does begin to lose control of his voice around the age of fifty, but that those who have been singing hard all along will keep their voices later than most. We shall see.

As Donald said in 1984 to reporter Steve Morse of The Boston Globe, "We're just going to take everything with a grain of salt. I don't think I can take anything as seriously as I used to anyway. In fact, I know I can't. After a point you just say, It's just rock 'n roll anyway. It's not a new Salk vaccine or something like that. It's a lot more fun, but it's not that important. The world would go right on turning without it."

Donald says of course that their technique and voices are much better now than they were back when they were so tremendously popular. "I'd hate to think that at twenty one I was the best I'd ever be," he once commented in a September 1984 edition of The San Francisco Chronicle.

Donald continues, "The music we've done, now when we go out on tour sometimes they use the word 'nostalgic sound'. To me it's not that nostalgic - it's still rock music and everything. We do produce that sound, the Everly Brothers as such. But as individuals we also have other directions in music other than the Everly Brothers because that happens to be a period in time that we still can do, yet continue on."

Apparently others are in awe of them, also. At times dubbed "The Emperors" by associates, Garrison Keillor has said that they were so famous they ought to be on stamps. He further complimented them by making up a song entitled, "Wouldn't It Be Everlys" which he sang on his show.

Singer-guitarist Glen Campbell told me that he thought they were "the best harmony singers in the business."

Legend Eddy Arnold remembered that "they had a distinctive and different sound. Their blend was very appealing ... I recognized their great talents. I admired them very much."

Andrew Lloyd-Webber, who today is probably the wealthiest human being in the field of music, was once secretary of the Everly Brothers' Fan Club.

Phil Cranham, Everlys' bass player, mentioned in talking to my husband that he felt pretty privileged to play with them, that they only hire the best that there is, and that they do their best to back themselves up with the best.

Their drummer, Larrie Londin, was honored by Ralph Emery on TNN's Nashville Now, as he said, "now Larrie Londin - we're talking about the best," told me a cute story about Donald which went like this: "When they were doing the Chet Atkins TV Special, Chet was on stage and surprised everyone by singing his special song, "My Dad" which he always sings with a hat on. I guess his father used to wear a hat. Only the hat he had on his head was Donald's, and Donald, if you know him at all, feels almost naked without his hat on. Well, backstage Donald was looking high and low for his hat, quite unaware that Chet was using it for a prop on stage."

The Everlys' steel guitar player, Buddy Emmonds, is considered by most to be the best steel guitar player there is, yet he continues to stick with the Everly Brothers year after year. When he is not on tour, he plays at Church Street Station in Orlando, Florida where I fortunately have a yearly pass, permitting me to go there every night if I so desire. I don't.

Whatever these beloved entertainers decide to do in the future, it will definitely not be to sit at home and retire. These men were raised to work and to work hard, and whether together or solo, they will definitely work in music. Imagine my surprise, therefore when I realized lately that they have basically done just that. In 1990, the Everlys were not much in evidence, although they continue to tour. No music was recorded, their publicity was nil, and they went into their career recluse bit. I don't really know how long this is to go on. Supposedly an album is to be put out in 1991.

Lately, there have been some changes in their road shows. Whereas several years ago Nanci Griffith opened their act, she was followed by Katy Moffat. In Tahoe, their opening act was a "clean" comedian (in Lake Tahoe?!) by the name of Alex Cole and Duane Eddy was a regular in the Nevada shows, as that is where he now lives. In 1990 their opening acts were either Carl Perkins or a very tame dulcimer player by the name of David Schnaufer.

Today's touring is very different from the old days, says Phillip. "We have about three times as many people on the road as we did in the old days. We would have just been with the band and a road manager, but now there's sound men, light men and all the technicians that are necessary. It's mostly technical things that have changed and the halls are nicer. There are a lot of good venues to play across the country that are really fun and pleasant. But outside that I don't think there is a lot of difference. The people are the same and they always are able to recognize when you are doing it right and they can tell when you're not. If I had my druthers, quite honestsly I would go back to the sound systems of the old days when you were balancing up against the house. Now it's like, you have an engineer running the monitor mix on stage, you have an engineer running the mix outside the hall so it's so technical now that you can hardly keep up with it."

He also stated that if it doesn't sound like fun, they don't do it, and he also doesn't consider a concert a success unless people give them standing ovations!

In December of 1989 Donald finally bought himself a home he should be proud of, a home he should live in. I think he has finally gotten a sense of himself.

Phillip has recently expressed an interest in sailing, although he readily admits that he doesn't know that much about the sport. He recently bought a used Ketch Motor Sailer which is about 43 feet in length, and was built in Taiwan around 1975 to 1980. He probably paid about $150,000 for this boat which would bring about $275,000 new. According to World Champion skipper Peter Godfrey, it is "OK but not a quality boat, at least not one that a knowledgeable sailer would have."

One thing that disturbs me is that they do not appear at any of the Nashville professional places, although Donald sometimes frequents various restaurants in and around Nashville, accompanied by his friends. But it seems that neither Donald nor Phillip contribute to those who are "coming up" in the business. After all, they had Chet Atkins to help them and of course the Bryants who became their surrogate family. Who have they ever been a Chet Atkins to? Never have I heard anyone say that the Everlys were their Chet Atkins. Although admired and copied by many, they are not thanked for helping anyone that I have heard other than the group Starbuck, and although many idolize their music, I am a firm believer of the old saying, "what goes around, comes around." In other words, as many of the artists stress time and time again, you must give of yourself to others in order to have that glow returned to you.

For example, we attend the Nashville Songwriters Association International Symposium every year and are grateful for the number of top songwriters, (such as the wonderful composing Nelson brothers, Gene and Paul and people like talented Taylor Dunn, etc.), producers, artists, radio people, agents and publishers who donate their time, energies and expertise in order to help others who may be struggling through the lower ranks of the business. The wonderful entertainers who give of their talents and contribute are too numerous to mention. Donald Everly lives in the same area of Nashville that the NSAI Symposium is conducted, and he has been a member of NSAI since 1977. I fail to understand, therefore, that with all his years of songwriting expertise as well as his extraordinary musical talents, he has not contributed. Yes, he is a star, but what is a star, really? Sylvester Stallone once said it's nothing more than a huge ball of gas.

I think the Everly Brothers are very proud of their accomplishments however, and they should be. Phillip remembered their beginnings: "The most asked question in the 1950s was, 'What are you going to do when it's all over?' I didn't foresee that it would last a lifetime. We had no idea. Looking back, if I had known, I would've enjoyed myself much more, relaxed more. We were always concerned with the next hit record. Rock has always been about going for it, about innovation, and we're part and parcel of that. I'm aware and I'm proud of our contribution. But it's also important for the music to mature. Our new music has the old spirit, but it also takes us a step beyond."

Donald once mused over this very subject, saying, "I'll be in the music business for the rest of my life. I don't think I'll just change and go into something else. First of all, I dislike business of any kind, you know. I don't like being with people and talking about money, about making money, and how we're going to make this and who is going to divide this up and percentages and all that. It just doesn't interest me. I think that the monetary system has got to change ... that's a whole big problem that I don't know anything about. I'm just going to go on working in music and art, if I can."

Phillip thinks in today's music, "There are technical advantages now that didn't exist before, a tremendous amount of synthesizers and things like that. They seem to be maintaining the basic element of rock 'n roll which is the feel of the music and as long as you have the good feelings in the music, I think it's fine. It doesn't matter what new sounds you add."

Music is constantly changing. The young people of today, even though some are climbing on a nostalgia bandwagon, come from a world of instant gratification. At times I think that "instant" is not even fast enough. One would think, therefore, that the music would be starting to tailor itself to this trend by making the songs shorter and by being more blatent with the lyrics. The youngssters of today can't seem to take the time to even listen to a long, complicated song and figure out all the ins and outs of the lyrics. They are in too much of a hurry, and want it stated straight out, quickly and without much fuss. Ah, so much for romance.

Phillip actually expected his voice to go, but so far it hasn't. His knee went, however, in 1985, and he was forced to undergo arthroscopic surgery. Yes, the knee went, but the voice is still there, strong and lilting.

247

When asked whether he hated today's business, Donald answered, "I don't really like to use the word hate. Because hate isn't going to stop it. You just have to look into it and learn about it. The record business is turning into a lawyer's business, I know that. And it's very difficult to start a record label in today's business. It's like starting a chain of hotels."

Has the business changed that much in recent years? Donald thinks that there is a lot more music around, but it really is not all that different than it used to be in the old days. The thing that has changed so much over the years in Nashville is the fact that the music business is now being controlled too much by executives who live in Los Angeles and New York. These people are basically out of touch with the performers and do not have a feel for the pulse of the industry. The longer these "absentee" bosses remain, the colder and more distant the country music industry becomes. Actually, the Grand Ole Opry people and the Music Row people are diametrically opposed. It is said many big shots on Music Row have never even been to the Grand Old Opry (or GOO) in their lives and have no intention of doing so. As far as I am concerned, country music would have all but disappeared if it was not for TNN and people such as Ralph Emery, Lorianne Crook and Charlie Chase, some of TNN's most powerful stars.

This does not mean, however, that the country music industry is unkind to older artists. On the contrary. It is the only industry I know of that so treasures its older talent. It also is blatently kind to those having legal, marital, or financial troubles. What a wonderful bunch of people!

It seems strange that the Everlys are not into diverse businesses, but they themselves admit they are not businessmen per se. Some other artists are, however, like Conway Twitty who has numerous corporations and businesses all over the south as well as Twitty City in Tennessee. I guess he just has a natural penchant for that sort of thing. Not everybody has, but it does create a bumper for any rough seas ahead. The Everlys do however, own thirteen small rental apartments in Nashville.

The music business is a rough one, and there are many casualties along the way. I am sure everyone can name lots of entertainers who did not survive. What you need to be to survive for many years in the entertainment business is simple. You need to be a tough hustler, and the Everlys apparently have filled that bill, or they would have been long gone by now. But are they tough hustlers? You bet your sweet bippy they are!

When on stage, I think the Everly Brothers are hysterically funny. Everly audiences love the hilarious stage banter which The Comedy Team of Don and Phil likes to ease into. Sometimes Donald will announce himself as the eldest Everly Brother, then introduce "the other one," his younger brother, Phillip, who is dressed just like him. He will urge the audience to give a hand to the one who sings the high part, which Phillip sometimes calls "the sissy part." Donald has been known to reassure his audiences that his brother will be with them again next year.

Donald's introduction of band members is equally as dry and humorous. He has called his bass player "one of the basest in music today," and in reference to the drummer, "our regular drummer is with us tonight. Our substitute couldn't make it this trip."

The Everly humor is very dry and matter-of-fact, not unlike that of Johnny Carson who I consider to be tops in his field. Donald does most of the talking on stage and gets most of the laughs, but I don't think for a moment that Phillip is lacking in the humor department. As a matter of fact he is superb, being very witty with his quick comebacks. It's a natural talent that both of them possess. For instance, if Donald thanks the audience, Phillip might answer with a "You're welcome!"

They sometimes begin a show by saying that it is a pleasure to be there, then add that they always say that and it's a pleasure to be anywhere at their ages. When ending a show, if they do an encore, Donald will thank the audience and add that they were planning to come back out again anyway.

One of the most amazing feats that the Everlys have pulled was when they were nominated in 1990 and 1991 for The TNN Music City News Country Awards. Every one of the other nominees had listed their current single, current album, record label, and what they were nominated for. The Everly Brothers were the only singers who just had a nomination under their names. They had no current single, album or label. This means that there are thousands of fans out there who just love them for who they are and what they have accomplished in the past. It seems like the Everly Brothers don't even have to perform to get nominated for music awards!

The Everly Brothers have confirmed that they get along fine now, as they think that they are probably too old to fight for long, and although they still argue, they know that each needs the other one.

Although Phillip admits he couldn't understand why people wanted to hear them in the beginning and he still can't, when asked if they see an end to their careers, Phillip said that if he could see an end to their profession, it would frighten him terribly, and went on to explain that due to the entertainer's basic nature, there aren't many who can see an end to their careers, whether they are a success or not.

Donald knows that by now he can do exactly what he wants in the recording business, and he doesn't really take much advice because he is the only one, he feels, who knows what's good. At any rate, all the record companies are interested in is making a lot of money. It's the name of the game.

In a radio interview by James Austin of Station KCSN in Los Angeles, when asked how their voices were holding up Phillip answered, "I think Don's voice is getting better but mine is a little more narrow, but I could still manage if I stand on a chair. I can still get most of the high notes."

As early as 1977, a more relaxed Donald stated in The Detroit Free Press as he looked at his straining stomach, "I'm laid back now. I'm not trying to prove anything any more." He said he doesn't like to have his picture taken any more because of the size of his stomach. "This? That's the result of being laid back. There was a time when I'd have worried myself sick about it. But not any more." Since 1977 his "result of being laid back" has grown a great deal, to alarming proportions.

What is wonderful about the Everlys now is reflected on by Phillip: "We sound like we sound. It still sounds like us no matter what the background music is."

In one of Donald's statements released by their publicist in California, he said, "Singers don't really hit their stride until their forties anyway. If you're singing about life, you have to live it. Experience and reflection are important ... that's something that youth doesn't really have. Good things don't end because you get older."

He also stated, "Brothers come before the act, now. It's in the proper perspective. That's really what we set out to do and that's what we succeeded in doing. We're going to be brothers for the rest of our lives." To which Phillip added, "Yeah. Guarantee that."

Both men have expressed the natural desire to pass on their music and both have taught their offspring to play guitar. They hope also that their grandchildren will play when they become old enough. Those grandchildren, however, have yet to appear on the scene.

When they were young, the Everly Brothers used to sing about falling in love. Nowadays the theme has changed more to songs about being in love. But the harmony remains, and the harmony is in itself a very special kind of love.

Back in their beginning years around 1958, however, even though the boys had not had any formal music lessons to speak of, *Look Magazine* reported that Donald thought of music as a normal pleasure. He simply stated, "There are just eight notes - that's all anyone has to work with." I guess it was an easy thing way back then in Kentucky. Donald has said that you almost had to play because there was nothing else to do. Also you have the theory that most of the best music comes from people who have difficult work loads such as coal miners and the slaves in the south. The melancholy seems to flow from these people because of the very hard lives they lead.

At one interview it was inferred that when they started out they had been rather young to be out working and singing on a regular basis, but neither of the men thought that their lives were particularly unique. To them, it seemed to be the norm. Phillip defended their apparent loss of childhood by saying, "Well ... we wouldn't have done it if our folks hadn't driven us down to the radio station, but we worked with our mom and dad and that's really where we got all of our musical training from. My father was quite an accomplished guitarist."

Donald elaborated defensively by saying, "It wasn't that uncommon. There was a couple of other families working in country music. In fact there's quite a few come to think of it. The Carter Family, the Hayden Family, the Masters Family. I mean in Gospel, it's a tradition. Family music." He really thinks that it's the norm, and that's OK, too.

The Everly Brothers

The Everlys definitely want to keep singing and to keep getting up in front of audiences until they are well into their seventies, if they are able. I think they are able. Will the Everly Brothers be performing in the year 2000? I think so. I certainly hope so.

Their concerts, however, need overhauling. I mean, how many times can fans listen to the same songs year after year after year? Granted, they are good. They are better than good, but new stuff has to be injected. I am convinced that Donald's voice is one of the very best, and Phillip's voice is downright uncanny, it is so beautiful when he has the right vehicle to ride with it. One of their favorite songs has always been "So Sad (To Watch Good Love Go Bad)" which they sing beautifully together. But has anyone heard Donald sing it solo? It is better than beautiful.

Many of the "easy listening" songs they do on records are not conducive to the stage. It's true that only certain songs come through to a live audience, but there are many songs that are adaptable to the stage but are never sung live. I really would like to see at least two solos, one sung by Phillip, the other by Donald, preferably two songs that they each wrote themselves. This would show the audience what superb songwriters and wonderful singers these two men are. Believe me, they can each hold their own. Unfortunately, since Donald sings the solo parts in their songs, some people don't know that Phillip has the talent that he has! Also, Donald's expertise on guitar could be shown with a solo instrumental.

Sometimes to make the audience feel more comfortable and relaxed, Donald will suggest a sing-along. (Phillip will sometimes answer, "Okay!") I do not like sing-alongs because I go to hear the Everlys sing, not to listen to a bunch of out-of-tune, off-beat amateurs. All is forgiven, however, when he asks for everyone to sing if they know the words but if they don't to just clap or do whatever they want to because "we've seen it all". Sometimes they will say if the audience wants to dance that's OK too, that there is room on the aisles. Once Donald said that the next song was a very fast fox trot and that if people were going to dance they had better begin right away!

I have always thought it would be fascinating for the Everlys and their very talented band to do one song with each man playing a secondary instrument. No one would expect it to be perfect, but I know super guitarist Albert Lee can play piano, someone could mark time with the drums, I know Donald enjoys the harmonica and electric guitar and I have seen Phillip playing the stand up bass fiddle. Both Everlys studied fiddle and mandolin as children. This would be a real show stopper and could turn out to be a lot of fun in addition to being a unique act. I doubt if the Everlys would go for something like this however, as they insist on total perfection, and an act like that would not appear as such. But at least it would be a change!

It is curious to note also that the Everlys have never recorded any religious music, which seems odd since they were raised Southern Baptists. I also keep wishing for a Christmas album with some interesting and unique Everly arrangements which only they could invent. A patriotic release would be timely, also.

These are just a few ideas, but ones that would add some new life into the old shows. I am not oldie bashing, I just think that singing "Bye Bye, Love" for thirty years could get a bit bromidic, don't you agree? In 1990, Donald announced that this year would be the "definitive Everly Brothers." Sadly, the "repetitive Everly Brothers" was closer to the truth.

In 1989 ex-Beatle drummer Ringo Starr performed a terrific publicity stunt by allowing all children twelve years old and under in free to his concerts as long as they were accompanied by an adult. In this way he secured fans from the pre-teens who would be certain to buy his records and support him through those music money years, the teen years. This was a very smart move and I think the Everlys could try something similar. After all, most of their fans are pretty old by now, myself included, and have moved on to other adult life pursuits. Adults do not attend many concerts. Most don't have either the money or the time as many of them are sending their own kids through college and/or pursuing their own careers.

I contend also that the Everly Brothers are not pro-moted well at all. I don't know who is responsible for this, but I know that they personally don't promote themselves and don't seem to want to take "center stage" when they aren't on stage. As Donald says, he doesn't like the business part. Well, that's obvious. They do, however, have a booking agent at Triad Artists, but there seems to be a steady decline in attention given to the Everlys each year. In 1989, it was practically non-existent. Triad is such a huge organization, and it represented at this writing, approximately two hundred and fifty eight artists who were being managed by twenty nine agents. If they are divid-ed up equally (which they are not), that amounts to about nine acts per agent. Now if that is all you have to do in life, wouldn't you do your best for your clients?

In perusing the latest Pollstar outputs, I noticed that in any releases from Triad in the Industry Hot Wire, the Everly Brothers were not mentioned. The Neville Brothers were men-tioned, as well as the Doobie Brothers, the Allman Brothers, the Smothers Brothers, as well as Larry Gatlin and The Gatlin Brothers. But no Everly Brothers. I searched for them in the Insider News Briefs, The Concert Pulse and the National Box Office Summaries. The only time they were mentioned in a promotional vein was in an announcement with fifty three other acts who would be available to play fair dates in 1990. This is promotion?

Apparently the Everlys didn't think they were getting a fair shake, either. Their publicity is being handled now in Nashville, although I think it is basically a very small operation. Their bookings remain with Triad.

Business dealings such as this are always in a constant state of flux, although I would think it would be healthier somehow to get with someone who would work consistently and hard for them year after year. Perhaps since they have already had that star treatment and adulation, they just don't want it any more. What a loss to everyone concerned.

It seems pop singer George Michael got into the same mode of thinking in 1990, when he refused to promote his new album due to the "stress of his celebrity status." This announcement was answered by a letter from none other than Frank Sinatra which was printed in The Los Angeles Times. Mr. Sinatra wisely wrote, "Those who have talent must hug it, embrace it, nurture it and share it, lest it be taken away from you as fast as it was loaned to you." Mr. Sinatra has learned quite a lot in seventy five years.

As far as the National Box Office Summaries went in 1989, the Everlys were not listed. I recalled that up until 1989, they were usually listed on the Top Fifty Artists list, hovering around the Number Thirty spot with an average gross of approximately $50,000.00 per concert. What happened? I don't understand. Most of their concerts are usually sold out.

In this report, the Everly grosses were reported, less the twenty-five to thirty percent merchandising fees and other expenses. All in all, I have my questions about why the Everlys hide from any major promotion of themselves. After all, all they have is themselves. I am not saying they don't make decent money, as I have seen fans clawing to see them and the residuals do keep streaming in, but the expense of a road show today is prohibitive! And not all entertainers can pull off unbelievable feats such as the Rolling Stones did in 1989. The Stones' average gross as stated in the November 20, 1989 Pollstar Concert Pulse, which is a computerized report ranking each artist by their average box office gross reported per venue, was $3,028,264 per concert. Wow.

The Everlys, however, are not the Rolling Stones, and they just keep on going as they always have. They insist that the basic element in rock 'n roll is change, so they do progress, but at their own rate and in their own way. Donald says, "We always used everything from acoustics to electric then. We did all on acoustic guitars. But we've never allowed too many vocal tricks because we are basically a duet but we'll take advantage of anything else."

In an January, 1984 interview by Jim Jerome in *People Weekly,* Donald gave some advice to newcomers as follows: "The best advice I have for someone coming into the music business now is: Learn to be an attorney or accountant first, then learn to sing." It seems the late Roy Orbison disagreed. His feeling was that if you have something to fall back on, you will. Both opinions deserve serious consideration.

All in all, the Everly Brothers have given us years of their talented selves. Their voices are outstanding and unequaled, Phillip's being so unique that it could never be copied, and although Donald once in The London Times quite accurately described his voice as sounding like "something a glacier has slithered over," his voice is still one of the very best I have ever heard. It sort of resembles scratchy velvet. If it is huskier than usual, Donald will sometimes explain to his audience that he has a bad throat, and he is warning the audience beforehand so that they will not think he is going through puberty again.

The Everly Brothers sing every kind of song imaginable: teenage laments, folk songs, English songs, protest songs, love songs, rock and roll, ballads, Beatles type songs, country songs, pop songs, rock, drinking songs, sad songs, depressing songs, happy songs, environmental songs, laments, harmony, solos, duets, male chauvinist pig songs, sexy songs, war songs, peace songs, love gone wrong songs, cruel songs, gentle songs, and they sing songs tracked on top of their own voices, harmonizing with themselves, sometimes. No one can compare with these guys!

Once on stage in the 1980s Donald explained to his audience, "We're here because our Daddy told us that we ought to sing." He then turned to his brother and said, "He also told us that we were supposed to sing together too, didn't he, Phil?" Their Daddy was a pretty smart guy!

One thing we can be fairly certain about is that the Everly Brothers are basically happy people (contrary to Donald's estimate of being happy about fifty percent of the time). I think that all human beings want to be famous, want to be noticed, and want to have an arena or venue or stage where they can speak out, sing out, or act out their innermost feelings. Those who lack that are unfortunately sometimes seen talking it out in their own heads on the street, labelled "crazy" by onlookers. Maybe they're not so crazy after all. Maybe they are just entertainers without a stage.

The Everlys will always have a stage, an audience and fans. And that would keep almost anybody happy, especially two men who were born and bred to do just that. It has to.

Listen to an Everly Brothers album when you yourself are happy and content. It should be done while sitting in front of a roaring fire on a frigid winter evening, wrapped in your favorite old bathrobe, snuggled up with someone you love and who adores you. The Everly Brothers' music is comfortable, safe, comfy, warm and cozy but heavily peppered with some real excitement.

In summing up their careers, Donald once gloated: "They tried to bury us, but we survived and now we're celebrating."

You're damn right you did!

EVERLY COMPOSITIONS

A Woman And A Man (P)
All Right Be That Way (P)
Angel Of The Darkness (P)
Asleep (D)

Back When The Bands Played In Ragtime (P)
Be My Love Again (D)
Better Than Now (P)
Born Yesterday (D)
Bowling Green (P)
Brown Eyes (P)
Buy Me A Beer (P)

California Gold (P)
Can't Get Over It (D)
Cathy's Clown (D)
Charleston Guitar (P)
Cornbread And Honey (P)
Cuckoo Bird (D & P)

Dancing On My Feet (P)
Dare To Dream Again (P)
Darling Talk To Me (P)
Detroit Man (P)
Don't Cha Know (P)
Don't Drink The Water (D)
Don't Let The Whole World Know (D & P)
Don't Say You Don't Love Me No More (P)
Double Trouble Love (P)
Draggin', Dragon (D) (Adrian Kimberly)

Evelyn Swing (D)
Eyes Of Asia (D)

Facts Of Life (D)
Feather Bed (P)
February 15th (D)
Follow Me (D)
Following The Sun (D)
Friends (P)

Gee, But It's Lonely (P)
Girls, Girls, Girls (Made To Love) (P)
Girls, Girls, Girls (What A Headache!) (P)
Give Me A Future (D & P)
Gee, But It's Lonely (P)
God Bless Older Ladies (For They Made
        Rock 'N Roll) (P)
Gone, Gone, Gone (D & P)
Green River (D & P)
Goodbye Line (P)

Hello, Amy (D)
Helpless When You're Gone (D)
Here We Are Again (D)
Human Race (D)

I Don't Want To Love You (D & P)
I Just Don't Feel Like Dancing (P)
I Think Of Me (D)
I Was Too Late For The Party (P)
I Wonder If I Care As Much (D & P)
Ich Bin Dein (I Am Yours) (P)
If Her Love Isn't True (D & P)

I'll Never Get Over You (D)
I'm Not Angry (Jimmy Howard)
I'm Thinking It Over (D)
I'm Tired Of Singing My Song In Las Vegas (D)
In Your Eyes (P)
Invisible Man (P)
It Only Costs A Dime (D & P)
It Pleases Me To Please You (P)
It Takes A Lot 'O Heart (P)
It's All Over (D)
It's True (P)

January Butterfly (P)
Jingo's Theme (P)

Keep A' Lovin' Me (D & P)
Kiss Your Man Goodbye (D & P)

La Divorce (P)
Lady Anne (P)
Let's Put Our Hearts Together (D)
Life Ain't Worth Livin' (D)
Life I Have To Live (D & P)
Lightening By Glove (D)
Lion And The Lamb (P)
Living Alone (P)
Lonely Days, Lonely Nights (P)
Love Will Pull Us Through (P)
Lover, Goodbye (P)

Man With Money (D & P)
Maybe Tomorrow (D)
Meet Me In the Bottom

Melodrama (P) (Keestone Family Singers)
Music Is The Voice Of Love (P)
My Baby (D)
My Friend (D)
My Little Yellow Bird (Micky Zellman)
My Love and Little Me (P)
Mystic Line (P)

Nancy's Minuet (D)
Never Gonna` Dream Again (P)
New Old Song (P)

Oh, Baby Oh (You're The Star) (P)
Oh, I'd Like To Go Away (D)
Oh, So Many Years (D & P)
Oh, What A Feeling (D)
Old Kentucky River (P)
Omaha (D)
One Too Many Women In Your Life (P)
Only Me (D)
Our Song (P)

Patiently (P)
Poisonberry Pie (P)

Real Love (P)
Red, White and Blue (P)
Ride The Wind (P)

Safari (D)
Should I Tell Him? (D)
Sigh, Cry, Almost Die (D)
Since You Broke My Heart (D)

Single Solitary Heart (D)
Snowflake Bombardier (P)
Some Hearts (D)
Something's Wrong (P) (Bernie Schwartz)
Somewhere South in Mexico (P)
So Sad (To Watch Good Love Go Bad) (D)
Step It Up & Go (Jimmy Howard)
Summershine (P)
Sweet Dreams Of You (D)
Sweet Grass County (P)
Sweet Music (P)
Sweet Pretender (P)
Sweet Southern Love (P)
Sweet Suzanne (P)

That's Just Too Much (D)
That's The Life I Have To Live (D & P)
The Collection (D)
The Drop Out (D)
The Facts Of Life (D)
The Fall of '59 (P)
The Price Of Love (D & P)
The Sun Keeps Shining (D & P)
They Smile For You (P)
Thou Shalt Not Steal (D)
Three Bands Of Steel (D)
('Til) I Kissed You (D)
Time To Spare (D) (Jack Pegasus)
Too Blue (P)
Turn The Memories Loose Again (D)

Up In Mabel's Room (P)

What's The Use, I Still Love You (P)
When I Stop Dreaming (D)
When I'm Dead And Gone (P)
When You Wish Upon A Star (D) (Adrian Kimberly)
When Will I Be Loved (P)
Wild Boy (P)
Words In Your Eyes (P)

You And I Are A Song (P)
You Broke It (P)
You Can Bet (P)
You Make It Seem So Easy (D)
You're My Girl (D & P)

MAJOR RECORD ALBUMS

A Date With The Everly Brothers
All They Had To Do Was Dream

Back Where It All Began
Beat 'N Soul
Born Yesterday
Both Sides Of An Evening
Brother Jukebox (solo)
Bye Bye Everlys

Chained To A Memory
Christmas With The Everly Brothers And
        The Boys Town Choir
Coke, Chrysler 'N Country

Don Everly (solo)
Don't Fight Girls, There's Two
Double Gold

EB '84
End Of An Era
Especially For You

15 Everly Hits
Folk Songs By The Everly Brothers
Foreverly Yours
Gone Gone Gone

Heartaches 'n' Harmonies
Home Again

In Our Image
Instant Party
In The Studio
It's Everly Time

La Grande Storia Del Rock #30
Living Alone (solo)
Living Legends
Louise (solo)

Mystic Line (solo)

Nice Guys
November 9, 1955

Original Greatest Hits (2 LP)

Pass The Chicken And Listen
Phil Everly (solo)
Phil's Diner (solo)
Pure Harmony

Reunion Concert
Rip It Up
Rock 'N Soul
Rockin' With The Everly Brothers
Rocking In Harmony
Roots

Some Hearts
Songs Our Daddy Taught Us
Star Spangled Springer (solo)
Stories We Could Tell

Sunset Towers (solo)

The Best Of The Everly Brothers
The Everly Brothers 1957-1960 (2 LP)
The Everly Brothers' Best
The Everly Brothers' Collection (3 LP)
The Everly Brothers' Golden Archives
The Everly Brothers' Greatest Hits
The Everly Brothers' Greatest Hits - Vol. I
The Everly Brothers' Greatest Hits - Vol. II
The Everly Brothers' Greatest Hits - Vol. III
The Everly Brothers' Original Greatest Hits
The Everly Brothers' Show
The Everly Brothers Sing
The Everly Brothers Sing Great Country Hits
The Everly Brothers' Story
The Everly Brothers: They're Off And Rolling
The Fabulous Style Of The Everly Brothers
The Golden Hits Of The Everly Brothers
The History Of The Everly Brothers (2 LP)
The Hit Sound Of The Everly Brothers
The Legends Of Rock
The New Album
The Very Best Of The Everly Brothers
20 Super Hits By The Everly Brothers
Two Yanks In England

Wake Up Again With The Everly Brothers (2 LP)
Walk Right Back

SONG TITLES

A Change of Heart
A Nickel For The Fiddler
A Voice Within
A Whiter Shade Of Pale
A Woman And A Man
Abandoned Love
Adestes Fideles
Ain't That Lovin' You Baby
All I Have To Do Is Dream
All Right Be That Way
All We Really Want To Do
Always Drive A Cadillac
Always It's You
Amanda Ruth
And I'll Go (unreleased)
Angel Of The Darkness
Angels From The Realms Of Glory (unreleased)
Aquarius
Arms Of Mary
Asleep
Autumn Leaves
Away In A Manger

Baby Bye Oh (Bernie Schwartz)
Baby What You Want Me To Do
Back When The Bands Played Ragtime
Ballad Of A Teenage Queen
Barbara Allen
Be-Bop-A-Lula
Be My Love Again
Better Than Now

Bird Dog
Black Mountain Stomp (Adrian Kimberly)
Blueberry Hill
Born To Lose
Born Yesterday
Bowling Green
Boy With The Blue Balloon (unreleased)
Brand New Heartache
Brand New Rock 'N Roll Band
Breakdown
Bring A Torch Jeannette Isabella
Brother Jukebox
Brown Eyes
Bully Of The Town
Buona Fortuna Amore Mio (So Sad) (Italy) (unreleased)
Burma Shave
Buy Me A Beer
Bye Bye Blackbird
Bye Bye, Love

C C Rider
California Gold
Can't Get Over It
Carol Jane
Carolina On My Mind
Caroline
Carolyn Walking Away (unreleased)
Casey's Last Ride (unreleased)
Cathy's Clown
Chained To A Memory
Chains
Charleston Guitar
Chloe

Christmas Eve Can Kill You
Chrysler/Plymouth Commercial
Claudette
Coca Cola Commercial
Coo Coo
Cornbread And Chitlings (Keestone Family Singers)
Cornbread And Honey
Crying In The Rain
Cuckoo Bird

Dancing In The Street
Dancing On My Feet
Danger, Danger
Dare To Dream Again
Darling Talk To Me
Deck The Halls (With Boughs Of Holly)
Deep Water
Del Rio Dan
Deliver Me
Detroit Man
Devoted To You
Did It Rain?
Do You?
Donna, Donna
Don't Ask Me To Be Friends
Don't Blame Me
Don't Cha Know
Don't Drink The Water (Drink The Wine)
Don't Forget To Cry
Don't Let The Whole World Know
Don't Run And Hide
Don't Say Goodnight
Don't Say You Don't Love Me No More

Don't You Even Try
Don't Worry Baby
Double Trouble Love
Down In The Willow Garden
Draggin', Dragon (Adrian Kimberly)
Du Bist Nicht Wie Die Andern (Germany) (unreleased)

Ebony Eyes
Eden To Cainin
Empty Boxes
Evelyn Swing
Even If I Hold It In My Hand (unreleased)
Every Time You Leave
Eyes Of Asia

Feather Bed
February 15th
Fifi The Flea
Follow Me
Following The Sun
Foolish Doubts (unreleased)
Friends
From The Realms Of Glory

Games People Play
Gee, But It's Lonely
Give Me A Future
Give Me A Sweetheart
Give Peace A Chance
Girls, Girls, Girls (Made To Love)
Girls, Girls, Girls (What A Headache!) (unreleased)
Glitter And Gold
God Bless America (Adrian Kimberly)

God Bless Older Ladies (For They Made Rock 'N Roll)
God Rest Ye Merry Gentlemen
Gone, Gone, Gone
Good Golly Miss Molly
Good Hearted Woman
Goodbye Line
Grandfather's Clock
Gran Mamou
Green River
Greensleeves (Adrian Kimberly)
Ground Hawg

Hard Hard Year
Hark! The Herald Angels Sing
Have You Ever Loved Somebody
Helpless When You're Gone
Hello Amy
Here We Are Again
Hernando's Hideaway (unreleased)
He's A Real Nice Guy (Bernie Schwartz)
He's Got My Sympathy
Hey, Doll Baby
Hey Jude
Hi-Heel Sneakers
Hi-Lili Hi-Lo
Honolulu
Hound Dog
House Of The Rising Sun
How Can I Meet Her
Human Race
Husbands And Wives

I Almost Lost My Mind

I Can't Say Goodbye To You
I Don't Want to Love You
I Got A Woman
I Just Don't Feel Like Dancing
I Know Love
I Think Of Me (unreleased)
I Used To Love You
I Walk The Line
I Want You To Know
I Was Too Late For The Party
I Wonder If I Care As Much
Ich Bin Dein (I Am Yours)
(I'd Be) A Legend In My Time
If Her Love Isn't True
If I Were A Carpenter
Illinois
I'll Mend Your Broken Heart
I'll Never Get Over You
I'll See Your Light
I'm Afraid
I'm Finding It Rough
I'm Gonna' Move To The Outskirts Of Town
I'm Here To Get My Baby Out Of Jail
I'm Movin' On
I'm Not Angry
I'm On My Way Home Again
I'm So Lonesome I Could Cry
I'm Taking My Time
I'm Thinking It Over
I'm Tired Of Singing My Song In Las Vegas
I'm Walking Proud (unreleased)
In The Good Old Days
In Your Eyes

Invisible Man
It Only Costs A Dime
It Pleases Me To Please You
It Takes A Lot O' Heart
It's All Over
It's Been A Long, Dry Spell
It's Been Nice
It's My Time
It's True
I've Been Wrong Before
Jack Daniels Old No. 7
January Butterfly
Jezebel
Jingo's Song
Julianne
June Is As Cold As December
Just In Case
Just One Time
Just To Show I Love You (unreleased)

Kansas City
Keep A Knockin'
Keep A' Lovin' Me
Kentucky
Kiss Your Man Goodbye

La Divorce
La Luna E Un Pallido Sole (Italy) (unreleased)
Ladies Love Outlaws
Lady Anne
Lay It Down
Lay, Lady, Lay
Leave My Girl Alone

Leave My Woman Alone
Legend In My Time
Less Of Me
Let It Be Me
Let's Go Get Stoned
Let's Put Our Hearts Together (Dead Cowboys)
Lettin' Go
Life Ain't Worth Livin'
Life I Have To Live
Lightening By Glove (unreleased)
Lightening Express
Like Every Time Before
Like Strangers
Lion And The Lamb
Little Bit Of Crazy (unreleased)
Little Hollywood Girl
Little Old Lady
Little Town Of Bethlehem
Living Alone
Living Too Close To The Ground
Lonely Avenue
Lonely Days, Lonely Nights
Lonely Island
Lonely Street
Lonely Weekends
Long Lost John
Long Time Gone
Lord Of The Manor
Louise
Love At Last Sight
Love Her
Love Hurts
Love Is All I Need

Love Is Strange
Love Is Where You Find It
Love Makes The World Go 'Round
Love Of My Life
Love Of The Common People
Love Will Pull Us Through
Love With Your Heart (unreleased)
Lover, Goodbye
Lovey Kravezit
Lucille

Maiden's Prayer
Mama Tried
Man With Money
Mandolin Wind
Mary Jane
Maybeline
Maybe Tomorrow
Meet Me In The Bottom
Melodrama (Keestone Family Singers)
Melody Train
Memories Are Made Of This
Mention My Name In Sheboygan
Mercy Mercy Mercy
Milk Train
Money
More Than I Can Handle
Morning
Mr. Soul
Music Is The Voice Of Love
Muskrat
My Baby
My Elusive Dreams (unreleased)

My Friend
My Gal Sal
My Grandfather's Clock
My Little Yellow Bird
My Love And Little Me
My Mammy
Mystic Line

Na, Na, Na (unreleased)
Nancy's Minuet
Nashville Blues
Never Gonna' Dream Again
Never Like This
New Old Song
Nice Guys
Nite Time Girl (unreleased)
No One Can Make My Sunshine Smile
Non Me Resti Che Tu (Italy) (unreleased)
Not Fade Away
Nothing But The Best (unreleased)
Nothing Matters But You
Nothing's Too Good For My Baby
Now Is The Hour

O Little Town Of Bethlehem
Oh, Baby Oh (You're The Star)
Oh, I'd Like To Go Away
Oh, Lonesome Me
Oh, My Papa
Oh, So Many Years
Oh, True Love
Oh, What A Feeling
Old Kentucky River (Caroline)

Omaha
On The Wings Of A Nightingale
One Too Many Women In Your Life
One Way Love
Only Me
Our Song
Outskirts Of Town

Paradise
Patiently (Jack Pegasus)
People Get Ready
Please Help Me, I'm Falling
Poems, Prayers and Promises
Poisonberry Pie
Pomp And Circumstance (Adrian Kimberly)
Poor Jenny
Portugese Bend (unreleased)
Pretty Flamingo
Problems
Put My Little Shoes Away

Radio And TV
Real Love
Red, White and Blue
Release Me
Ride The Wind
Ridin` High
Ring Around My Rosie
Rip It Up
Rock 'N Roll Music
Rockin` Alone In An Old Rockin' Chair
Rocky Top
Rovin' Gambler

Running Out

Safari
Sag Auf Wiedersehn (Germany) (unreleased)
Sea Of Heartbreak
Send Me The Pillow That You Dream On
Shady Grove
She Means Nothing To Me
She Never Smiles Anymore
Should We Tell Him?
Sigh, Cry, Almost Die
Signs That Will Never Change
Silent Night
Silent Treatment
Silver Threads And Golden Needles
Since You Broke My Heart
Sing Me Back Home
Single Solitary Heart
Sleepless Nights
Slippin` & Slidin'
Snowflake Bombardier
So Fine
So How Come (No One Loves Me)
So It Will Always Be
So Lonely
So Sad (To Watch Good Love Go Bad)
Some Hearts
Some Sweet Day
Somebody Help Me
Somebody Nobody Knows
Something Wrong (Bernie Schwartz)
Somewhere South In Mexico
Southern California

Stained Glass Morning
Step It Up And Go (Jimmy Howard)
Stick With Me Baby
Sticks And Stones
Stories We Could Tell
Summershine
Summertime
Susie (Germany) (unreleased)
Susie Q
Sweet Dreams
Sweet Grass County
Sweet Memories
Sweet Music
Sweet Pretender
Sweet Southern Love
Sweet Suzanne

T For Texas
Take A Message To Mary
Takin' Shots
Talking To The Flowers
Temptation
That Silver-Haired Daddy Of Mine
That Uncertain Feeling
That'll Be The Day
That's Just Too Much
That's Old Fashioned
That's The Life I Have To Live
That's What You Do To Me
The Air That I Breathe
The Brand New Tennessee Waltz
The Collector
The Devil's Child

The Doll House Is Empty
The Drop Out
The End
The Everly Family 1952
The Everly Family 1953
The Facts Of Life
The Fall of '59
The Ferris Wheel
The First In Line
The First Noel
The Girl Can't Help It
The Girl Sang The Blues
The House Of The Rising Sun
The Last Song I'm Ever Going To Sing
The Last Thing On My Mind
The Party's Over
The Power Of Love
The Price Of Love
The Sheik Of Araby (unreleased)
The Story Of Me
The Sun Keeps Shining
The Thrill Is Gone
The Way You Remain
The Wayward Wind
The Words In Your Eyes
There's Nothing Too Good For My Baby
These Shoes
They Smile For You (unreleased)
Thinkin' 'Bout You
Thinking It Over
This Little Girl Of Mine
Thou Shalt Not Steal
Three-Armed Poker-Playin' River Rat

Three Bands Of Steel
Time To Spare (Jack Pegasus)
('Til) I Kissed You
Too Blue
Torture
Trouble
Trouble In Mind
Trains And Boats And Planes
True Love
Tumbling Tumbleweeds
Turn Around
Turn The Memories Loose Again

Up In Mabel's Room

Ventura Boulevard
Wake Up Little Susie
Walk Right Back
Walking The Dog
Warming Up The Band
Warum (Germany) (unreleased)
Watchin' It Go
We Can Change The World (unreleased)
Wenn Du Mich Kusst (Germany) (unreleased)
We Wish You A Merry Christmas
We're Running Out
What About Me
What Am I Living For
What Child Is This
What Kind Of Girl Are You?
Whatever Happened To Judy
What's The Use, I Still Love You
When Eddie Comes Home (unreleased)

When I Grow Too Old To Dream
When I Stop Dreaming
When I'm Dead And Gone
When It's Night Time In Italy (It's Wednesday Over Here)
When Snowflakes Fall In The Summer
When Will I Be Loved
When You Wish Upon A Star (Adrian Kimberly)
Who's Gonna' Keep Me Warm
Who's Gonna' Shoe Your Pretty Little Feet
Why Not?
Why Worry
Wild Boy
Wo Sind Die Schoenen Tage (Germany) (unreleased)
Woman Don't You Try To Tie Me Down
Yesterday Just Passed My Way Again
You And I Are A Song
You Broke It
You Can Bet
You Done Me Wrong
You Make It Seem So Easy
You Send Me
You Thrill Me
You're Just What I Was Looking For Today
You're My Girl
You're The One I Love
Yves

Zwei Gitarren Am Meer (Germany) (unreleased)

CHRONOLOGY

1935

8/31: Ike and Margaret Everly marry

1937

2/1: Isaac Donald Everly is born in Brownie, Kentucky. His mother was 17 years old, his father was 28.

1939

1/19: Phillip Everly is born in Cook County Hospital, Chicago, Illinois.

1945

1945: Donald (8) and Phillip (6) debut on Station KMA in Shenandoah, Iowa

1949

1949: Donald (12) and Phillip (10) become regulars on the show. The family earned $75 a week

1950

1950: The Everly Family Show was born
1951

1951: The Everly Family Show moved to Evansville, Indiana at Radio WIKY

1953

1953: The family worked on Station WROL in Knoxville, TN. They were fired because the station manager didn't like their "bobby soxer" music. After they became famous, he claimed he "discovered" them

1954

1954: Donald wrote "Thou Shalt Not Steal" (Another Man's Wife). Kitty Wells had a top 10 hit with it.

1955

6/55: Donald graduated from West High School in Knoxville, Tennessee

1955: Donald and Phillip went to Nashville

1955: Recording contract signed with Columbia Records

1956

Feb.: "Keep A Lovin' Me/The Sun Keeps Shining/If Her Love Isn't True/That's The Life I Have To Live"

1957

3/1: Donald and Phillip sign a 3 year contract with Cadence Records. Wesley Rose becomes their manager

3/25: Donald and Mary Sue Ingraham elope to Ringgold, Georgia. She was 19, he was 20 and Phillip was best man.

5/10: First Grand Ole Opry appearance

May: "Bye Bye, Love/I Wonder If I Care As Much"

6/1: Become members of Grand Ole Opry

June: The Ed Sullivan Show

Aug.: The Ed Sullivan Show

9/6: Irvin Feld Tour, 11 weeks, 78 cities

Sept.: "Wake Up Little Susie/Maybe Tomorrow"

Sept.: The Ed Sullivan Show

10/10: Donald and Mary Sue's infant, Mary E. Everly, was born and died

1957: Bill Monroe's Grand Ole Opry Tent Tour

1957: Phillip receives high school diploma in the mail

1957: The Julius La Rosa Show

1957: The Perry Como Show

1957: The Vic Damone Show

1957: *Billboard Magazine*'s Award for Most Promising Country and Western Vocal Group

1957: *Cashbox* Award - Best New Pop Group

1957: Awarded *Country & Western Jamboree's* Best New Singing Group

1957: "Bye Bye, Love" voted Best Vocal Record of the Year

1957: The Biggest Show of Stars in NYC

1957: Alan Freed's Christmas Jubilee at the Paramount Theatre in NYC

1958

Jan. "This Little Girl of Mine/Should We Tell Him?"

April: "All I Have To Do Is Dream/Claudette"

April: LP - *The Everly Brothers (They're Off And Rolling)*

July: "Bird Dog/Devoted To You"

Nov.: "Problems/Love Of My Life"

Dec.: LP - *Songs Our Daddy Taught Us*

1958: U.S. Tour - 480 cities

1959

1/16: Tour of Europe, incl. England, Belgium, Holland, Sweden, Germany, Luxembourg and France with Andy Williams and the Chordettes

1/16: Cool for Cats Show - BBC TV

March: "Take A Message To Mary/Poor Jenny"

March: LP - *The Everly Brothers' Best*

April: Tour of Australia

5/16: Venetia Ember, Donald's daughter, is born in Nashville, Tennessee

Aug: "(Til) I Kissed You/Oh, What A Feeling"

1960

Jan.: "Let It Be Me/Since You Broke My Heart"

March: "Cathy's Clown/Always It's You"

May: LP - *The Fabulous Style Of The Everly Brothers*

May: LP - *It's Everly Time*

June: "When Will I Be Loved/Be Bop A Lula"

Aug.: "So Sad (To Watch Good Love Go Bad)/Lucille"

Oct.: LP - *A Date With The Everly Brothers*

1960: Donald and Phillip leave Cadence Records, sign on with Warner Brothers Records. Signed the first million dollar contract in recording history, guaranteeing them $100,000 per year.

1960: LP - *Folk Songs By The Everly Brothers*

1960: In California, enroll at Peyton Price's drama class at Warners and decide to live in L.A. permanently

1960: "Like Strangers/Brand New Heartache" (U.S.A.)

1960: "Like Strangers/Leave My Woman Alone" (Britain)

1960: World Tour

1961

Jan.: "Ebony Eyes/Walk Right Back" (Banned by BBC)

5/23: Donald and Mary Sue divorce with his tasteless comment, "Babe, you just ain't Hollywood."

May: "Temptation/Stick With Me Baby"

Aug.: LP - *Both Sides Of An Evening*

Oct.: "Muskrat/Don't Blame Me"

11/25: Join U.S. Marine Corps Reserves

Dec.: "Crying In The Rain/I'm Not Angry"

1961: Wesley Rose fired as manager, who later sued for breach of contract. Jack Rael becomes new manager

1961: Calliope Records formed

1961: Alma Cogan Show, BBC TV

1961: Tour of U.S.A. and the Orient

1962

Jan.: LP - *Instant Party*

2/13: Graduate from boot camp, Camp Pendleton, CA

2/13: Donald marries Venetia Stevenson at Camp Pendleton. The remainder of their Marine training was at Twenty Nine Palms in the southern California desert

2/15: The Ed Sullivan Show

5/24: Marine Corps stint finished. Donald became Squad Leader, Phillip was Private First Class

May: "That's Old Fashioned/How Can I Meet Her?"

June: LP - *The Golden Hits Of The Everly Brothers*

10/13: Donald hospitalized in London from drug overdose. Phillip bravely continues the tour alone

Oct.: "No One Can Make My Sunshine Smile/Don't Ask Me To Be Friends"

Oct.: "I'm Here To Get My Baby Out Of Jail/Lightning Express"

Oct.: LP - *15 Everly Hits*

Oct.: LP - *Christmas With The Everly Brothers And The Boys Town Choir*

1962: Tour of Europe

1962: Cumulative record sales in excess of 35 million singles, 26 of which made it to the charts

1963

1/12: Phillip marries Jacqueline Alice Ertel. Donald is best man. Nashville honeymoon, then L.A. to live

Jan.: "It's Been Nice/I'm Afraid"

March: "So It Will Always Be/Nancy's Minuet"

5/5: Anastasia Dawn (Stacy), Donald's daughter, born in L.A.

Aug.: Venetia sues Donald for divorce. They reconcile

Oct.: LP - *The Everly Brothers Sing Great Country Hits*

Nov.: "The Girl Sang The Blues/Love Her"

1963: Toured Britain on Don Arden Tour with Bo Diddley and the Rolling Stones

1963: Saturday Club, BBC Radio

1964

March: "Hello Amy/Ain't That Lovin' You Baby"

June: "The Ferris Wheel/Don't Forget To Cry"

Aug.: "You're The One I Love/Ring Around My Rosie"

Aug.: LP - *The Very Best Of The Everly Brothers*

Oct.: "Gone Gone Gone/Torture"

Dec.: "You're My Girl/Don't Let The Whole World Know"

1964: LP - *For Everly Yours* (Holland)

1964: U.S. Tour

1965

Jan.: LP - *Gone Gone Gone*

Jan.: Hullabaloo, Paul Anka's TV show

Jan.: "Donna, Donna/Made To Love"

Feb.: "That'll Be The Day/Give Me A Sweetheart"

Feb.: Shindig, U.S. TV show

March: LP - *Rock 'N Soul*

April: "The Price Of Love/It Only Costs A Dime"

June: Saturday Club, BBC Radio

Aug.: LP - *Beat 'N Soul*

Aug.: "I'll Never Get Over You/Follow Me"

Sept.: Saturday Club, BBC Radio

Sept.: Star Scene 65 Tour (England)

Oct.: "Love Is Strange/Man With Money"

Oct.: "Baby Bye Oh/Something Wrong"

11/8: Erin Invicta, Donald's daughter, born in L.A.

Dec.: "It's All Over/I Used To Love You"

Dec.: "You're My Girl/Don't Let The Whole World Know"

1965: Spring Promotional Tour of England, Italy, Germany and France

1965: Hullabaloo, U.S. TV (2)

1965: Shindig, U.S. TV (2)

1965: American Bandstand, U.S. TV

1965: Tour of Midwestern U.S.A.

1966

Feb.: "The Doll House Is Empty/Lonely Kravezit"

March: "(You Got) The Power Of Love/Leave My Girl Alone"

April: Tour of Ireland, also perform at U.S. Army bases

April: LP - *In Our Image*

May: U.S. Tour (five months)

July: LP - *Two Yanks In England*

9/9: Phillip Jason, Phillip's son, born in New York City

Sept.: "Somebody Help Me/Hard Hard Year/I've Been Wrong Before"

1966: "Release Me/Sweet Dreams"

1966: Tour of Orient, incl. Manila

1967

Jan.: "Fifi The Flea/Like Every Time Before"

Feb.: LP - *The Hit Sound Of The Everly Brothers*

Feb.: Snowed in in Chicago for 2 days during worst snow storm in history

March: "The Devil's Child/She Never Smiles Anymore"

April: "Oh, Boy!/Good Golly Miss Molly"

May: "Bowling Green/I Don't Want To Love You"

May: Expo 67 in Montreal. Stacy, age 4, gets her first chance to see Daddy and Uncle Phil perform and she joins them on stage

Aug.: LP - *The Everly Brothers Sing*

Aug.: "Mary Jane/Talking To The Flowers"

Oct.: "Love Of The Common People/A Voice Within"

1967: Tour of U.S. and Canada (Germany and England tours are cancelled)

1968

April: "It's My Time/Empty Boxes"

July: "Milk Train/Lord Of The Manor"

8/15: Edan Donald, Donald's son is born in Burbank, California

Dec.: LP - *Roots*

1968: The Latin Quarter, NYC

1968: The Mike Douglas Show, U.S. TV

1968: The Merv Griffin Show, U.S. TV

1968: Carrier Enterprise, U.S. TV

1968: County Fair, U.S. TV

1968: Tour of Tokyo, Bangkok, Taiwan, Okinawa, Manila, Germany, Paris, England

1968: Tour of Australia

1969

Jan.: "T For Texas/I Wonder If I Care As Much"

May: "I'm On My Way Home Again/Cuckoo Bird"

July: Newport Folk Festival (R.I.)

Aug.: "Carolina On My Mind/My Little Yellow Bird"

1969: The Glen Campbell Good Time Hour, U.S. TV

1969: The Kraft Music Hall, U.S. TV

1969: The Smothers Brothers Show, U.S. TV

1969: Hollywood Palace, U.S. TV

1969: Music Scene, U.S. TV

1969: Donald and Venetia snowed in in cabin and miss opening night of tour originating in Boulder, Colorado

1969: Tour of Hawaii, taking their families and those of band with them

1970

2/23: Jackie files for divorce from Phillip

4/8: Venetia files for divorce from Donald

July: LP - *The Everly Brothers Show*

July: LP - *Original Greatest Hits*

Nov.: "Tumbling Tumbleweeds/Only Me"

Dec.: The Johnny Cash Show, U.S. TV

Dec.: "Yves/Human Race"

Dec.: LP - *Don Everly* (solo)

1970: LP - *Chained To A Memory*

1970: Jimmie Rodgers Show, U.S. TV

1970: The Dean Martin Show, U.S. TV

1970: The Petula Clark Show, U.S. TV

1970: The Ed Sullivan Show, U.S. TV

1970: Leave Warner Brothers, sign new contract with RCA Records

1970: Johnny Cash Presents The Everly Brothers Summer Replacement Show

1970: Tour of South Africa and London

1971

1/14: Donald's and Venetia's divorce finalized

Jan.: LP - *End Of An Era*

Feb.: The Ed Sullivan Show, U.S. TV

May: Knott's Berry Farm, California

6/4: Magic Mountain, California

6/24: Tullamarine Jetport, Melbourne, Australia, Festival Hall

June: Hippies With Money, Australian TV

9/3: Knott's Berry Farm

9/10: Eindhoven, Holland

9/11: Ahoy Pop Festival, Rotterdam

1971: Tour of U.S and Europe

1971: Royal Albert Hall with Ike

1971: LP - *The Everly Brothers Story*

1971: AFN Interview (Germany)

1971: Jack Rael fired as personal manager

1971: Scene and Heard, BBC radio

1971: The Old Grey Whistle Test, BBC TV

1971: Jan Donkers' Aloha Interview

1972

2/7: Jackie and Phillip's divorce finalized

March: Stand Up And Cheer, U.S. TV

March: The Merv Griffin Show, U.S. TV

March: Phoenix, Arizona

April: Popsmuk, Dutch radio

April: Palomino Club, North Hollywood

5/8: Philharmonic Hall, NYC

5/20: Miss America Pagent, U.S. TV

May: The Dick Cavett Show, U.S. TV

May: The David Frost Show, U.S. TV
Donald meets Karen Prettyman

May: "Ridin' High/Stories We Could Tell"

May: Montreal/Ottawa, Canada

6/24: Orange County Fairgrounds

7/15: Phillip marries Patricia Mickey, a former Dean Marin Golddigger

8/19: Midnight Special, U.S. TV

9/4: Bartley Variety Club, BBC TV

9/19: Old Grey Whistle Test, BBC TV

9/23: Kenny Rogers' Rollin' Show, U.S. TV

10/13: Cine Roma, Antwerp, Belgium

10/14: Musis Sacrij, Arnhem, Holland

10/15: Stadsschouwberg, Sittard

Oct.: Weekend World, AFN Radio, Germany

Oct.: USA Country Coach, German radio

Oct.: Musikladen, German TV

Oct.: Birmingham - Barbarella's Club

Nov.: Talk Of The South, Southend

Nov.: "Paradise/Lay It Down"

1972: Promotional tape for *Pass The Chicken And Listen*

1972: LP - *Stories We Could Tell*

1972: Tour of U.S., Belgium, Germany, Holland and England

1973

March: LP - *Pass The Chicken And Listen*

April: Knott's Berry Farm, California

April: "Ladies Love Outlaws/Not Fade Away"

June: Las Vegas

June: LP - *Star Spangled Springer* (solo)

7/13: Knott's Berry Farm

7/14: Knott's Berry Farm (The Breakup)

1973: Phillip hosts In Session, U.S. TV

1973: LP - *The History Of The Everly Brothers*

1973: LP - *Star Collection*

1973: LP - *The Most Beautiful Songs Of The Everly Brothers*

1973: LP - *Bye Bye Everlys*

1973: Donald tours a bit with the Crickets and Heads, Hands & Feet

1974

Aug.: Cilla Black Show, BBC TV (P)

9/25: Christopher Isaac, Phillip's son is born in L.A.

1974: The Story of Pop, BBC radio

1974: All American Heroes, BBC radio

1974: Sounds Like The Navy (P)

1974: LP - *Sunset Towers* (solo)

1974: Donald leaves California for Nashville, Tennessee

1974: LP - *Phil's Diner* (solo) (called *There's Nothing Too Good For My Baby* in Britain)

1974: LP - *Don & Phil's Fabulous Fifties Treasury* (UK)

1974: LP - *The Best Of The Everly Brothers*

1974: LP - *The Everly Brothers* (Holland)

1974: LP - *The Everly Brothers' Original Hits* (France)

1974: LP - *Wake Up Again With The Everly Brothers*

1974: Phillip and Patricia return to L.A. from living in England

1975

5/5: Donald marries Karen Prettyman

10/22: Ike dies from pneumonia, following lung surgery

Oct.: LP - *Mystic Line* (solo)

1975: LP - *The Exciting Everly Brothers*

1975: LP - *Songs Our Daddy Taught Us*

1975: LP - *The Everly Brothers Sing!* (Japan)

1975: LP - *All About The Everly Brothers* (Japan)

1975: LP - *Double Gold*

1975: LP - *Magical Golden Hits Of The Everly Brothers*

1975: Phillip receives BMI's prestsigious Robert J. Burton Award for "When Will I Be Loved," as The Most Performed Song Of the Year.

1975: LP - *Walk Right Back With The Everly Brothers* (UK)

1976

3/6: Sound Stage, U.S. TV

March: "Oh, I'd Like To Go Away/Deep Water" (D)

March: Dick Clark's Solid Gold, U.S. radio

4/20: Popreconstructie, Dutch radio

5/29: "Moonlight Feels Right" (Starbuck)

1976: LP - *Brother Jukebox* (solo)

1976: "Jingo's Song" - Black Oak Conspiracy (film)

1976: "Detroit Man" - Moving Violation (film)

1976: LP - *The Everly Brothers' Best* (Japan)

1976: LP - *Portrait*

1977

March: See You Later Alligator, Hamburg

4/11: Wembley Country Festival (D)

4/17: Jimmy Saville Show, BBC TV

April: David Hamilton Show, BBC TV

5/21: "Everybody Be Dancin'" (Starbuck)

6/77: Coca Cola Story (France)

11/14: Patricia files for divorce from Phillip

12/10: VIP Show, Holland radio

1977: Donald receives BMI award for one millionth airing of his So Sad (To Watch Good Love Go Bad)

1977: LP - *The New Album* (UK)

1977: LP - *Living Legends*

1977: LP - *The Best Of The Everly Brothers*

1977: Sing Country, Wembley TV

1977: All You Need, BBC TV

1978

1/29: See You Later Alligator, Hamburg

2/6: See You Later Alligator, Hamburg

3/25: Wembley, 1978 (D)

Sept.: Country Style, U.S. TV

12/22: Patricia and Phillip's divorce is finalized

1978: Sing Country, Wembley TV (D)

1978: LP - *Back Where It All Began*

1978: LP - *Coke, Chrysler 'N Country*

1978: Cameo in Every Which Way But Loose (film) (P)

1978: Cameo in Any Which Way You Can (film) (P)

1978: Tour of UK with Mary Robbins (D)

1979

1/24: Meer Muziek, Antwerp

2/7: Dean Reed TV Show (E. Germany) (P)

Feb.: LP - *The Sensational Everly Brothers*

3/1: Open House, BBC radio (P)

4/6: Hammersmith Odeon (D)

9/9: Ronnie Prophet Show, BBC TV (D)

9/14: Hammersmith Odean, Buddy Holly Week

1979: LP - *Living Alone* (solo)

1979: LP - *Take Off The 70s*

1979: "Ich Bin Dien" (P)

1980

1/5: The Palomino Club (P)

3/29: Frankfurt, Germany (D)

4/1: Hippodrome de Paris, French TV (D)

4/6: Country Festival, Rotterdam (D)

4/12: Solid Gold, US TV (P)

April: Wembley, BBC radio (D)

April: Country Festival, Swiss TV (D)

5/2: Palomino Club (P)

5/3: Palomino Club (P)

5/5: Palomino Club (P) (A benefit performance with Emmylou Harris)

6/28: Palomino Club (P)

7/3: Musis Sacrum Arnhem, Dutch radio (D)

7/4: Tunes Van Toen, Dutch radio (D)

7/4: Gouda, Holland (The Dead Cowboys)

July: Don Everly Special (Dutch)

8/1: The Venue, London (D)

9/6: Palomino Club (P)

11/14: Palomino Club (P)

Nov.: "Dare To Dream Again/Lonely Days, Lonely Nights" (P)

1980: Donald with The Dead Cowboys

1980: Sing Country, BBC TV (D)

1980: Chet Atkins Special, U.S. TV (D)

1980: The John Davidson Show, U.S. TV

1980: "She Means Nothing To Me" (P)

1981

3/14: Dave Edmunds Interview, BBC radio

4/24: Round Table, BBC radio (P)

June: Cardiff Radio (D)

8/31: Dean Reed Show, E. Germany (P)

Aug.: Weet-Je-Nog-Van Toen Show, Dutch TV

Sept.: "Let's Put Our Hearts Together/So Sad" (UK)

11/5: Caerfilly, Wales (D)

1981: LP - *La Grande Storia Del Rock* (Italy)

1982

6/19: Lincoln, England (The Dead Cowboys)

Oct.: Radio Luxembourg (P)

Nov.: Star Choice, BBC radio (P)

Dec.: LP - *Love Hurts*

1982: Palomino Club (P)

1983

3/8: Karen and Donald's divorce becomes finalized

7/2: Stephanie Lawrence Show, BBC TV (P)

7/5: The Today Show, NBC TV

7/5: Good Morning America, CBS TV

7/6: The Today Show, NBC TV

9/22: Reunion Concert, Royal Albert Hall, London, England

9/23: Reunion Concert, Royal Albert Hall, London, England

Sept.: British Reunion News

11/29: PISA, Dutch TV

Nov.: "The Price Of Love/Devoted To You/Ebony Eyes/Love Hurts" (7" disc)

Nov.: "Devoted To You/Ebony Eyes/Love Hurts/Baby What You Want Me To Do" (12" disc)

1983: Nationwide Show - BBC TV (P)

1983: Video - *The Reunion Concert*

1983: LP - *Phil Everly* (P)

1984

July: Entertainment Tonight

Aug.: Entertainment Tonight

Sept.: LP - *EB '84*

Sept.: KRTH Radio (P)

Sept.: LP - *Nice Guys* (British)

Sept.: French TV (D)

10/10: AVRO's Platengala, Dutch TV

10/20: Wembley Arena (D)

10/22: AM-TV, BBC TV

10/24: Interview, Cardiff, Wales

Oct: The Des O`Connor Show

11/2: Arena Special, BBC TV

Dec.: LP - *Phil's Diner* (P)

1984: LP - *The Everly Brothers' Reunion Concert*

1984: Video - *Rock 'N Roll Odyssey*

1984: Video - *Album Flash*

1084: Laser Video - *Reunion Concert*

1984: LP - *Louise* (P)

1984: CD - *EB '84*

1984: Tour of U.S., Canada and Europe

1984: Lake Tahoe - Joined by Edan

1985

1/26: Dick Clark's Rock, Roll & Remember

7/28: Valley Forge Music Fair, Devon, PA

8/24: Lookin' Back, Toronto, Canada

Aug.: Dutch radio interview

11/10: Live On Her Majesty's, BBC TV

11/25: Hammersmith Odeon, London

1985: LP - *Born Yesterday*

1985: CD - *Born Yesterday*

1985: LP - *Home Again*

1985: LP - *All They Had To Do Was Dream*

1985: CD - *Their 20 Greatest Hits*

1985: World Tour - U.S., Canada, Honolulu, Australia, Great Britain

1986

1/17: FM Hall of Fame, CBS TV

1/19: Today in Music History, Toronto

1/19: Spotlight, Toronto, Ont., Canada

1/23: Inducted into Rock And Roll Hall of Fame at Waldorf Astoria, NYC

1/86: Tennessee Homecoming, U.S. TV

2/86: KHSL Radio, Chico, California (D)

3/5: Nashville Now, U.S. TV

6/17: CBS Morning News

6/28: Trump Palace, Atlantic City, NJ

7/5: Shenandoah, Iowa Homecoming Celebration. July 5 pronounced Everly Brothers Day in Iowa

7/18: Hilton Hotel - Las Vegas, NV

8/20: Valley Forge Music Fair, Devon, PA

10/2: Awarded 1,834th Star on Hollywood's "Walk of Fame"

10/11: Country Notes, TNN, US TV

10/19: Harrah's, Atlantic City, NJ

11/9: Walt Disney World's 15th Anniversary Celebration

12/36: In Session, Canadian TV

1986: LP - *The Best of the Everly Brothers* (6 record set)

1986: LP - *The Everly Brothers' Greatest Recordings*

1986: LP - *Susie Q*

1986: Teledisc/USA Radio - commercial

1986: LP - *Born Yesterday*

1986: Tour of U.S.A.

1987

3/13: Beach Boys Concert, Hawaii, ABC TV

5/16: A Prairie Home Companion Show

6/25: Boudleaux Bryant dies

1987: CD - *The Everly Brothers: 1957-1962*

1987: CD - *Susie Q*

1987: CD - *Louise* (P)

1987: CD - *Brother Jukebox* (D)

1987: Film, A Rock 'n Roll Odyssey with Chet Atkins

1987: Phillip commissions the D-50 guitar as 50th birthday present for Donald

1987: Tour of USA and England

1988

6/4: A Prairie Home Companion Show: The 2nd Annual Farewell Performance, Radio City Music Hall, NYC

1988: First Annual Central City Everly Brothers Music Festival

1988: LP - *Some Hearts*

1988: CD - *They're Off And Rolling*

1988: CD - *Songs Our Daddy Taught Us*

1988: CD - *The Fabulous Style of the Everly Brothers*

1988: CD - *All They Had To Do Was Dream*

1988: CD - *Nice Guys*

1988: CD - *The Golden Hits Of The Everly Brothers*

1988: CD - *The Very Best Of The Everly Brothers*

1988: CD - *Lil' Bit Of Gold - The Everly Brothers* (Mini)

1988: CD - *The Everly Brothers, Vol. 2*

1988: CD - *Some Hearts*

1988: Fan Fair '88 - surprise appearance

1988: Tour of USA and Europe

1989

1/19: Donald gives Phillip a rebuilt 1960 Cadillac Coupe de Ville (which was his car originally), for a 50th birthday present

8/12: Second Annual Central City EB Music Festival

8/89: LP - *Hidden Gems*

10/8: Nominated for CMA Award for "Vocal Event of the Year" along with Johnny Cash and Rosanne Cash for their rendition of "Ballad of a Teenage Queen"

1989: Tour of USA, Europe and Australia

1989: Three weeks in Las Vegas, NV

1990

2/16: Tennessee Ernie Ford's 50th Anniversary Special, US TV

2/21: Harrah's South Shore Room, Lake Tahoe, NV (5 days)

4/29: Erin Everly marries W. Axl Rose of the rock band, Guns N' Roses

5/30: W. Axl Rose sues Erin for divorce. They reconcile.

6/4: Nominated for "Duo of the Year" at the TNN Music City News Country Awards

6/29: 1990 USA Tour begins

9/1: Third Annual Central City EB Music Festival

10/9: Donald honored at BMI's 50th Anniversary TV Show. He was presented with the Robert J. Burton Award for The Most Performed Song of the Year for "Cathy's Clown"

10/9: Nashville Now, US TV (D)

10/10: Crook & Chase, US TV (D)

11/1: Amusement & Music Operators Association (AMOA) Jukebox Awards, New Orleans, LA. Inducted into the Jukebox Legends Hall of Fame.

1990: Video - *Born Yesterday*

1990: Everlys' contract dropped by Mercury/Polygram

1991

1/91: Axl and Erin's marriage is annulled

9/91: Fourth Annual Central City EB Music Festival

1991: Book - *The Everly Brothers: Ladies Love Outlaws* by Consuelo Dodge

BIBLIOGRAPHY

Amburn, Ellis. *Dark Star: The Roy Orbison Story.* New York: Carol Publishing Group, 1990.

Anderson, Nancy. "A Legend Changes Course," The Sacramento Union, March 20, 1976.

Bane, Michael. *The Outlaws: Revolution In Country Music.* A Country Music Magazine Press/Doubleday/Dolphin Books, 1978.

Bartlett, John. *Bartlett's Familiar Quotations,* Thirteenth and Centennial Edition. Boston and Toronto: Little, Brown & Company, 1955.

Belz, Carl. *The Story of Rock.* New York: Oxford University Press, 1969.

Blanche, Ed. "The Sound of One Everly," The Detroit Free Press, May 3, 1977.

Bolander, Donald O., and Dolores D. Varner, Gary B. Wright, Stephanie H. Greene. *Instant Quotation Dictionary.* Illinois: Career Publishing, Inc., 1988.

Bragg, Melvyn. *Richard Burton: A Life, 1925-1984.* Boston: Little, Brown & Co., 1988.

Carr, Patrick. "Bye Bye Blues - Hello Happiness," *Country Music Magazine,* November/December, 1986, pp. 43-46.

Citron, Stephen. *Songwriting: A Complete Guide To The Craft.* New York: William Morrow and Company, Inc., 1985.

Clark, Dick. *Rock, Roll & Remember.* Popular Library: 1976.

Cohen, Martin. "New Career Switch For The Everlys."

Cohn, Ed. *Newsday,* March 30, 1966, p. 9.

Cross, Wilbur and Michael Kosser. *The Conway Twitty Story.* Garden City, New York: Doubleday & Company, Inc., 1986.

Daily Express, "Going Solo - The Everly Brother." June 4, 1974.

Davis, Bette, with Michael Herskowitz. *This 'n That.* New York: G. P. Putnam's Sons, 1987.

Dellar, Fred and Roy Thompson. *The Illustrated Encyclopedia of Country Music.* New York: Harmony Books, 1977.

Donahue, Michael, The Hawk Eye, "Everly Brother Enjoys New Fame," August 8, 1986.

Detroit Free Press, May 3, 1977.

The Evansville Courier, 1983.

Everly, Ike, "Father Calls Mother Secret of Amazing Success," *Country and Western Jamboree,* 3, No. 5 (August 1957): 15, 34

Ibid. 4, No. 1 (Summer 1958): 10-16, 33, 38.

Fisher, Eddie. *Eddie: My Life, My Loves.* New York: Harper & Row, 1981.

Fournier, Lou. "The Everlys: In Harmony Once Again," The Washington Times, 1986.

Goldrosen, John and John Beecher, *Remembering Buddy: The Definitive Biography of Buddy Holly.* New York: Penguin Books, 1986, Page 173.

Grooves Magazine, "Rock History From 'A to Z'," 1979.

Hennessy, Val, "Everlasting Appeal of The Everlys," The Times, November 22, 1985.

Hensley, Dennis E. "Don Everly," *Country Musician's Magazine,* GPI Publications, 1987, Page 38.

Heymann, C. David. *A Woman Named Jackie,* Secaucus, New Jersey: Lyle Stuart Books, 1989.

Hilburn, Robert. "Everly Brothers Give Nostalgia A Fresh Edge," The Los Angeles Times.

Isler, Scott. "The Everlys: Brothers In Arms," *Musician Magazine,* July 1986, No. 93.

Jerome, Jim. "Don and Phil Everly End A Discordant Decade Apart to Harmonize Sweetly Again," *People Weekly,* January 23, 1984, p. 73.

Karpp, Phyllis. *Ike's Boys,* Pierian Press, 1988.

Kelley, Kitty. *Elizabeth Taylor: The Last Star.* New York: Simon and Schuster, 1981, pp. 174-175.

Kelley, Kitty. *Jackie Oh!* Secaucus, New Jersey: Lyle Stuart Books, 1978.

Lewis, Myra with Murray Silver. *Great Balls of Fire!* New York: St. Martin's Press, 1982.

The London Times, September 23, 1983.

The Los Angeles Times, July 16, 1973.

Ledgerwood, Mike. *Disc & Music Echo,* September 13, 1971.

Loder, Kurt. *Rolling Stone Magazine,* Issue #473, May 8, 1986, p. 61.

Look Magazine, "The Everly Brothers: Fast Spin to Success," April 15, 1958.

McLean, Hope. "What Chance Does This Marriage Have?" *Photoplay,* 1961.

McTavish, Brian. "1980s Easy After Hostile '50s," Kansas City Star, August 7, 1986.

Malone, Bill C. and Judith McCulloh, Editors, *Stars of Country Music,* University of Illinois Press, Urbana, Chicago, London, 1975, p. 233.

Morse, Steve, "Everly Brothers Glad To Be Back," Boston Globe. August 21, 1984.

The New Yorker Magazine, February 22, 1969.

The New Yorker Magazine, August 31, 1987, pp. 24-25.

Newsday, July 7, 1986.

Norman, Phillip. "The Everly Brothers: Growing Apart."

Penn, Jean. "Everybody and His Brother," *Playboy Magazine,* January 1986, pp. 118-119.

People Weekly, January 23, 1984, Vol. 21, No. 3, p. 73.

People Weekly, Review, December 19, 1988, Vol. 30, No. 25, p. 28.

Playboy, January, 1968.

Playboy, 1986, Vol. 33, Issue 1, p. 194.

Reynolds, Debbie with David Patrick Columbia. *Debbie: My Life,* New York: Pocket Books, 1988.

Rolling Stone Magazine, August 16, 1973.

Rolling Stone Magazine, September 13, 1984, pp. 47-8.

Sellers, Pat. "Joan Rivers," *Cosmopolitan,* December, 1989, p. 213.

Selvin, Joe, The San Francisco Chronicle, September 13, 1984.

Shaw, Arnold. *The Rockin' '50s, The Decade That Transformed The Pop Music Scene.* New York: Hawthorne Books, Inc., 1974.

The Shenandoah Evening Sentinel. Shenandoah, Iowa, June 17, 1986.

Surkamp, David. "Everly Brothers Show Is Strictly First Rate," St. Louis Post-Dispatch, August 28, 1985.

Tillis, Mel, with Walter Wager. *Stutterin' Boy.* New York: Rawson Associates, 1984.

Time Magazine, "The Everly Brothers In Arms," March 17, 1986, Vol. 127, Page 74.

Ullman, L. P. and Krasner, L. *A Psychological Approach To Abnormal Behavior,* Englewood Cliffs, N.J.: Prentice-Hall, 1975.

The Vancouver Sun. Vancouver, July 8, 1986.

The Wall Street Journal. New York, February 2, 1987.

Wallace, Irving, David Wallechinsky, Amy Wallace and Sylvia Wallace, *The People's Almanac Presents The Book of Lists, No. 2.* New York: William Morrow & Co., Inc., 1980.

Ward, Ed, Geoffrey Stokes and Ken Tucker. *Rock of Ages: The Rolling Stone History of Rock & Roll.* New York: Rolling Stone Press/Summit Books, 1986.

White, Charles. *The Life and Times of Little Richard.* New York: Harmony Books, 1984.

Wilson, Susan, The Boston Globe, April 10, 1987.

World Almanac and Book of Facts, 1979.

Wortman, Camille B. and Elizabeth F. Loftus. *Psychology.* New York: Alfred A. Knopf, 1981.

Zimbardo, Phillip G. *Psychology and Life.* Glenview, Illinois: Scott, Foresman and Company, 1985.

INDEX

THE EVERLY BROTHERS

ORDER FORM

CIN-DAV, Inc.
Rt. 1, Box 778
Starke, Florida 32091

Please send me _____ copies at $14.95 each book $ _____

Shipping/Handling U.S.A. and Canada   _____

$3.00 first book   _____

$2.00 additional books   _____

Other countries: $25.00 flat fee (U.S. currency only)   _____

Floridians please add 6% sales tax ($0.90 per book)   _____

                                      TOTAL   _____

Name _____

Address _____

City _____ State _____

Zip Code/Country _____

Telephone _____

Use This Form (or a photocopy) To Order Your Book.

THE EVERLY BROTHERS

ORDER FORM

CIN-DAV, Inc.
Rt. 1, Box 778
Starke, Florida 32091

Please send me _____ copies at $14.95 each book $ _____

Shipping/Handling U.S.A. and Canada   _____

$3.00 first book   _____

$2.00 additional books   _____

Other countries: $25.00 flat fee (U.S. currency only)   _____

Floridians please add 6% sales tax ($0.90 per book)   _____

                       TOTAL   _____

Name _____

Address _____

City _____ State _____

Zip Code/Country _____

Telephone _____

Use This Form (or a photocopy) To Order Your Book.

THE EVERLY BROTHERS

ORDER FORM

CIN-DAV, Inc.
Rt. 1, Box 778
Starke, Florida 32091

Please send me _____ copies at $14.95 each book $ _____

Shipping/Handling U.S.A. and Canada   _____

$3.00 first book   _____

$2.00 additional books   _____

Other countries: $25.00 flat fee (U.S. currency only)   _____

Floridians please add 6% sales tax ($0.90 per book)   _____

                                   TOTAL   _____

Name _____

Address _____

City _____ State _____

Zip Code/Country _____

Telephone _____

Use This Form (or a photocopy) To Order Your Book.

THE EVERLY BROTHERS

ORDER FORM

CIN-DAV, Inc.
Rt. 1, Box 778
Starke, Florida 32091

Please send me _____ copies at $14.95 each book $ _____

Shipping/Handling U.S.A. and Canada   _____

$3.00 first book   _____

$2.00 additional books   _____

Other countries: $25.00 flat fee (U.S. currency only)   _____

Floridians please add 6% sales tax ($0.90 per book)   _____

                              TOTAL   _____

Name _____

Address _____

City _____ State _____

Zip Code/Country _____

Telephone _____

Use This Form (or a photocopy) To Order Your Book.

The name rings a bell.

They used to be pretty good didn't they?

I used to love them but they broke up and disappeared.

I think a ~~folksy~~ folksy type of music and were somewhat popular.

They sang something in the 50's

You much in love with "Him" Everly I was ...in high school

Aren't they all washed up?

Too young to remember — Age 23